Understanding
ADHD
—■—

*Dedicated, with appreciation and love,
to the memory of my friend and colleague,
Willis H. Ploof.*

Understanding ADHD

— ■ —

Attention Deficit Hyperactivity Disorder and the Feeling Brain

Sandra K. Woods
Willis H. Ploof

SAGE Publications
International Educational and Professional Publisher
Thousand Oaks   London   New Delhi

For information:

SAGE Publications, Inc.
2455 Teller Road
Thousand Oaks, California 91320
E-mail: order@sagepub.com

SAGE Publications Ltd.
6 Bonhill Street
London EC2A 4PU
United Kingdom

SAGE Publications India Pvt. Ltd.
M-32 Market
Greater Kailash I
New Delhi 110 048 India

Printed in the United States of America

Library of Congress Cataloging-in-Publication Data
    Woods, Sandra K.
        Understanding ADHD: Attention deficit hyperactivity disorder
    and the feeling brain / by Sandra K. Woods and Willis H. Ploof.
            p.   cm.
        Includes bibliographical references and index.
        ISBN 0-8039-7422-1 (cloth: acid-free paper). — ISBN
    0-8039-7423-X (pbk.: acid-free paper)
        1. Attention-deficit hyperactivity disorder.   I. Ploof, Willis H.
    II. Title.
    RJ506.H9W68 1997
    616.85'89—dc21   97-4853

This book is printed on acid-free paper.

97 98 99 00 01 02 03 10 9 8 7 6 5 4 3 2 1

Acquiring Editor:	Jim Nageotte
Editorial Assistant:	Kathleen Derby
Production Editor:	Sherrise M. Purdum
Production Assistant:	Denise Santoyo
Typesetter/Designer:	Danielle Dillahunt
Indexer:	Teri Greenberg
Cover Designer:	Lesa Valdez
Print Buyer:	Anna Chin

Contents

SECTION 2. BACKGROUND

SECTION 3. BRAIN REWARD AND PUNISHMENT MECHANISMS: A CLOSER LOOK

Preface

This work is a point-of-view endeavor representing an integration of some of the basic research findings drawn largely from the field of neuroscience and behavior, with the observations and insights garnered from clinical practice. Our hope is that it will both inform and stimulate future thinking and research on the biological underpinnings of attention deficit hyperactivity disorder (ADHD).

At the heart of the model lies our capacity as humans for psychic feeling—the ability to attach meaning to the events, people, ideas, and objects in our lives—to complex them with feelings of psychic pain and psychic pleasure. And the notion that there are natural, heritable differences in this capacity is key. Although this may make intuitive sense, we are often surprised and perplexed when confronted by obvious deviations in this capacity as expressed in word or deed. How can you be so insensitive, we ask. Have you no feeling, we exclaim. While giving lip service to the idea of individual differences, we secretly expect conformity. It disturbs us when others do not feel as we expect them to, especially when such feeling, or lack thereof, is reflected in action. We may even try to "convince" people to feel differently, an often fruitless and frustrating endeavor. Yet our frustration and confusion might be tempered, perhaps even eliminated, if we could learn to view this capacity in the same light as we view other human traits—traits that vary and have a natural, heritable component but that also may be modified by experience. In so doing, we will deepen our understanding and appreciation for the symptoms and internal suffering of those afflicted with ADHD, for these are individuals who appear to have considerable difficulty imprinting the feeling component of experience.

A few comments about the organization of the book, which is divided into four main sections. The first section introduces the model; then we discuss related neurobehavioral processes and the relevance of temperament to our understanding of the disorder.

The second section consists of an overview of some of the background literature, emphasizing the body of work that has informed and guided our own practice and thinking. Here we present a brief introduction to the disorder, describing symptoms, prevalence rates, and the evidence for its persistence into adulthood. We then take a fairly in-depth look at the mechanisms of action of the psychomotor stimulants, as these remain the drugs of choice in the treatment of symptomatology. Next, we review some of the research specifically related to ADHD and monoamine function and pose questions related to a potentially fruitful line of study.

The third section reviews the literature on brain reward and punishment mechanisms in greater detail. It is the delicate workings of these systems, collectively referred to as "the feeling brain"—along with hypothesized inherited variations in their functioning—which form the foundation for the model.

The final section is devoted to treatment. The practices described reflect common sense and most are standard in the field. To these we have added our own clinical observations, insights, and speculations.

At the end of the book are two appendixes. Appendix A is a description of the Pupil Adjustment Program as originally presented to the Springfield School Department, Springfield, Massachusetts, in May 1970. Appendix B is a summary of the basic concepts and treatment strategies contained in the text but simplified as a handout for parents and teachers.

Acknowledgments

We would like to thank the following friends and colleagues for reading parts of the manuscript and for their many helpful comments and suggestions: Sue Anne Assimon of the Food and Drug Administration and Robert S. Feldman and Jerrold S. Meyer of the Neuroscience Department, University of Massachusetts at Amherst. Dr. Feldman, in particular, invested considerable time reading and commenting on the neuroscience material.

We especially want to acknowledge Richard J. Lombard and the late Donna R. Montessi for their steadfast dedication and contribution to the success of the Pupil Adjustment Program.

Finally, thanks to the following parent, Everett C. Hume, for reading and commenting on the entire manuscript, and to Susan D. Wyant for her careful drawings of some of the figures.

Section 1

The Model

1

Introduction

■ **OPENING COMMENTS**

The exact biobehavioral basis of attention deficit hyperactivity disorder (ADHD) is not entirely known. After more than 50 years of research, we have yet to come up with an integrated, biologically reasonable explanation—one that ties together information about the natural or inherited properties of the human brain; the various neurotransmitter systems and brain structures subserving complex processes such as attention and impulse control, and the complex of behaviors and symptoms known as ADHD. Although some important initial clues were provided long ago by the medications that have proven to be the most useful in treatment—Dexedrine® and Ritalin®—current theory is hampered by our incomplete understanding of the mechanisms of action of these compounds, the exact brain structures affected, and the precise behavioral functions subserved by these structures. Even if these things were thoroughly understood, we would still have to question the relative contribution of heredity and environment.

That said, there have been some important advances in our knowledge and understanding. For example, researchers are now looking at the ventral striatum and the frontal cortex as areas whose functioning might be "normalized" by stimulant pharmacotherapy. Also, with the advent of the human genome project, the future promises to provide us with important clues about the identity of biologically reasonable candidate genes that may make one individual more susceptible than another.

3

The magnitude of the task notwithstanding, we and others remain committed to finding the explanation of best fit. This is what this book is about. Personal bias and prejudice acknowledged, we believe that the ideas contained herein represent the most parsimonious explanation of ADHD available. We have been working on it for what seems like a lifetime—applying it in our clinical practice and research and refining it as warranted, as our understanding of genetics, brain processes, and drug effects improves. Many of the details have yet to be worked out, but the basic theoretical model is in place and from a clinical perspective— albeit our own—it has withstood the test of time.

Some of the ideas contained in this work were originally conceived in the late 1960s and early 1970s as an outgrowth of the Pupil Adjustment Program—a program developed for the Springfield School Department, Springfield, Massachusetts, to treat children with symptoms of this disorder. A description of this early work is contained in the appendixes. Our colleagues and many of our patients have been pushing us to make our perspective public so that others might benefit. We offer it now for consideration with the full awareness that only time and further study will tell if it is the most fitting.

■ **EARLY CLUES**

Our initial thinking regarding the underlying neurophysiological and biobehavioral basis of ADHD was guided by the early theoretical speculations and research of Larry Stein (1964). Drawing upon the work of early learning psychologists, most notably Tolman and Mowrer, who were the first to suggest that reinforcement acts via an expectancy mechanism, Stein proposed that ongoing behavior is either repeated or avoided because of the *expectation* of reward or punishment, and not because of their actual occurrence.

According to this view, reward and punishment play a critical but *indirect* role in behavior, that of establishing and maintaining the expectation. Because expectancy can only exist if there is some associated memory from the past, Stein (1964) theorized that the mechanism of expectation is a Pavlovian conditioned reflex resulting in the activation of the medial forebrain bundle, in the case of reward, and the periventricular system of the diencephalon and midbrain, in the case of punishment. Whereas activation of the reward system provides facilitating feedback to ongoing behavior, activation of the punishment system provides inhibitory feedback.

Accordingly, by the mechanism of expectation, past behavior that led to rewarding consequences will tend to be repeated. Similarly, behavior that was previously punished will tend to be inhibited. In this manner, ongoing behavior comes under the reciprocal control of a response-facilitating "go" mechanism and a response-suppressant "stop" mechanism, which feed continuously into motor mechanisms and jointly determine the net effect, either facilitation or inhibition, on ongoing behavior. When one system is activated, the other is suppressed. Similarly, if one system is suddenly deactivated, the other will go through a brief period of rebound activity. This may explain why we feel sad when "the party's over," or why it feels so good when we stop banging our heads against the proverbial wall.

In Pavlovian terms, response-related stimuli are the conditioned stimuli and reward and punishment, the unconditioned stimuli. The unconditioned response, either psychic pain or psychic pleasure, is a direct result of the activation of one or the other system. Response-related cues, either external (originating within the environment) or internal (originating within the organism), which forecast impending reward or punishment are responsible for directly engaging and activating these systems. Presumably, liminal activity in one or the other system would exert only a mild incentive or deterring effect on ongoing behavior, whereas the full-blown excitation of either system would exert a powerful motivating influence.

Once again, the important points to be emphasized are:

1. Activation of these systems takes place *before* the actual occurrence of a punishing or pleasurable consequence and is therefore a mechanism for *expectation.*
2. The participation of both systems can be felt even in situations that may appear upon first glance to be pure "heaven" or "hell."
3. These systems are mutually inhibitory; that is, when you feel good, you can't simultaneously feel bad.

Obviously, in the young organism, the need for direct experience with its associated consequences—whether painful or pleasurable—is a necessary prerequisite for the development of this higher-level anticipatory reflex.

Extrapolating to the behavior of humans, it is possible to imagine how by repeated, consistent stimulation of the reward systems of the brain in response to a specific behavior, we reinforce that behavior by associating it with a pleasurable feeling tone, which is then stored together with the behavior in memory—creating what we have termed a *memory-feeling tone complex.* To obtain, once again, the delicious feeling of reward, the individual will repeat the associated behavior.

Conversely, consistent, repeated stimulation of the punishment systems of the brain would result in the storage of unpleasant or painful feeling tones along with the behavior that elicited them. This behavior will tend to be inhibited in the future. In a similar manner, salient stimuli that have in the past been consistently associated with the experience of psychic pleasure or psychic pain are either sought or avoided because of what they portend. This reflexive resurgence of psychic feeling associated with the original event is what appears to endow these previously neutral stimuli with reinforcing qualities of their own. In light of this explanation of behavior, the *expectancy reflex* appears to be as fundamentally a part of the mammalian brain as the orienting reflex.

■ SPECULATIONS REGARDING THE NEUROPHYSIOLOGICAL BASIS OF ADHD

We have previously hypothesized that the mechanism of expectancy, as conceptualized by Stein (1964), is related to an organism's development of an appreciation of time in its three dimensions of past, present, and future, and we have suggested how the symptomatology presented by the ADHD child might be accounted for by a dysfunction in this mechanism (e.g., see Appendix A: The Pupil Adjustment Program, and/or Woods, 1990). Accordingly, if we think of future time as expectancy and past time as the stored memory complex of behavior and its associated psychic feeling tones, one can see how the past and the future are brought into play in the present behavior of the organism.

When this mechanism is working properly, we see an individual who is organized in time and in behavior. Immediate stimuli are screened with reference to a future goal. Inner impulses are checked with reference to a future punishment. The individual can relate past to future and thus determine his or her behavior in the present. Furthermore, having the capacity to experience deeply, that is, to attach the appropriate psychic feeling to events, behavior, objects, and people, the individual is able to identify and empathize with the feelings of others, leading to the development of a feeling-bond with them, an essential prerequisite for functioning adequately in a social setting.

Assuming, however, that this mechanism is not functioning properly, that for some reason the threshold for activation of the reward and punishment systems of the brain is extremely high, a situation would exist whereby the usual intensity of stimulation of these systems would have little or no effect on ongoing behavior. Consequently, conditioning in this sense would not occur; there would be little or no psychic feeling complexed with a particular behavior, person, event, or object in memory and, therefore, little or no *expectancy* of either reward or punishment. Robbed, so to speak, of both anticipatory pleasures and anticipatory anxieties or punishers, and lacking an adequate feeling-bond with others, this type of individual may be said to be truly socially and emotionally deprived.

■ IMPLICATIONS FOR UNDERSTANDING THE DEVELOPMENT OF ADHD SYMPTOMATOLOGY

The consequences of such a situation might well be responsible for the symptoms manifested by the ADHD child. Impulsivity, for example, might be due to a failure to check impulses with reference to future rewards and punishments. Attentional deficits and distractibility, both cardinal symptoms, might be thought of as the pathological inertia of the orienting reflex or the perseveration of reflexive, involuntary attention—once again due to the lack of a meaningful reference point (that is, a stored memory complex of events and associated feeling tone)—so that each event or environmental stimulus is reacted to as if it were novel, leaving the child unable to concentrate and complete assigned tasks. The inability to delay gratification is similarly brought into perspective when viewed as the failure to develop a meaningful conceptualization of the future (expectation of reward or punishment) and the past (stored memory complex of behaviors and associated feeling tones). Having no expectation of reward, the individual is bound to the present moment, seeking instant gratification of immediate needs and desires. Similarly, having no expectation of punishment, the individual is bound to repeat the same behaviors that in the past led to unpleasant consequences.

This might account for the reports of parents and teachers that punishment does not serve to deter the misconduct of ADHD children. Although these children often "remember" on a purely cognitive level what behaviors are likely to lead to punishment, the motivational component (adequate feeling tone) of the memory-feeling-tone complex is missing and therefore does not serve to inhibit the inappropriate behavior. Feeling little or no guilt or remorse for past transgressions, these children come into continuous conflict with authority figures who attempt to set limits on behavior, thus leaving the impulse-ridden, stimulus-bound children with a negative self-image. Forever at the mercy of external and internal stimuli, it is easy to see how children with this problem may be hyperactive.

Finally, the frequently reported descriptions of these children as self-centered, bossy, bullying, and persistent in getting their own way regardless of the feelings of others may be understood as the failure to develop an adequate feeling-bond with others, the basis of empathic responding. Children (or adults) whose brains can't process psychic pain and psychic pleasure "normally" are apt to go to extremes in order to awaken the feeling brain. Pushing others with inappropriate behavior is especially likely to generate a feeling response, and may be seen as the children's attempt to stimulate their own reinforcement systems. Put simply, what ADHD children (or adults) may be saying when they provoke others with socially unacceptable behavior is "please help me feel"—although the "please" is very likely to be omitted. But it remains to place this symptomatology in the proper context, that is, within the framework of the overall development of the individual, on the one hand, and the maturation of the brain, on the other, so that it might be more fully understood.

■ ADHD SYMPTOMATOLOGY AND PSYCHOSOCIAL DEVELOPMENT

Initially, in the very young organism, behavior is primarily reflexive and random in nature. Through conditioning, a process that is dependent on the functional integrity of the reward and punishment systems of the brain, or what we will refer to as the *feeling brain,* the behavior of the young organism eventually loses its random quality and is replaced with more purposeful, goal-directed behavior. Obviously, this is a gradual process. Beginning with the early affect-laden experiences of childhood, a memory bank of behaviors, events, people, and associated feeling tones is accumulated slowly, only gradually evolving into a meaningful reference point for comparing past to future and thus determining behavior in the present.

The process may be said to begin with the early attempts of mothers and fathers to enculturate children and keep them alive, an often painful but necessary process involving, among other things, parental attempts to get children's behavior to conform to the cultural expectations of the society in which they live. Out of necessity, certain behaviors must be encouraged and others prohibited. Consistent feeling feedback from parents and other significant authority figures plays a crucial role in this process. Behavior that is rewarded one day and punished the next leaves the child feeling confused regarding what is expected and acceptable, forcing the child to push the parents—often with unacceptable behavior—to determine what the limits are. For the young organism, these are critical lessons to be learned, lessons that will ensure his or her continued survival and adaptation in the outside world. They are lessons born out of *direct* experience with the environment under the guiding tutelage of the feeling brain.

Gradually, paralleling the maturation of higher cortical functions along with the brain structures that provide their physiological basis (especially, medial prefrontal cortex), children begin to anticipate the consequences of their actions without having to experience them directly. Reason and logic make their appearance, becoming a more observable aspect of behavior during adolescence.

Drawing heavily on past experience and associated feeling tones, actions in the present are now screened with an eye to expected outcomes. Plans and intentions are formulated, and the relevant behavior is set into motion; progress toward the goal is verified, and subsequent behavior is fine-tuned with reference to the original intention.

Eventually, in mature adults, it becomes possible for phenomena in the real world to become "knowable" through the world of ideas and fantasy without the need for direct experience (e.g., Einstein). Activity in the reward and punishment systems of the brain plays a crucial role in this process, particularly early in development, transforming, as it were, "the cold light with which we see into the warm light with which we feel" (MacLean, 1973, p. 42). But for ADHD children, this transformation does not occur or occurs only minimally. This diminished capacity for imprinting feelings of psychic pain and psychic pleasure may be said to disrupt the normal course of conditioning, delaying (or, in the extreme case, preventing altogether?) the development of the expectancy reflex and the appearance of the more organized, goal-directed behavior characteristic of the mature organism.

To better understand how this might happen, it is first necessary to explore the neurophysiological bases for certain brain processes that appear to be closely linked, functionally, to the workings of the reward and punishment systems of the brain. Here we refer specifically to brain mechanisms for wakefulness, attention, habituation, planning, and foresight. These mechanisms will be discussed with particular emphasis on their relationship to the development of purposeful goal-directed behavior, which in the ADHD child is conspicuous by its virtual absence. Much of the work that will be presented has come from Soviet psychology, especially from the investigations of the late A. R. Luria and colleagues, pioneers in the field of neuropsychology.

Following this is a discussion of the model from the perspective of temperament. As will be seen, we have come to view the ADHD individual as falling at one extreme of a naturally occurring—perhaps normally distributed—temperament continuum.

2

Associated
Neurobehavioral Processes

■ **THE WAKING STATE AND
SIMPLE FORMS OF ATTENTION**

Obviously, the waking state is necessary before any goal-directed activity can occur. The brain structure thought to play a focal role in maintaining wakefulness and general cortical tone, that is, arousal, is the brain stem reticular formation. Identified in 1949 by Moruzzi and Magoun (see details in Magoun, 1969), the reticular formation consists, not of isolated neurons that obey the all-or-none principle of excitation, but rather

> has the structure of a nerve net, among which are scattered the bodies of nerve cells connected with each other by short [axonal] processes. Excitation spreads over the net . . . not as single, isolated impulses . . . but gradually, changing its level little by little and thus modulating the whole state of the nervous system. (Luria, 1973, p. 46)

Located in the medial parts of the medulla, pons, and midbrain, the reticular formation is a complex, intricate neural network where influences from diverse areas of the brain (e.g., spinal cord, cerebellum, thalamus, hypothalamus, limbic cortex, orbitofrontal cortex) converge and interact to alter states of arousal and to modify the reactivity of the organism. The connectivity of each neuron in this network is rich and extensive; it is estimated that each cell in this net may receive inputs from over 4,000 neurons and in turn may send inputs to over 25,000 other cells (Noback & Demarest, 1977). The unified influences of this system on higher (e.g., thalamus, orbitofrontal cortex) and lower (e.g., spinal cord) structures of the central nervous system are conveyed via identifiable ascending and descending reticular pathways.

In humans and other mammals, the reticular formation represents the evolved product of a phylogenetically ancient system of fiber tracts. In addition to its role in consciousness and associated states—from sleep to drowsiness to alertness and attention—the reticular formation has an important background role to play in the modification of the perception, conduction, and discrimination of sensory input (Noback & Demarest, 1977). Stimulation of descending corticoreticular pathways arising primarily from the medial portions of the prefrontal cortex, for example, has been shown to lower the threshold of discrimination for sensory stimuli (Luria, 1973). Once considered an amorphous network of cells, with a diffuse organization and no modally specific function, the reticular formation is now recognized as a well-organized neural network with specific functions to fulfill in addition to the function of nonspecific arousal.

With respect to nonspecific arousal, the ascending reticular activating system (ARAS)—acting primarily through its connections with the intralaminar nuclei of the thalamus—is thought to play a focal role in *transitioning* between various states of arousal and vigilance. In humans, these differing states of consciousness can be distinguished by the pattern of the electroencephalogram (EEG) and also by changes in cerebral blood flow and oxygen consumption. For example, when an individual goes from a sleepy, drowsy state to one of wakefulness, or to more intense states of arousal (e.g., selective attention, vigilance, hypervigilance), there are distinct changes in the background frequency of the EEG. Specifically, the frequency changes from low (e.g., 6 to 7 Hz) to high (e.g., 20 to 25 Hz), depending upon the degree of arousal (Roland, 1993). These EEG changes in frequency are accompanied by decreases in the amplitude of the EEG. At the same time, there are corresponding increases in cerebral blood flow (CBF) and in the rate of cerebral oxygen consumption (Roland, 1993).

The behavioral and EEG changes that accompany the transition from a drowsy or relaxed state to one of arousal are reproduced when the primary nuclei (e.g., central tegmentum, nucleus cuneiformis, parabrachial nucleus) of the ascending reticular formation of the midbrain are stimulated (Steriade, 1984). These nuclei project to various nuclei of the thalamus (e.g., ventromedial, dorsal medial nucleus, zona incerta), but not directly to the cortex (Steriade, 1984). Thus activation of the cortex by direct stimulation of these nuclei takes place indirectly, through thalamic connections with the cortex (see Figure 2.1).

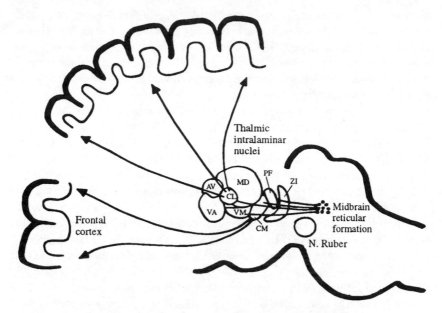

Figure 2.1: Schematic Drawing of Mammalian Midbrain Reticular-Thalamic System Important for General Attention. Activation of the cortex takes place indirectly via connections with the intralaminar nuclei of the thalamus. Shown are the anterior ventral nucleus (AV), central lateral nucleus (CL), central medial nucleus (CM), medial dorsal nucleus (MD), parafascicular nucleus (PF), ventral anterior nucleus (VA), and the zona incerta (ZI).

Source: Adapted from P. E. Roland (1993), *Brain Activation,* New York: Wiley-Liss. Reprinted with permission from John Wiley & Sons, Inc.

Using changes in regional cerebral blood flow, as measured by positron emission tomography (PET), Roland and coworkers (Kinomura, Larsson, Gulyas, & Roland, 1996) recently confirmed the involvement of the midbrain reticular nuclei and the intralaminar nuclei of the thalamus in higher states of arousal and vigilance. Specifically, regional blood flow to the midbrain tegmentum and intralaminar region of the thalamus was found to be significantly increased in human subjects ($N = 10$) during the performance of two attention-demanding visual and somatosensory reaction-time tasks, compared to the resting condition. Furthermore, these increases were found to be independent of the sensory modality that provided the alerting signal.

Finally, the reticular formation is known to comprise a number of distinct neurochemical systems that project widely, yet quite specifically, to destinations in the forebrain. These include noradrenergic (NE), dopaminergic (DA), serotonergic (5-HT), and cholinergic systems (ACh). Evidence suggests that each of these neurochemical systems has a unique role to play in more complex forms of behavioral arousal—namely, in selective attention (e.g., Robbins, Everitt, Muir, & Harrison, 1992).

To investigate the possible contributions made by these systems to selective attention, Robbins and coworkers employed a five-choice, serial reaction-time task (see details in Robbins et al., 1989). Briefly, this task required rats to discriminate brief (0.5 seconds) flashes of light presented randomly at the rear of one of five apertures located in a specially designed testing apparatus. Correct responding consisted of any insertion of the snout into the illuminated aperture from the time of the initial 0.5 second flash of light to the end of the 5-second trial. Incorrect responding consisted of responses in nonilluminated apertures, responses during a 5-second intertrial interval of darkness, and failure to respond during a given trial. Correct responses were rewarded by the delivery of a food pellet. Incorrect responses were punished with a 5-second period of darkness (time out). Any additional errors during a given time-out period, or any responses made during a given intertrial interval restarted the time-out clock. Once a particular animal met the established criterion—at least 80% correct responses and less than 20% omissions for five consecutive 30-minute test sessions—the targeted neurochemical system was selectively destroyed via infusion of neurotoxin. Following a period of recovery, the animal was retested.

The performance of sham-operated versus neurochemically lesioned animals was compared using the following behavioral measures: accuracy or the number of correct responses/total number of responses, speed of response or the latency to respond, anticipatory responses or the number of responses in the aperture during the intertrial interval, errors of omission or the number of trials in which no response was made, and perseverative responses or the number of additional responses in the aperture following the initial response in the aperture. In some experiments, the experimental procedure included the presentation of brief (0.5 seconds) bursts of distracting white noise (e.g., see Muir, Dunnett, Robbins, & Everitt, 1992, for specifics).

The findings from their extensive body of work were summarized in a recent report (Robbins et al., 1992) and are illustrated in Figure 2.2. As can be seen, rats that underwent neurochemical destruction of the locus coeruleus via infusion of the neurotoxin, 6-hydroxydopamine (6-OHDA) were found to be more distractible than sham-operated animals. In contrast, depletion of mesolimbic dopamine (DA)—via 6-OHDA—led to a reduction in the overall speed or latency of responding (termed the incentive-motivational component) on this same task. Reduction of ACh by 70% led to difficulties discriminating the visual

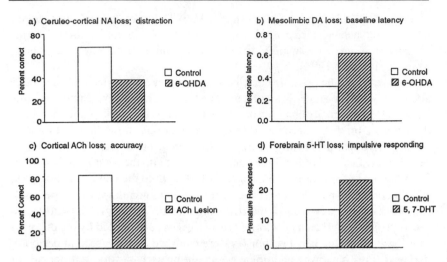

Figure 2.2: Illustration of Some of the Main Effects of Depletion of Chemically Defined Neurotransmitter Systems of the Reticular Core on the Five-Choice Attentional Task. (a) Following ceruleo-cortical depletion via infusion of 6-OHDA, no effects were seen on accuracy or speed of responding, but when distracting white noise was interpolated just prior to presentation of the visual targets, accuracy was impaired to a greater extent than in controls. (b) Following mesolimbic DA depletion via infusion of 6-OHDA, the largest effect was on measures of response vigor (incentive/motivational component). Specifically, chemically lesioned animals took longer to respond in comparison to controls. (c) Following 70% loss of neocortical ACh resulting from damage to the cells of the nucleus basalis of Meynert, accuracy of responding was impaired to a greater extent than in controls. (d) Depletion of forebrain 5-HT via infusion of 5,7-DHTA led to greater premature or impulsive responding compared to controls.

Source: Adapted and reprinted from T. W. Robbins, B. J. Everitt, J. L. Muir, & A. Harrison (1992), "Understanding the Behavioral Functions of Neurochemically Defined Arousal Systems," *International Brain Research Organization News, 20,* 7, with kind permission from Elsevier Science Ltd, The Boulevard, Langford Lane, Kidlington OX5 1GB, UK.

targets and suggests that ACh may be involved in enhancing the signal-to-noise ratio of salient stimuli. Finally, depletion of forebrain 5-HT via intraventricular infusion of 5,7 dihydroxytryptamine (5,7-DHTA) led to impulsive or premature responding on this task, and is consistent with other work (e.g., Soubrie, 1986; Wise, Berger, & Stein, 1973), suggesting a pivotal role for 5-HT systems in behavioral inhibition.

Based on such findings, Robbins and coworkers and others have argued that the old concept of nonspecific arousal should be thrown out in favor of a more specific definition, in which the role played by each of these systems is taken into consideration.

■ THE ORIENTING REFLEX

Once awake, we are naturally in a better position to receive and evaluate environmental stimuli, providing, of course, that they have first attracted our attention. One of the most elementary forms of attention is involuntary in nature and serves as the basis for simple investigative activity. Originally studied and later identified by Pavlov (1928) as the "orienting reflex," this type of activation of the brain is directly linked to the arrival of novel or potentially biologically significant stimuli from the outside world; in humans and other mammals, it consists of a turning of the eyes and head in the direction of the stimulus and the cessation of all other irrelevant forms of activity. It is what involuntarily happens, for example, when a loud noise suddenly interrupts our evening meal. We are immediately alert and automatically orient our bodies and our senses to the source of the stimulus, checking it out for familiarity and meaning. If the stimulus is neutral in meaning, requiring no special investigative reaction or approach or avoidance response, we gradually "forget" about the noise, returning our attention to the task at hand. Any change in the intensity of the stimulus, however, may cause us to promptly reinvestigate.

The process by which a repeatedly presented stimulus gradually loses its novelty or meaningfulness, no longer requiring or eliciting an orienting or investigative response, is termed *habituation.* In everyday language, one becomes accustomed to something, so that it gradually fades into the background. Microelectrode recordings of certain nonmodally specific nuclei of the reticular formation and limbic system (hippocampus) have shown that these nuclei compose the physiological substrate for habituation, becoming active with the appearance of novel stimuli and quiescent with the development of habituation to old, previously encountered stimuli (Luria, 1973). This capacity of the brain to compare old and new stimuli, and to habituate with repeated presentations of the same nonmeaningful stimulus (that is, to forecast neither pleasurable nor painful consequences for the organism), appears to be the means by which the orienting reflex is closely linked functionally to activity in the reward and punishment systems of the brain, on the one hand, and to brain mechanisms for memory, on the other.

But, as Luria (1973) has pointed out, it would be foolish to assume that the child's attention can only be attracted by novel or biologically meaningful stimuli. In addition to this involuntary, reflexive form of attention, Luria and colleagues identified a higher form of attention, voluntary in nature, which appears much later in development.

■ SOCIAL ORIGINS OF VOLUNTARY ATTENTION

This higher form of attention is essentially social in origin, for its vestiges lie in the child's relationships with parents and other adult caretakers (Luria, 1973). From infancy, the child is surrounded by adult members of the species, who use language, gestures, and other means to direct the child's attention to important environmental stimuli. In the process, objects and other stimuli begin to stand out from the rest of the environment.

According to Luria (1973), this capacity of a word or gesture from an adult to direct and control a child's attention is not fully acquired by children until shortly before they are ready to begin school. Later in development, as children's capacity for language and symbolic representation matures, they will acquire the ability to name objects and other environmental stimuli and thereby begin to exert more control over their attentional processes. Gradually, the function that was formally shared between the young organism and the adult members of the species will mature into an internalized, self-regulating process—the basis of the highest forms of voluntary attention. But it is this initial arrival of stimuli from the outside world in association with the most elementary forms of investigative activity, from the orienting reflex, on the one hand, to socially organized attention, on the other, and the evaluation of (attachment of meaning to) these stimuli by the feeling brain that set the stage for the development of voluntary attention and the more complex forms of purposeful, goal-directed behavior.

■ THE FRONTAL CORTEX:
AN IMPORTANT ROLE IN THE DEVELOPMENT
OF HIGHER FORMS OF ATTENTION
AND GOAL-DIRECTED BEHAVIOR

According to Luria (1973), these higher forms of attention and goal-directed behavior have their origins not in the external environment, but rather in the internal life of the individual as they arise from the plans and intentions formulated by the individual in association with language and other secondary signaling systems, for example, gestures, nonverbal thought, visual imagery, and so on. This most complex form of attention and organized goal-directed behavior makes its appearance much later in ontogeny and requires the integrity of the latest structure of the brain to be acquired during phylogeny, the frontal cortex, especially its basal and medial portions, which are closely linked to both the limbic cortex and the reticular formation of the brain.

There is a saying in the biological sciences that ontogeny recapitulates phylogeny, meaning that the development of the individual from conception to adulthood parallels the stages of the evolution of the species. Although this is not meant to be taken literally, it has relevance for the current discussion, for as is the case with the evolution of the species, the frontal cortex is the last brain structure to mature during the development of the individual.

A full appreciation of the importance of the role played by the frontal cortex in behavior was slow in emerging. As previously mentioned, much of the data regarding human frontal lobe function is due to the pioneering research of Luria and colleagues. In Western society in the not so distant past (1930s to 1950s), the frontal lobes were considered almost expendable, and frontal lobotomies were commonly performed on psychotic patients to provide much needed symptom relief (Freeman & Watts, 1950). In this procedure, the thalamo-cortical projections to the frontal lobes were severed. The notion that the frontal cortex—long acknowledged as the seat of rational thought and other forms of creative intellectual activity—could be virtually sequestered from the rest of the living brain with relative impunity was extraordinary, even for that time period.

As we now know, tests of "general intelligence" in use at that time, for example, Binet, Wechsler-Bellevue, were relatively insensitive to the effects of this procedure. Postoperatively, patients reportedly exhibited no measurable cognitive or sensory-motor deficits. Fortunately, a handful of concerned researchers decided to take a closer look at these patients, using a more sensitive measure of frontal lobe functioning—the Porteus Maze Test (Porteus, 1973). Their efforts revealed obvious postoperative losses in foresight, rehersal, and planning abilities (Porteus, 1973). This is consistent with the results of animal research (Pribram, 1961, 1973, and references cited therein), and with the research of Luria and colleagues (Luria, 1973, 1980) on patients with local lesions of the frontal lobes, research that was begun well over 50 years ago but was slow to be appreciated by the Western scientific community.

Evidence suggests that the maturation of the frontal cortex takes place over a protracted period of time. In humans, the rate of increase in the surface area of the frontal regions of the brain rises steeply until between 7 and 8 years of age, after which it slows considerably (Luria, 1973). Although there is evidence that the process can continue well into and possibly beyond the fourth decade of life, due to a protracted cycle of myelination (Yakovlev & Lecours, 1967), the rate of increase is considerably more gradual in nature. According to Luria, it is around 7 to 8 years of age that children acquire the rudiments of voluntary attention in stable enough form so that a spoken instruction from an adult directing the child's attention to a particular stimulus is easily obeyed. Before this age, the immature organism is more easily influenced by distracting, irrelevant stimuli. It is also around this time that children's behavior begins to be subordinated to plans and intentions formulated with the aid of language and other secondary signaling systems. Naturally, these more complex forms of behavior associated with voluntary, selective attention develop only gradually. And it is not until around the age of 12 to 15, at a time when distinct and reliable changes appear in the electrophysiology of the frontal cortex, that they become a more stable and salient aspect of behavior (Luria, 1973).

■ EXPECTANCY WAVE PHENOMENA

One electrophysiological indicator of maturity in the prefrontal cortex is the reliable appearance of expectancy waves (Grey Walter, 1973). Expectancy waves, also called E-waves or contingent negative variation (CNV), are distinctive slow waves that appear initially in the prefrontal cortex of normal adults and then spread to other regions of the brain in response to a stimulus that has come to serve as a *warning* that an expected event (the imperative stimulus) is about to happen, which will require a response on the part of the subject. CNVs develop even if the required action is inhibitory in nature, as when a subject is asked, for example, to refrain from pressing a button. CNVs associated with this state of anticipation or expectation have been reliably observed both in primates and humans (Fuster, 1980).

Electrophysiological recordings of neurons in the prefrontal cortex reveals that most are activated during the delay that occurs between the warning and the anticipated event (Fuster, 1980, 1981). Glucose utilization, as determined by the ^{14}C-2-deoxyglucose method, has been shown to be selectively increased in the prefrontal cortex of monkeys trained in this type of delayed response task (Bugbee & Goldman-Rakic, 1981).

Once established, expectancy waves reportedly persist as long as the subject's interest is sustained and he or she remains motivated to perform. When the probability of the occurrence of the imperative stimulus is low, for example, during extinction trials, expectancy waves gradually subside and eventually disappear. The rate and magnitude of this attenuation has been found to vary both between individuals and also to some extent within individuals from one time to the next (Grey Walter, 1973). Furthermore, the rate of attenuation has been found to be greatest for repeatedly presented tactile stimuli, moderate for visual stimuli, and least for auditory stimuli.

Although expectancy waves are rare in children between 3 and 10 years of age, their development can be stimulated in the experimental situation under certain conditions: through the development of a relationship with the experimenter and the use of social reinforcement, for example, praise, reassurance. Under such conditions, expectancy waves may develop, but they are relatively unstable, unlike the expectancy wave patterns found in normal adults. The role of social reinforcement in the development of expectancy waves is particularly evident in children between the ages of 5 and 15 years, as well as in young adults, where their appearance is reportedly highly sensitive to the social influences that permeate the experimental situation (Grey Walter, 1973).

For example, a single, accurate, and reliable instruction on the part of the experimenter that the expected event will not materialize, or that a response need not be made, will cause the expectancy wave to subside immediately. In one sense, such trustworthy information coming from the experimenter may be seen as equivalent, in terms of mathematical probability, to several incidents of direct experience to this effect on the part of the subject. On the other hand, this same instruction coming from a stranger or from someone who is likely to mislead or tease the subject may have an inverse effect. In the extreme case—in suggestible subjects who are easily and deeply hypnotized—the individual may be persuaded to respond to entirely imaginary associations between stimuli, in which case expectancy wave patterns develop in response to the suggestions made by the experimenter, rather than to objective reality. Social factors such as tone of voice and the actual gestures and words used by the experimenter may even be as effective as objective associations between stimuli in the development of the CNV in young adults, particularly when they are studied in the group situation (Grey Walter, 1973).

The reliable appearance of expectancy wave phenomena in the maturing prefrontal cortex seems to indicate that the neurophysiological and biochemical machinery that allow one to integrate disparate information (sensory and otherwise) arising from both external (within the environment) and internal sources (within the organism) in *anticipation* of taking some organized, relevant action in both the immediate and distant future is finally in place and is beginning to become a more conspicuous aspect of the individual's behavior.

Of interest here is research suggesting that ADHD children do not benefit from warning stimuli that signal immediately forthcoming events designed to aid in task performance (e.g., Douglas, 1983). This finding is consistent with the more general finding that the capacity for anticipation is fully matured only later in ontogeny; nevertheless, in comparison to normal controls, it suggests that, in ADHD children, even the early vestiges of this capacity may be developmentally delayed. Furthermore, given the continuing difficulties with anticipatory responding that many ADHD adults have, one must question whether those with extreme symptoms ever develop the mature adult CNV. Certainly, the study of expectancy wave phenomena in ADHD adults is an area worth exploring.

Based on his work with patients with local lesions of the frontal lobes, Luria (1973, 1980) identified four basic functions played by the frontal cortex in goal-directed behavior. The first is that of regulating the state of arousal depending upon the task to be accomplished. Patients with lesions of the medial or basal portions of the frontal lobes were said to exhibit the most profound disruptions in this function. Such patients rarely exhibited any obvious sensory, motor, or cognitive deficits; rather, they were easily and quickly fatigued, and their performance was carried out in a behavioral state closely resembling stupor.

The second important function is motivational in nature and involves the formation of plans that are strong enough to withstand the influence of distracting, irrelevant stimuli. A disturbance of this function was found to be most apparent in patients with lesions in the medial portions of the frontal lobes. Although such patients retained the intention to complete a given task, involuntary orienting reactions to irrelevant stimuli made the actual achievement of the task unlikely.

A third important function identified by Luria involves the conscious verification of ongoing, goal-directed behavior: ascertaining that progress toward a predetermined goal has been made and ultimately that the goal itself has been achieved. Anokhin (cited in Luria, 1973) first described this feedback mechanism as the action-acceptor function, and numerous investigations both in monkeys (Pribram, 1961) and humans have confirmed that the most complex forms of "action acceptor" are subserved by the frontal cortex. In the performance of even simple intellectual tasks, patients with extensive bilateral lesions of the medial portions of the frontal lobes failed to notice their mistakes and were therefore unable to correct them. Although the assigned task was frequently retained in memory, the lack of an internal, self-regulating feedback mechanism made the successful execution of the task impossible (Luria, 1973, 1980).

■ THE FRONTAL CORTEX AND THE CONTROL OF EMOTIONAL BEHAVIOR

The fourth critical function subserved by the frontal cortex is control over what Luria (1973) called the "inclinations and emotions." Patients with lesions of the mediobasal portions of the frontal cortex reportedly exhibited the most profound changes in affective states (Luria, 1973). Such changes were characterized by a generalized lack of self-control, leading to extremes in the expression of feeling—from complete indifference, on the one hand, to expressions that were highly charged and dramatic in quality (e.g., rage). According to Luria, the uncontrollable impulsiveness and disinhibition of thought processes reflective of this generalized loss of self-control precluded the execution of any organized, planned intellectual activity.

As previously indicated, the mediobasal portions of the frontal cortex are richly connected to thalamic, limbic, and reticular structures. Superimposed over these phylogenetically ancient structures of the brain, the frontal cortex not surprisingly has an important role to play—not only in general arousal and more complex forms of voluntary attention and goal-directed behavior—but also in the control of emotion.

Research suggests that the prefrontal cortex, in association with the dorsome-dial nucleus of the thalamus, which relays emotional information to the frontal cortex, forms a critical functional unit in the performance of goal-oriented, delayed-response tasks (e.g., see Fuster, 1973). And work by Porrino and coworkers suggests that this nucleus may form part of the brain reward circuitry (Porrino, Esposito, et al., 1984). Thus, information conveyed to the prefrontal cortex via its connections with this nucleus may provide essential motivational information, which, in the mature organism, is then placed in the service of the plans and intentions of the individual, in line with the goal to be achieved. Naturally, such emotional control is not an immediate aspect of the behavior of the young child, whose emotions are more readily available for expression. In line with Luria's thinking, this higher form of control evolves out of and is initially dependent upon the functional integrity and maturation of brain structures laid down early in phylogeny (e.g., limbic structures and associated reward and punishment pathways), becoming a more consistent, salient aspect of behavior only later in ontogeny.

In summary then, any purposeful goal-directed activity requires the participation of a number of brain structures, all working in concert, with each structure making a unique contribution (Luria, 1973). The reticular formation of the brain and associated cortical and subcortical structures provide the necessary cortical tone and energy; the limbic system (especially the reward and punishment systems) provides the meaning or relative importance; and the frontal cortex subserves an executive function, controlling and recruiting subcortical structures of the brain and brain stem as well as other areas of the cortex as it guides behavior toward completion. Throughout, the influence of the environment is felt, providing the organism with the necessary stimulation (e.g., sensory, emotional, social, cultural) and reinforcement it needs for development to take its normal course.

■ ADHD AND FRONTAL LOBE DYSFUNCTION

Considering the importance of the frontal cortex—especially prefrontal regions—in voluntary attention and goal-directed behavior, as well as in self-regulation and the control of emotion, areas of functioning that have long been recognized as problematic in ADHD individuals, it is not surprising that interest in the frontal cortex as a possible etiological factor has increased over the last several years. Although an early review of the literature (see Barkley, Grodzinsky, & DuPaul, 1992) revealed marked inconsistencies and inconclusive findings with respect to this notion, techniques have been refined, research has intensified, and the latest evidence is strongly supportive of this view. Some of the most recent findings are presented below.

To evaluate the appropriateness of the idea of frontal lobe dysfunction as a potential factor in the etiology of ADHD, Shue and Douglas (1992) administered two batteries of neuropsychological tests to a group of ADHD children ($N = 24$) and a matched group of normal controls ($N = 24$). One battery was sensitive to deficits in frontal lobe functioning, and the other to deficits in memory associated with temporal lobe functioning. In comparison to normal controls, ADHD children differed significantly on measures of frontal lobe functioning, but not on tests measuring temporal lobe functioning. More specifically, ADHD children appeared to be delayed in the development of skills, that is, motor control and problem solving, associated with frontal lobe functioning—performing more like 6- to 7-year-olds, despite a minimum age of 8 and a mean age of 10.

More recently, ADHD patients ($N = 10$) were found to have less activity in the left frontal and left parietal regions of the brain than a control group consisting of non-ADHD psychiatric patients ($N = 6$), as measured by single-photon, emission-computed tomography (SPECT) (Sieg, Gaffney, Preston, & Hellings, 1995). On the other hand, activity in the temporal regions of the brain was similar between groups.

Finally, in the largest and most comprehensive brain imaging study carried out to date using magnetic resonance imaging (MRI), Rapoport and coworkers have provided the strongest morphological evidence for frontal lobe involvement, particularly the prefrontal region in association with the nuclear complexes of the basal ganglia (Castellanos et al., 1996). More specifically, ADHD children ages 5 to 18 ($N = 57$) were distinguished from a matched group of normal, healthy controls ($N = 55$) by the following: a significant loss of the normal right > left asymmetry in the caudate nucleus, a smaller right globus pallidus, a smaller right prefrontal region, a smaller right cerebellum, and a reversal of the normal lateral ventricular asymmetry. A similar MRI study using ADHD girls is currently under way.

3

Temperament and Psychic Illness

Relevance of Temperament to the Model

■ **ADHD: AN EXTREME OF A TEMPERAMENT CONTINUUM?**

We know that much of brain development is dependent upon environmental stimulation. Although there is still some debate regarding the relative importance of nature versus nurture, most psychologists would agree that behavior is a result of an interaction between the genetic or inherited qualities of the brain and the demands placed on the organism over the course of development as a result of interacting with the environment. In this sense, the development of ADHD symptomatology can be seen as an interaction between the fundamental (innate) temperament of the child and the stimulation forthcoming from the environment as represented by parents, teachers, and significant others, as well as the cultural milieu into which the child is born.

For example, it is well-known that ADHD children condition with difficulty; compared to normal children, the anticipation of rewards and punishments plays little part as a motivator of their behavior. Assuming that the capacity to be conditioned is a fundamental (inherited) quality of the human nervous system, a trait we share in common with other species, one might logically conclude that there is some degree of variability among individual members of the species— and between species as well—in their responsiveness to the conditioning process. To the extent that effects of conditioning are dependent upon the functional integrity of the reward and punishment systems of the brain, one might further speculate that individuals are born with a varying capacity for imprinting feelings of psychic pain and psychic pleasure. Assuming that this capacity could be measured in the population as a whole and the data treated statistically, this variability might well take the form of a normal distribution curve, with most individuals falling somewhere in the middle—having an average or "normal" capacity—and a small percentage of individuals falling at either extreme—having too much or too little capacity.

Depending on how close we might be to either end of the continuum, we might well imprint the feeling component of experience, that is, psychic pain or psychic pleasure, too readily or conversely, with great difficulty. In the first instance, even liminal stimulation of the reward and punishment systems of the brain would lead to their full-blown excitation, stamping events, objects, and people with too much meaning, so to speak. Moreover, if rewards and punishments do act via an expectancy mechanism, as hypothesized by Stein (1964) and elaborated by us, past events and associated feeling tones would weigh heavily as determinants of the ongoing behavior of such individuals. Having a highly developed expectancy reflex, they would tend to be overly cautious in committing word or deed to behavior, always testing the waters in anticipation of the possible consequences of their actions. Already overly sensitive to the feeling tones attached to their behavior by parents and other authority figures, children of this temperament would require almost no discipline; that is, even a mild disapproving glance would have the desired effect on behavior.

Such individuals may be said to possess a deep reservoir of psychic feeling underlying approach versus avoidance responses—the yes versus no decisions of everyday life. At times, this reservoir may be so filled to capacity that the individual becomes stuck or mired in the feelings so to speak, making movement increasingly difficult. To find some relief from this heavy processing (burden) of psychic feeling, this type of individual may seek to withdraw from the banquet of social experience from time to time. In the extreme case, the emotional coloration of experience may be so great that loss of contact with reality occurs. With persistent high-intensity stimulation of these areas over time, one can see how perceptual disturbances might develop (e.g., auditory hallucinations) and how thinking might become delusional (e.g., paranoid ideation). Such delusional thinking arises out of the individual's need to make sense out of—to give a reason for—the feelings he or she is experiencing. Although such rationalizations don't fit the reality of the situation, the underlying feelings that they are based on are real.

At the opposite end of the continuum, we would have the complement of this temperament—children in whom even strong stimulation of the reward and punishment systems of the brain produces only liminal excitation, with little or no attachment of feeling tone to experience. In this case, objects remain objects (e.g., a rose is a rose is a rose), and events remain events rather than rich, meaningful experiences, that is, memories complexed with psychic feeling. The inner life of such children may be said to be cold and empty indeed; the reservoir of psychic feeling, shallow. Unable to draw on a meaningful past to determine behavior in the present, such children are at the mercy of the immediate stimuli impinging from within and from without. Unlike their naturally cautious complement, children of this temperament would tend to speak and act without thinking—to barge full steam ahead—with little or no concern for the fitness of their actions. For this type of child, appreciation of feeling consequences arises from the doing, not beforehand. And with only liminal imprinting of psychic feeling associated with ongoing activity, the tendency to repeat the same mistakes over and over again would exist. Such children would be extremely dependent on external authority for behavioral control.

In its extreme form, the picture presented is that of active ADHD children as previously described. Already insensitive, relatively speaking, to the positive and negative feedback of parents and others, this type of individual would require much supervision and discipline. Those factors known to be important in the formation of conditioned responses now take on new meaning when one considers the discipline (socialization) and enculturation of children with this temperament. Immediate reinforcement, for example, becomes a crucial part of the process, ensuring that the feeling component of experience is appropriately attached to the concomitant behavior. Any delay of reinforcement for children who live largely in the world of the present moment (that is, have a poorly developed expectancy reflex) might lead to the attachment of feeling tone to the wrong behavior. Similarly, repetition and consistency become important components of the process. A consistent and constant (enduring stability in terms of place and parental attitude) environment would naturally be expected to facilitate learning and the process of socialization and enculturation. Failure to provide such an environment would tend to keep children at an infantile level of development, both emotionally and socially.

Furthermore, those medications that are known to enhance the activity of the reward and punishment systems of the brain become an especially important treatment consideration, as they may lower the thresholds for stimulating these systems, thereby enhancing the effectiveness of conditioning by facilitating the attachment of psychic feeling tone to behavior, events, and people. Conversely, those medications (e.g., neuroleptics) that reduce the activity of these systems would be expected to provide some relief from the symptoms suffered by those who represent the extreme complement of this temperament by ensuring a more usual intensity of activation of these systems in response to external and internal stimulation.

Before leaving this section, we would like to share our thoughts regarding the temperaments of those falling more toward the middle of the hypothesized continuum. We have proposed the existence of two more balanced types where the tendencies seen in the two extremes would still exist, but in milder form, and where behavior would be adaptive. It is possible that these two more milder forms require the mellowing influence of age and experience, which in turn implies that there may be only two fundamental types. (If so this would also suggest that a bimodal distribution might be a more accurate mathematical representation of the variable of temperament, rather than the normal distribution curve.) This mellowing might happen early in childhood through the idealized positive influences of the parents, as well as the social and cultural influences that pervade the child's early milieu, or much later in development, after a lengthy and perhaps very difficult conditioning history extending well into adulthood.

■ AN ANCIENT CONCEPT
WITH ENDURING SIGNIFICANCE

The question of temperament has a long and colorful history, dating back to ancient times, when personality was thought to be an emergent property of the four ancient bodily humors (see Table 3.1). Depending upon the relative proportions of these fluids within the body, individuals were said to possess a choleric, melancholic, sanguine, or phlegmatic nature. The choleric individual was characterized by a pugnacious, passionate, and irritable nature—all due to an excess of yellow bile. An excess of black bile was said to be responsible for the sad, dejected, and pessimistic nature of the melancholic; an excess of blood, for the confident, optimistic, and energetic nature of the sanguine. And the slow, calm, and deliberate nature of the phlegmatic type was thought to arise from a preponderance of phlegm. Although we now know that temperament isn't rooted in blood, or bile, or phlegm, we still don't know what makes one individual naturally more quiet and shy, and another more lively and uninhibited. And although natural differences in temperament are still commonly perceived and acknowledged, especially among mothers and other caretakers of the young, the idea of temperament has yet to be widely accepted by the scientific community.

Translating a concept such as temperament into objective terminology so it can be quantified and measured is difficult. Some important piece of information is always lost in the translation. But in the world of science where logic and reason predominate, concepts frequently have to be proven in the statistical sense

TABLE 3.1 Ancient Temperament Types

Type	Characteristics	Excess Bodily Humor
Melancholic	Sad, dejected, pessimistic	Black bile
Choleric	Pugnacious, passionate, irritable	Yellow bile
Phlegmatic	Slow, calm, deliberate	Phlegm
Sanguine	Confident, optimistic, energetic	Blood

before they are accepted as valid. With so-called psychical concepts such as temperament, the task can be formidable, for even in the "objective" world of science, antiquated attitudes and prejudices exist that make the resolution of this question difficult. For ages, mind and matter were thought of as separate entities, and temperament, which was considered to be a purely mental or psychical phenomenon, wasn't considered a proper pursuit for scientists studying "real" events in the natural, physical world. This belief severely restricted the disciplines and tools that were brought to bear on the study of personality. Today, many psychologists still believe that the human psyche can be separated from the living tissue it is embedded in—exempt from the laws governing the natural, physical world. Vestiges of this mind/body dualism can even be found among those of us who work in the neurosciences and are more accustomed to thinking about behavior from the perspective of brain function. But slowly all of us in the broad field of human psychology—clinicians, behaviorists, and neuroscientists alike—are being pushed, begrudgingly at times, to the realization that every so-called mental or psychic phenomenon, including human temperament, has its material basis in the living tissue of the brain.

Identifying the biological underpinnings of temperament will not be easy. Scientists must first agree on how temperament should be defined. For us, temperament has come to mean that quality of the mammalian brain—conserved over the course of evolution—which forms the physiological basis for our ability to benefit from the effects of conditioning, that is, to attach meaning to the people, ideas, objects, and events in our lives—to color, imprint, or complex them with feelings of psychic pain and psychic pleasure. Moreover, there appear to be inborn differences in this capacity, which are observable from birth but may be modified to some degree by nurture, and by certain psychotropic medications that alter the neurochemistry and therefore the functional activity of those brain structures involved. In the global sense, temperament can be seen as the emotional template upon which all of the activity of the individual is superimposed. Reading that template will be difficult and will require the skills and techniques of the molecular scientist and the behavioral geneticist.

■ THE EARLY CONTRIBUTIONS
OF IVAN PAVLOV

The first to demonstrate that temperament could be studied objectively in the laboratory and understood as an emergent property of the central nervous system was the Russian physiologist, Ivan Pavlov. Pavlov's interest in temperament developed during the course of his work on the simple conditioned reflexes in dogs. More specifically, Pavlov (1928) was impressed by how seemingly natural differences in the demeanor or constitution of his subjects away from the laboratory seemed to predict how they would respond in the experimental situation. Dogs that were naturally "shy and cautious" in their usual surroundings, for example, adapted very slowly to the experimental procedures but, once adjusted, performed "like a perfect machine." "Especially notable is the stability of the inhibitory conditioned reflexes—when conditioned agents call forth not the process of excitation but of inhibition" (p. 364). This inhibition was said to be so extreme that the slightest change in the experimental surroundings prevented the conditioned response from occurring; that is, not one drop of saliva could be measured even in the presence of a well-established conditioned stimulus.

Away from the laboratory, the natural timidity and cautiousness of this type of dog necessitated a gentle approach to discipline, for at the slightest threatening look or gesture, the animal would "slink off as if from dangerous enemies" (Pavlov, 1928, p. 364). Pavlov called these animals specialists in inhibition because it appeared that the inhibitory capacities of the nervous system governed their general behavior.

At the opposite pole were dogs that were highly excitable as well as aggressive around humans. In contrast to the inhibitory type, dogs exhibiting this natural excitability and aggressive nature required a firm approach to discipline, for threatening looks or gestures were without effect. In the laboratory situation, these animals were said to have extreme difficulty inhibiting the conditioned response in the presence of extraneous stimuli; that is, although salivation may have been greatest in the presence of the conditioned stimulus, there was always some measurable amount of saliva in response to stimuli that had never been paired with food. Pavlov (1928) called these animals specialists in excitation because it appeared that the excitatory capacities of the nervous system predominated.

Between these two extremes stood two balanced or whole types—animals in which the processes of excitation and inhibition were said to be "constantly active and in equilibrium" (Pavlov, 1928, p. 375). Yet despite such seeming inner harmony, the external demeanor of these two balanced types was very different. Away from the laboratory, one was said to be quiet, sedate, and self-contained, "peculiarly indifferent to external happenings, but always on the alert" (p. 390); the other to be "very lively and active, running here and there, sniffing at

TABLE 3.2 Pavlov's Temperament Types

Type	Characteristics	Dominant Cortical Process
Inhibitory	Timid, cowardly, cautious	Inhibition
Excitatory	Stimulus seeking, easily irritated, aggressive	Excitation
Balanced	Type I: active, lively, curious	Both processes
	Type II: quiet, self-contained, sedate	in equilibrium

everything" (p. 376), but quickly falling asleep in the absence of stimulating conditions. In the experimental situation, these two well-balanced types were reportedly distinguished by the following: In the quiet type, the delicate switching from excitation to inhibition was accomplished with relative ease, allowing a conditioned reflex, once formed, to remain stable, that is, to be consistently manifested under certain experimental conditions and consistently inhibited under others. In the lively type, this delicate balancing of the processes of excitation and inhibition was accomplished with some difficulty, "just avoiding pathological breakdown" (p. 375). Pavlov's temperament types, along with their defining characteristics, are presented in Table 3.2.

The pathological breakdowns referred to in the previous paragraph were characterized by Pavlov (1928) as "nervous breakdowns," analogous to the nervous breakdowns or neuroses seen in humans. Such "breakdowns" could be experimentally induced in his extreme types under the following experimental conditions: presenting a well-established conditioned stimulus and a stimulus differing only slightly from it in rapid succession. To perform successfully, the animal would have to manifest the conditioned response one moment and inhibit it the very next. Pavlov found that after one or more trials of this procedure, "the dog becomes ill" (p. 375). In the excitatory type, conditioned inhibition proved to be impossible—the animal could not refrain from salivating to the extraneous stimulus. In the inhibitory type, conditioned inhibition prevailed—the animal did not salivate in response to either stimulus.

Pavlov (1928) considered these disturbances to be serious illnesses, continuing sometimes for months, and ones for which treatment was necessary. The "curative measures" used to restore these dogs to their previous level of functioning differed depending on the temperament type. For the inhibitory type, there was often "no other cure than to let them rest for five or six months or even more from the experiments" (p. 375). For the excitatory type, Pavlov found "bromides and calcium salts very useful; in a week or two the animals return to normal" (p. 375). Thus it became apparent that dogs of the opposite temperament subjected to one and the same experience developed "diseases of the opposite nature." This same experimental procedure, when applied to the two central or equilibrated types, was reportedly without effect; the animals "remain healthy."

Pressed by his observations and experimental findings, Pavlov (1928) concluded that temperament "is the most fundamental characteristic of the nervous system, a characteristic which colors and pervades all the activities of every individual" (p. 390). More specifically, Pavlov saw temperament as an emergent property of the cerebral cortex which, in his view, was the only organ in the brain that could possibly subserve, in the executive sense, the formation of the conditioned reflexes.

Extrapolating to the behavior of higher organisms, Pavlov (1928) concluded that analogous temperaments existed in humans—temperaments much like those observed in his dogs and similar to those proposed by Hippocrates, but whose origins could be found, not in blood or bile or phlegm, but rather in the delicate relations between the cortical processes of excitation and inhibition. The melancholic—seeing only the dark side of life and expecting the worst—was equivalent to his inhibitory type of dog; the choleric—hot-tempered and combative—to his excitatory type. And "in the golden middle" stood the phlegmatic and sanguine types, "well-equilibrated and therefore healthy, stable, and real living nervous types, no matter how different or contrasted the representatives of these types may seem outwardly" (p. 377). Pavlov hypothesized further that there were separate excitatory and inhibitory substances underlying these opposing processes of excitation and inhibition. This speculation was indeed far-sighted, considering what we now know about neurotransmitters and brain function.

In his closing years, just prior to his death in 1936, Pavlov began to apply his experimental findings and conditioning principles to the field of psychiatry. He spent long hours visiting and observing patients committed to local mental hospitals, and even made suggestions for particular "pharmaceutical remedies." Had he been alive to witness the advent of modern psychotropic medicines, we wonder what pharmaceutical remedies he might have used with his dogs. When one considers the symptom profile of Pavlov's excitable type, one can't help but see analogous symptoms in the ADHD child, for example, the natural excitability, the high activity level, the extreme difficulty with inhibition and self-control, the relative insensitivity to discipline resulting in the need for a firm hand. Had Pavlov observed any of these children during his day, would he have been tempted to recommend bromides? Certainly, if he were alive today, he would have taken satisfaction in the knowledge that certain excitable "hyperactive" dogs, for example, the Telomian-beagle hybrid, are calmed by the same pharmaceutical remedy, d-amphetamine, that calms the symptoms of hyperactivity in humans (Arnold, Kirilcuk, Corson, & Corson, 1973; Bareggi, Becker, Ginsburg, & Genovese, 1979a, 1979b).

Like Pavlov, we have come to view temperament as an essential property of the central nervous system—a property that colors and pervades all of the activity of the individual organism—whether human or animal. Moreover, like Pavlov, we think that the origins of psychic illness can be found in the delicate interplay of temperament with environment. But in contrast to Pavlov, we believe the origins of temperament lie, not in highest levels of the cerebral cortex, but rather in the deeper, more medial areas of the brain, or more specifically, in the reward and punishment systems of the brain. Assuming, as we have, that there are natural, heritable variations in these systems—variations that may provide the topography or form of temperament—we were eager to review the published research in the field of genetics. Specifically, we were curious to see if any genetically associated variations in these systems had been identified. Among the work that caught our attention was the research of Donald Reis and colleagues of Cornell University and Dwight German and colleagues of the University of Texas Southwestern Medical Center. This and related work is summarized below.

■ **TEMPERAMENT, GENETICS,
AND BRAIN DOPAMINE SYSTEMS**

Some of the information that follows is rather technical. Readers may wish to move to the concluding paragraphs of this subsection.

In the mid 1970s, Reis and coworkers began investigating the cellular mechanisms underlying the newly discovered finding by Ciaranello, Barchas, Kessler, and Barchas (1972) of genetically linked differences in whole brain tyrosine hydroxylase (TH) activity in inbred strains of mice. More specifically, mice of the BALB/cJ strain had been found to exhibit significantly greater whole brain TH activity than mice of the CBA/J strain. Reis and colleagues first tried to determine if this difference was restricted to DA neurons, or if this was also characteristic of NE neurons (e.g., locus coeruleus) (Reis, Baker, Fink, & Joh, 1979; Ross, Judd, Pickel, Joh, & Reis, 1976).

As illustrated in Table 3.3, the higher TH activity of BALB/cJ mice was found to be restricted to DA cell groups (e.g., substantia nigra, VTA) and their terminal regions (e.g., striatum, n. accumbens, olfactory tubercle), with all dopaminergic systems being comparably affected. That this was a specific property of dopaminergic, and not noradrenergic, neurons was further supported by the finding that the activity of dopamine-beta-hydroxylase, the enzyme that converts DA to NE in noradrenergic neurons, did not differ between the two strains in either locus coeruleus or hypothalamus (Ross et al., 1976).

Obviously, such differences in TH activity could result from variations in the amount of enzyme, or from differences in the catalytic activity of the enzyme

TABLE 3.3 Regional Tyrosine Hydroxylase (TH) in Brain of BALB/cJ
and CBA/J Mice

			Strain			
Area	*BALB/cJ*	*n*	*CBA/J*	*n*	*CBA/BALB*	*p*
Substantia nigra-A10	3.98 ± 0.07	32	3.19 ± 0.04	32	0.80	<0.001
A9	6.28 ± 0.89	6	3.60 ± 0.47	6	0.57	<0.05
A10	17.76 ± 1.89	5	9.96 ± 1.01	6	0.56	<0.01
Corpus striatum	12.49 ± 0.39	30	10.31 ± 0.21	30	0.82	<0.001
Nucleus accumbens	4.43 ± 0.29	6	3.66 ± 0.18	5	0.83	<0.01
Olfactory tubercle	3.48 ± 0.13	6	2.56 ± 0.37	5	0.74	<0.05
Hypothalamus	2.67 ± 0.07	5	1.58 ± 0.02	5	0.59	<0.001
Olfactory bulb	15.41 ± 0.64	8	10.47 ± 0.34	8	0.68	<0.001
Retina	.766 ± 0.04	8	.313 ± 0.01	8	0.41	<0.001
Locus ceruleus	12.4 ± 3.3	5	10.9 ± 2.0	5	0.88	NS

Source: Reis et al. (1981), in *Genetic Research Strategies in Psychobiology and Psychiatry,* edited by E. S.
Gershon, S. Matthysse, X. O. Breakefield, & R. D. Ciaranello. Reprinted by permission of Boxwood Press.
Note: TH activity was expressed as nmole/dopa/substantia nigra/hour for the substantia nigra and as
nmole/dopa/mg/protein/hour for all other brain areas.

molecule. Reis and his group were able to establish that the observed differences
were due to differences in the amount of enzyme protein; the catalytic activity
per neuron was equal between strains (Ross et al., 1976) (see Table 3.4). Later
work determined that strain-dependent differences in the amount of enzyme
protein were entirely accounted for by genetically related variations in the
number of DA neurons, with mice of the BALB/cJ strain having between 20%
and 25% more TH-staining neurons in substantia nigra-VTA regions than mice
of the CBA/J strain (Baker, Joh, & Reis, 1980). Moreover, these differences in
neuronal number were found to be restricted to the most medial parts of these
regions (see Figure 3.1).

Strain-dependent differences in the number of DA neurons were subsequently
found to be widespread throughout the brain, involving, for example, the A12
group of the arcuate nucleus, the A13 group of the zona incerta, and the A14
group of the preoptic region (Reis, Fink, & Baker, 1983) (see Table 3.5). In these
cell groups, differences of 49% to 74% were observed (Baker, Joh, Ruggiero,
& Reis, 1983).

Interestingly, strain-dependent differences in DA neuronal number were also
found to be correlated with differences in the size of the target organs (e.g., mice

TABLE 3.4 Number of Neurons Stained for Tyrosine Hydroxylase (TH) and Their Estimated Enzyme Activity in Substantia Nigra-A 10 Regions of BALB/cJ and CBA/J Mice

	BALB/cJ	n	CBA/J	n	CBA/BALB	p
Number of neurons	$7,849 \pm 487$	6	223 ± 151	5	0.79	<0.01
TH activity	3.98 ± 0.07	32	3.19 ± 0.04	32	0.80	<0.001
TH activity/ neuron (nmole dopa/hour/ neuron $\times 10^4$)	5.07		5.13		0.99	NS

Source: Reis et al. (1981), in *Genetic Research Strategies in Psychology and Psychiatry,* edited by E. S. Gershon, S. Matthysse. X.O. Breakfield, & R. D. Ciaranello. Reprinted by permission of Boxwood Press.

of the BALB/cJ strain have a significantly larger striatum) innervated by substantia nigra-VTA regions (e.g., Fink & Reis, 1981). Yet despite the larger striatum of BALB/cJ mice, there was apparently no difference between strains in the number of midbrain neurons innervating a given unit of striatal tissue, suggesting that the organization of the infrastructure of the striatum is the same in both strains. Thus, in both BALB/cJ and CBA/J mice, 1 mm^3 of striatum receives input from approximately 800 midbrain DA cells (Mattiace, Baring, Manaye, Mihailoff, & German, 1989).

The discovery of such widespread differences in brain between BALB/cJ and CBA/J mice in DA neuronal number and TH activity raised obvious questions about how these two strains might differ in the physiological and behavior processes known to be mediated by DA systems. One of the most widely studied and well-understood physiological processes regulated by DA is the synthesis and secretion of prolactin in the pituitary. Specifically, DA release from hypothalamic neurons of the arcuate nucleus (A12 group)—the origin of the tuberoinfundibular DA system—functions to inhibit prolactin synthesis (Maurer, 1980) and secretion (Gudelsky, 1981). As predicted from the difference in DA neuronal number in the arcuate nucleus, Reis and colleagues found that BALB/cJ mice had greater TH activity in hypothalamus and significantly less serum and pituitary prolactin than CBA/J mice (Sved, Baker, & Reis, 1985). Consistent with this finding, the number of prolactin-staining cells in the pituitary, as determined by standard immunocytochemistry, was also greater in CBA/J versus BALB/cJ mice (Baker, Sved, Tucker, Alden, & Reis, 1985).

As expected, Reis and colleagues also found strain-dependent differences in DA cell number and TH activity to be accompanied by differences in both the naturalistic and drug-induced behaviors known to be mediated—in large part— by DA systems of the midbrain (Fink & Reis, 1981; Fink, Swerdloff, Joh, &

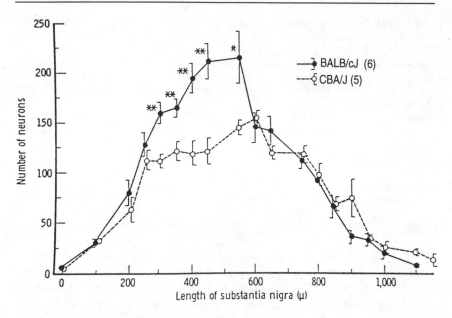

Figure 3.1: Strain-Dependent Differences in Neuronal Number in the Ventral Tegmentum (Including Substantia Nigra-A10 and A8 Regions) of BALB/cJ and CBA/J Mice. The most rostral section containing immunocytochemically stained tyrosine hydroxylase neurons is indicated as 0 μ. As shown, strain-dependent differences were restricted to the mid-regions of the ventral tegmentum from 200-600 μ.
Source: Baker, Joh, & Reis (1980). Reprinted by permission of D. J. Reis.
*$p < 0.05$; **$p < 0.01$.

Reis, 1979; Reis et al., 1979, 1983). More specifically, BALB/cJ mice were found to be more sensitive to the effects of DA agonists (d-amphetamine) and antagonists (neuroleptics) than CBA/J mice (Reis et al., 1983). Under low doses of amphetamine (< 5 mg/kg), for example, mice of the BALB/cJ strain exhibited both a lower threshold for the locomotor-stimulating effects of this drug and a greater magnitude of amphetamine-induced motor activity than mice of the CBA/J strain. BALB/cJ mice also exhibited a lower threshold for the induction of stereotyped behaviors (e.g., sniffing, grooming, and gnawing) associated with higher doses of amphetamine, as well as more intense stereotypy over the entire range of tested doses (5 to 20 mg/kg) than did CBA/J mice.

The greater magnitude of amphetamine-induced behaviors in BALB/cJ mice was paralleled by a greater magnitude of spontaneous behaviors known to be mediated by midbrain DA systems. Thus BALB/cJ mice exhibited more intense exploratory behavior, as well as more intense spontaneous motor activity in the

TABLE 3.5 Number of Neurons Stained for Tyrosine Hydroxylase (TH) and Their Estimated Enzyme Activity in Brain Regions of BALB/cJ and CBA/J Mice

	BALB/cJ	n	CBA/J	n	CBA/BALB	p
Substantia nigra (A10)						
Number of neurons	7,849 ± 487	6	6,223 ± 151	5	0.79	<0.01
TH activity	3.98 ± 0.07	32	3.19 ± 0.04	32	0.80	<0.001
TH activity/ neuron (nmole dopa/hr/neuron × 10^{-4})	5.07		5.13		0.99	ns
Locus ceruleus						
Number of neurons	780 ± 6	4	774 ± 26	4	0.99	ns
TH activity	12.4 ± 3.3	5	10.9 ± 2.0	5	0.88	ns
TH activity/ neuron (× 10^{2})	1.58		1.41		0.89	ns
Hypothalamus						
Number of neurons	6,607 ± 400	6	4,451 ± 313	5	0.67	<0.002
TH activity	0.59 ± 0.03	5	0.365 ± 0.02	5	0.62	<0.001
TH activity/ neuron (× 10^{4})	0.892		0.820		0.92	ns
ZI and posterior periventricular nucleus						
Number of neurons	3,257 ± 237	5	2,008 ± 141	6	0.62	<0.002
TH activity	0.47 ± 0.021	8	0.307 ± 0.014	8	0.65	<0.001
TH activity/ neuron (× 10^{4})	1.443		1.528		1.06	ns
Arcuate nucleus (A12)						
Number of neurons	3,621 ± 265	5	2,695 ± 151	6	0.74	<0.002
TH activity	0.274 ± 0.010	8	0.141 ± 0.006	8	0.51	<0.001
TH activity/ neuron (× 10^{4})	0.757		0.523		0.69	ns
Preoptic region (A14)						
Number of neurons	3,949 ± 338	6	1,929 ± 175	5	0.49	<0.002
TH activity	0.189 ± 0.015	8	0.104 ± 0.008	8	0.55	<0.001
TH activity/ neuron (× 10^{4})	0.479		0.539		1.12	ns

Source: D. J. Reis, S. J. Fink, & H. Baker, H. (1983), "Genetic Control of the Number of Dopamine Neurons in the Brain: Relationship to Behavior and Response to Psychoactive Drugs," in S. S. Kety, L. P. Rowland, R. L. Sidman, & S. W. Matthysse (Eds.), *Genetics of Neurological and Psychiatric Disorders* (pp. 55-75). Reprinted by permission of Raven Press.

TABLE 3.6 Dopamine-Mediated Drug-Induced and Spontaneous Behaviors in
BALB/cJ and CBA/J Mice

Drug-induced behavior	n	Strain		p
		BALB/cJ	CBA/J	
D-Amphetamine				
Locomotion				
(squares crossed,				
3.5 mg/kg)	10	326 ± 52	110 ± 40	<0.001
Stereotypy score (7.5 mg/kg)	10	16.0	7.5	<0.050
Spiroperidol				
Catalepsy scores				
(second/300-minute				
test, 1 mg/kg)	10	849 ± 239	131 ± 85	<0.05
Haloperidol				
Catalepsy scores (second/				
300-minute test, 4 mg/kg)	10	755 ± 292	39 ± 26	<0.05
Spontaneous behaviors				
Exploration				
Approaches to object	10	8.6 ± 1.80	2.6 ± 0.8	<0.001
Duration of investigation				
(seconds)	10	10.3 ± 1.9	5.2 ± 1.9	<0.01
Activity				
Locomotion (squares crossed)	20	55 ± 5	32 ± 4	<0.01
Rears	20	15 ± 2	6 ± 5	<0.001

Source: Reis et al. (1981), in *Genetic Research Strategies in Psychobiology and Psychiatry,* edited by E. S.
Gershon, S. Matthysse, X. O. Breakefield, & R. D. Ciaranello. Reprinted by permission of Boxwood Press.
Note: Data are presented as mean ± SEM except for the stereotypy scores, which are expressed as medians.

test chamber as compared to CBA/J mice (Reis, Baker, Fink, & Joh, 1981; Reis
et al., 1983) (see Table 3.6). And consistent with the greater sensitivity of
BALB/cJ vs CBA/J mice to d-amphetamine, the magnitude of the catalepsy
induced by drugs of the neuroleptic class (e.g., haloperidol, spiroperidol) was
significantly greater in BALB/cJ versus CBA/J mice (see Table 3.6).

BALB/cJ mice have also been found to possess a greater number of striatal
D_2 receptors than CBA/J mice (Boehme & Ciaranello, 1981; Helmeste &
Seeman, 1982; Severson, Randall, & Finch, 1981), a finding predicted from the
greater volume of the striatum, and one that is consistent with the greater
magnitude of response to the neuroleptics. The greater number of D_2 receptors
in BALB/cJ mice has also been associated with an amphetamine-induced
hypolocomotion (Helmeste & Seeman, 1982). Interestingly, autoreceptor sensitivity and baseline firing rate of DA neurons of the VTA (A10 group) have

recently been shown to be similar in both strains despite a large difference (BALB/cJ mice have 30% more DA neurons in the VTA) in the number of DA cells (Bernardini, Gu, & German, 1991). This is further evidence suggesting that neuronal number, and not some other factor, for example, DA autoreceptor sensitivity, may underlie the variability between strains in the biochemical and behavioral responses mediated by DA.

Related work by Reis and coworkers established that the strain-dependent differences in DA cell number and TH activity were not present at birth, but rather developed postnatally and, once established, persisted into adulthood (e.g., Baker, Joh, & Reis, 1982; Reis et al., 1983). Furthermore, differences in cell number and TH activity were found to precede rather than to follow the observed differences in spontaneous and drug-induced behaviors, suggesting that the biochemical and cellular events subserve such behavioral differences and are not caused by them. The mechanism accounting for such postnatal differences in DA cell number and TH activity could be either postnatal cell loss, or alternatively, the failure of DA neurons to maintain the phenotypic expression of TH.

In an attempt to differentiate between these two possibilities, Baker and Reis (1986) looked at the development of strain-dependent differences in DA cell number and TH activity in the substantia nigra in the neonate (day 5) versus the adult (day 56). The results showed that in both strains, the number of TH-stained neurons in adults was significantly greater than the number of TH-stained neurons in neonates. This finding essentially ruled out programmed postnatal cell death as a factor, but rather favored the alternative explanation, that is, loss of the phenotypic expression of TH. Loss of the phenotypic expression of TH may, in turn, be related to the observed variability between strains in the size of the target organ (Baker & Reis, 1986). In CBA/J and BALB/cJ mice, the substantia nigra (A9 cell group) makes contact with the striatum at about postnatal day 8, just prior to the time (on postnatal day 9) when strain differences first appear in midbrain TH activity (Baker et al., 1982). Thus CBA/J mice—with a smaller striatum—would have fewer neurons, relative to BALB/cJ mice, expressing the dopaminergic phenotype because CBA/J mice have fewer sites available for synaptic contact.

Alternatively, afferent input from striatum to substantia nigra may be necessary for TH expression. Related work in the olfactory bulb supports this idea. In both mouse and rat species, peripheral deafferentation of the olfactory bulb reportedly results in the loss of TH enzyme in juxtaglomerular DA neurons without any apparent cell death (Baker, Kawano, Margolis, & Joh, 1983). Upon reafferentation, juxtaglomerular neurons express the DA phenotype again, suggesting that DA neurons require such input to induce TH synthesis. Thus, in the absence of environmental input such as afferent stimulation, DA neurons may synthesize another neurotransmitter (Baker & Reis, 1986).

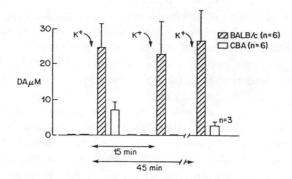

Figure 3.2: Comparison of Striatal K$^+$-Stimulated DA Release in BALB/cJ and CBA/J Mice. As shown, K$^+$-stimulated DA release was greater in BALB/cJ versus CBA/J mice. Note that in BALB/cJ mice, DA release could be evoked every 10 to 15 minutes, whereas in CBA/J mice DA release could not be evoked until 45 minutes after the initial stimulation, and then in only three of six animals.

Source: Reprinted from M. K. Sanghera, F. Crespi, K. F. Martin, D. J. Heal, W. R. Buckett, & C. A. Marsden (1990), "Biochemical and in Vivo Voltammetric Evidence for Differences in Striatal Dopamine Levels in Inbred Strains of Mice," *Neuroscience, 19,* 649-656, with the kind permission of Elsevier Science Ltd., The Boulevard, Langford Lande, Kidlington OX5 1GB, UK.

Other studies were carried out to see if BALB/cJ mice actually synthesize and release more DA than CBA/J mice, as would be predicted by the finding of more DA neurons and greater TH activity in the BALB/cJ strain. The rate of DA synthesis in striatum was assessed using two measures: (1) DOPA accumulation following the inhibition of DOPA decarboxylase, and (2) the rate of decline of DA following synthesis inhibition (Sved, Baker, & Reis, 1984). As expected, the synthesis of DA in striatum was found to be significantly greater in BALB/cJ vs CBA/J mice (e.g., 40 ng/mg protein/hr versus 24 ng/mg protein/hr, respectively). Later work by a different group of researchers demonstrated that not only do BALB/cJ mice synthesize more DA in striatum, they also apparently release more DA than CBA/J mice (Sanghera et al., 1990). Using the technique of in vivo voltammetry, Sanghera et al. measured DA release in the striatum of living animals in response to K$^+$ infusion. As expected, K$^+$-stimulated DA release was found to be significantly greater both in magnitude and frequency in BALB/cJ (*N* = 6) versus CBA/J mice (*N* = 6). In fact, in BALB/cJ mice, DA release could be evoked every 10 to 15 minutes with successive infusions of K$^+$, whereas in CBA/J mice, K$^+$-stimulated release could not be evoked until 45 minutes after the first stimulation, and then in only three of the six animals tested (see Figure 3.2).

The above findings of Sanghera et al. extend the earlier findings of Reis and colleagues by providing evidence in support of the hypothesis that the observed differences in naturalistic behaviors existing between strains—behaviors that are known to be dependent on the integrity of midbrain DA systems for their expression—are related not only to naturally occurring differences in the number of DA neurons, but to naturally occurring differences in *functional,* that is, extracellular, levels of DA.

Taken together, the above research findings suggest a new principle governing the magnitude or variability of behavior—the number of neurons of a particular chemical class. The actual mode of inheritance of differences in DA neuron number and the accompanying behavioral (and physiological) correlates are currently unknown; however, genetic analysis of TH activity in substantia nigra and striatum of the CXB recombinant inbred strains indicated that only a few genes were involved in the observed strain-dependent differences in enzyme activity (Vadasz, Baker, Joh, Lajtha, & Reis, 1982). And although two traits may be associated by chance, the studies summarized above strongly suggest that DA neuronal number and the specific physiological processes, for example, pro-lactin secretion, and spontaneous behavioral responses, for example, locomotor activity, that are known to be mediated by DA systems are controlled by similar genes or gene products. In other words, there is considerable evidence suggesting that these traits cosegregate.

As suggested by Reis and colleagues (e.g., Reis et al., 1983), the existence of genetically determined differences in DA cell number raises intriguing possibilities with respect to expression of diseases that are associated with alterations in DA neurotransmission. For example, could such variations in cell number be one genetic component in schizophrenia, or in Parkinson's disease, or in ADHD, for that matter? It is well-known that the brains of schizophrenics studied at autopsy contain an increased number of D_2 receptors in striatum, n. accumbens, and olfactory tubercule. Using PET, this increase in D_2 receptors has now been demonstrated in living patients who have never been treated with antipsychotic drugs, an indication that the greater number of D_2 receptors is not a secondary effect of drug treatment (Kandel, 1991). Given the evidence suggesting that DA cell number and the number of D_2 receptors may cosegregate, perhaps this would be an important line of investigation in the etiology of ADHD.

From our perspective, an even more intriguing question—a question also raised by Reis and coworkers—is whether variations in cell number subserve the expression of traits collectively referred to as human temperament? Obviously, modern science is just in its infancy with respect to genetic research, especially the work now being conducted at the molecular level. And the discovery of the gene or genes associated with human temperament will no doubt take a back seat to the identification of those genes involved in various disease states. But, just as there is a growing body of evidence that there is a genetic component to diseases such as schizophrenia and ADHD (e.g., Cook et al., 1995; Faraone et al., 1992; Hechtman, 1994; Lombroso, Pauls, & Leckman, 1994;

Stevenson, 1992), for example, there is a growing body of evidence in support of the heritability of human temperament, especially of specific traits such as activity level, excitability (Cloninger, Adolfsson, & Svrakic, 1996), and social introversion versus extroversion (Goldsmith, 1983).

Given the high activity level and excitability of ADHD children, as well as associated problems with impulse control—which may indeed show up in behavior as a more extroverted demeanor—temperament is one factor that could lead to another potentially fruitful line of investigation in the etiology of ADHD. As suggested by the work of Reis and colleagues, a good starting place might be heritable differences in the number of neurons of a particular chemical class, particularly those belonging to the neurotransmitter systems widely thought to play a role in ADHD symptomatology: DA, 5-HT, and NE. Further work in a wide variety of mammalian species could determine whether cell number and the behavioral traits known to be dependent upon the particular neurochemical system in question cosegregate.

Careful studies looking at the morphology (i.e., size and shape) of human brain structures, for example, striatum, n. accumbens, and medial prefrontal cortex, using techniques such as MRI might also provide useful data. Some of this work is already being done (e.g., Castellanos et al., 1994; Hynd et al., 1993; Hynd, Semrud-Clikeman, Lorys, Novey, & Eliopulos, 1990). Attempting to integrate the findings from the MRI studies that have been carried out to date can be difficult, as often they are not directly comparable. In addition to the problems of small sample size and diagnostic inclusion criteria, the anatomic boundaries of the particular target structure in question may vary from one study to the next. For example, some researchers have included only the head of the caudate in their measurements, whereas others (e.g., Castellanos et al., 1996) include both the head and the body of the caudate. As the technology improves and researchers begin to standardize the precise anatomic boundaries to be included in their measurements, the reliability of MRI findings will no doubt improve.

In the largest and most comprehensive morphological MRI study carried out to date, Castellanos et al. (1996) found decreased volume—predominantly on the right side—in several brain structures widely thought to be involved in the pathophysiology of ADHD, for example, prefrontal cortex, caudate nucleus, and globus pallidus. Additional studies along these same lines may reveal further morphological differences between normal controls and ADHD children in regions of the brain thought to play a focal role in ADHD symptomatology. Obviously, it would be important to extend the findings of Castellanos et al. to ADHD girls.

Recently, two independent research groups reported in *Nature Genetics* that they had discovered a link between the dopamine D4 receptor gene and the normally distributed personality trait of novelty seeking (Benjamin et al., 1996; Ebstein et al., 1996). Like other temperament traits that show a considerable

TABLE 3.7 Tridimensional Personality Questionnaire (TPQ) Personality Factor Scores in Subject Groups Sorted by D4DR Allele and Genotype[1]

Subject Group	Novelty Seeking	Reward Dependence	Persistence (RD2)	Harm Avoidance
7 allele absent (n = 90)	15.45 ± 0.47	13.73 ± 0.36	5.02 ± 0.21	12.53 ± 0.61
7 allele present (n = 34)	17.94 ± 1.04[2]	14.06 ± 0.57[4]	5.21 ± 0.35[4]	13.00 ± 1.04[4]
4,4 genotype (n = 70)	15.40 ± 0.55	13.81 ± 0.49	4.91 ± 0.23	12.68 ± 0.64
4,7 genotype (n = 29)	17.89 ± 1.11[3]	13.76 ± 0.59[4]	5.10 ± 0.37[4]	12.89 ± 1.05[4]

Source: Ebstein et al. (1996), p. 78. Reprinted by permission of *Nature Genetics* and R. P. Ebstein.
Note: Mean raw scores for Reward Dependence and Persistence (RD2) have been corrected from original article per correspondence from RP Ebstein.
1. TPQ results are reported as mean raw scores ± SEM.
2. $F = 6.34, p = 0.013$.
3. $F = 5.11, p = 0.026$.
4. $p > 0.05$.

heritable component, novelty seeking can be reliably measured by self-report rating scales such as Cloninger's tridimensional personality questionnaire (TPQ). Individuals who score higher-than-average in this trait are characterized as excitable, impulsive, exploratory, quick-tempered, and extravagant compared to lower-than-average novelty seekers, who tend to be reflective, stoic, cautious, slow-tempered, and frugal.

It has been proposed that individual variations in this trait are mediated by variations in dopamine neurotransmission (Cloninger, Svrakic, & Przybeck, 1993). The dopamine D4 receptor gene was considered an attractive candidate for the quantitative trait locus of novelty seeking because, among other factors, it contains an unusually polymorphic 16-amino acid repeat region in the exon III segment. Furthermore, the most frequently occuring long form of this receptor, the 7-repeat allele (D4.7 receptor), and the least common form containing only 4 repeats (D4.4 receptor) have been shown to exhibit different ligand-binding characteristics. Allelic association studies, such as the two summarized below, are quickly emerging as the method of choice in attempts to detect relatively small gene effects contributing to complex traits such as human personality (see Lander & Kruglyak, 1995).

In the Ebstein et al. (1996) study, individuals with the long 7-repeat allele in the exon III 16-amino acid repeat region had significantly higher scores in novelty seeking—as measured by the TPQ—compared to individuals lacking this allele. Similar results were found when the data were grouped either by genotype, 4,4 versus 4,7 (see Table 3.7), or by allele length, long (6 to 8 repeats) versus short (2 to 5 repeats) alleles. Furthermore, this association was found to be independent of the age, sex, and ethnicity of the subjects ($N = 124$).

This link between novelty seeking and the longer dopamine D_4 repeat alleles was corroborated in a subsequent study by Benjamin et al. (1996), who estimated that approximately 10% of the genetic variance mediating this normally distributed trait can be attributed to the D_4 receptor gene. Considering the similarity between the behavioral profile of the ADHD individual and the behavioral profile of the higher-than-average novelty seeker, it seems reasonable to consider the D_4 receptor as a biologically attractive candidate locus for future allelic studies, as heritable differences in the structure of this receptor may also underlie part of the genetic susceptibility to ADHD. This idea is supported by recent work indicating an association between ADHD symptoms in children and polymorphic variation in the gene encoding the D_4 receptor (LaHoste, Swanson, Wigal, Glabe, Wigal, King, & Kennedy, 1996). Specifically, LaHoste et al. found that the D_4, 7-repeat allele occurred significantly more frequently in ADHD children ($N = 39$) than in controls ($N = 39$) matched for gender and ethnicity.

Another attractive candidate locus for allelic association study is the gene that codes for the dopamine transporter. The dopamine transporter recaptures dopamine that has been released into the synapse and transports it back into the neuron. Recently Cook and colleagues (1995) found a link between ADHD and a variant of this gene, specifically the 10-repeat allele. Interestingly, elevated levels of the dopamine transporter molecule have been found in the brain of patients with Tourette's disorder (Malison et al., 1995).

In conclusion, we have proposed that ADHD is an extreme variant of a naturally occuring temperament continuum, the origins of which may lie in our ability to benefit from the effects of conditioning, that is, to complex events, ideas, objects, and people with feelings of psychic pain and psychic pleasure. The idea that there are inborn variations in this capacity is key, as is the notion that temperament may be modified to some degree by nurture and by certain psychotropic medications which alter the functioning of the critical brain structures involved. Research in the field of mammalian genetics has provided us with clues as to where to look for the potential underpinnings of temperament, starting, for example, with genetically-linked variations in the number of dopaminergic cells in key brain sites such as the ventral tegmental area. Further research is needed to determine the validity of this model.

Section 2

Background

4

Brief Description of the Disorder

Since it was first recognized in the 1940s, ADHD has been known by a variety of terms, including minimal brain dysfunction and hyperkinetic syndrome. According to the American Psychiatric Association (APA, 1987), the disorder is characterized predominantly by developmentally inappropriate inattention, impulsivity, and hyperactivity. Associated features vary as a function of age and may include: a problem delaying gratification (e.g., see Sonuga-Barke, Taylor, Sembi, & Smith, 1992), mood lability, a low frustration tolerance, poor self-esteem, oppositional behavior, stubbornness, bossiness, bullying, obstinacy, temper outbursts, and a lack of response to discipline. "Soft" neurological signs such as clumsiness, as well as perceptual-motor dysfunctions, for example, poor eye-hand coordination, problems with spatial orientation, and visual memory deficits, may also be present.

There are also a number of children who manifest many symptoms of ADHD yet who are hypoactive and listless. In the early 1970s, Wender (1971) argued that these children should be included in this diagnostic category, not only because they possess many other characteristics of the syndrome, but also because they respond similarly to medication. This is consistent with our observations. It is now commonly accepted that hyperactivity need not be present in order for the diagnosis to be made.

TABLE 4.1 *DSM-IV* Diagnostic Criteria for Attention Deficit/Hyperactivity Disorder

A. Either (1) or (2):

   (1) six (or more) of the following symptoms of **inattention** have persisted for
        at least 6 months to a degree that is maladaptive and inconsistent with
        developmental level:

   Inattention

   (a) often fails to give close attention to details or makes careless mistakes in
        schoolwork, work, or other activities
   (b) often has difficulty sustaining attention in tasks or play activities
   (c) often does not seem to listen when spoken to directly
   (d) often does not follow through on instructions and fails to finish
        schoolwork, chores, or duties in the workplace (not due to oppositional
        behavior or failure to understand instructions)
   (e) often has difficulty organizing tasks and activities
   (f) often avoids, dislikes, or is reluctant to engage in tasks that require
        sustained mental effort (such as schoolwork or homework)
   (g) often loses things necessary for tasks or activities (e.g., toys, school
        assignments, pencils, books, or tools)
   (h) is often easily distracted by extraneous stimuli
   (i) is often forgetful in daily activities

   (2) six (or more) of the following symptoms of **hyperactivity-impulsivity** have
        persisted for at least 6 months to a degree that is maladaptive and
        inconsistent with developmental level:

   Hyperactivity

   (a) often fidgets with hands or feet or squirms in seat
   (b) often leaves seat in classroom or in other situations in which remaining
        seated is expected
   (c) often runs about or climbs excessively in situations in which it is
        inappropriate (in adolescents or adults, may be limited to subjective
        feelings of restlessness)
   (d) often has difficulty playing or engaging in leisure activities quietly
   (e) is often "on the go" or often acts as if "driven by a motor"
   (f) often talks excessively

   Impulsivity

   (g) often blurts out answers before questions have been completed
   (h) often has difficulty awaiting turn
   (i) often interrupts or intrudes on others (e.g., butts into conversations or
        games)

Recent nomenclature (*Diagnostic and Statistical Manual of Mental Disorders,* 4th ed., *DSM-IV*; APA, 1994) distinguishes between those individuals with predominant symptoms of inattentiveness and distractibility and those with predominant symptoms of hyperactivity and impulsivity. *DSM-IV* also provides for the diagnosis of a combined type—the child with symptoms of inattention

TABLE 4.1 *Continued*

B. Some hyperactive-impulsive or inattentive symptoms that caused impairment were present before age 7 years.
C. Some impairment from the symptoms is present in two or more settings (e.g., at school [or work] and at home).
D. There must be clear evidence of clinically significant impairment in social, academic, or occupational functioning.
E. The symptoms do not occur exclusively during the course of a Pervasive Developmental Disorder, Schizophrenia, or other Psychotic Disorder and are not better accounted for by another mental disorder (e.g., Mood Disorder, Anxiety Disorder, Dissociative Disorder, or a Personality Disorder).

Code based on type:

314.01 Attention-Deficit/Hyperactivity Disorder, Combined Type: if both Criteria A1 and A2 are met for the past 6 months

314.00 Attention-Deficit/Hyperactivity Disorder, Predominantly Inattentive Type: if Criterion A1 is met but Criterion A2 is not met for the past 6 months

314.01 Attention-Deficit/Hyperactivity Disorder, Predominantly Hyperactive-Impulsive Type: if Criterion A2 is met but Criterion A1 is not met for the past 6 months

Source: American Psychiatric Association (1994). Reprinted by permission.

plus hyperactivity (see Table 4.1), which probably accounts for the majority of children referred for services.

Previous *DSM* classification schemes tended to place the emphasis on either hyperactivity (*DSM-II*; APA, 1968), or attentional difficulties (*DSM-III*; APA, 1980) in making the diagnosis. *DSM-IV* represents a more balanced weighting of the two most salient and widely accepted features of the disorder. This would allow the "quieter" type to be recognized more easily and to be referred for treatment. For the purposes of simplicity, the term ADHD is used throughout the text with one exception—when the research cited is specific to one of the putative subtypes.

Symptoms of ADHD range from mild to severe, and it is rare for them to be present in every situation. The individual often does very well in one-to-one situations, perhaps because personal needs for feeling attention and external control are easier to satisfy. Depending upon the degree of structure, stability, and consistency within a particular environment, children may evidence most of their difficulties at home, in school, or in both situations. Frequently the diagnosis is not made until children enter school, at a time when more age-appropriate behavior is expected. In the classroom setting, the problems of ADHD children often stand out in bold relief against the behavior of peers who are better at sitting quietly, waiting their turn, applying themselves to the task, and playing cooperatively.

■ PREVALENCE

Prevalence rates for ADHD vary from 3% to 5% (APA, 1994) to as high as 5% to 10% of prepubertal children (Wender, 1975). Prevalence rates for adolescents and adults have not been definitively established.

Although the disorder is most often associated with boys, recent reports suggest that symptoms are just as likely to occur in girls (McGee, Williams, & Silva, 1987), and moreover, that the genders share a common biological substrate (Faraone, Biederman, Keenan, & Tsuang, 1991). Girls, however, may still be underrepresented (Berry, Shaywitz, & Shaywitz, 1985) with respect to being referred for evaluation—perhaps because associated symptoms of the more troublesome type, for example, aggressiveness, are less likely in girls; thus boys tend to be overrepresented in clinical samples.

A recent survey of secondary school children in Baltimore County, Maryland, found that the ratio of girls to boys being treated with stimulant medication for the control of ADHD symptoms narrowed from 1:12 in 1981 to 1:6 in 1993 (Safer & Krager, 1994).

■ PERSISTENCE OF SYMPTOMS
INTO ADULTHOOD

Although traditionally thought of as disorder of childhood, reports in the literature over the 25 years provide strong evidence for ADHD's persistence into adolescence (Barkley, Fischer, Edelbrock, & Smallish, 1990; Gittelmann, Mannuzza, Shenker, & Bonagura, 1985) and adulthood (e.g., Amado & Lustman, 1982; Bellak, 1977, 1979; Klein & Mannuzza, 1991; Mannuzza, Klein, Bessler, Malloy, & LaPadula, 1993; Weiss & Trokenberg-Hechtman, 1986; Wender, Reimherr, & Wood, 1981). It is estimated that up to 50% of children with ADHD will continue to manifest symptoms in adolescence and early adulthood.

Especially disturbing are reports suggesting that untreated ADHD children may be at risk for the development of the more troublesome symptoms of sociopathy (Huessy, Cohen, Blair, & Rood, 1979; Satterfield & Cantwell, 1975; Satterfield, Hoppe, & Schell, 1982; Weiss & Trokenberg-Hechtman, 1986), alcoholism (Vaeth et al., 1988), and drug abuse (Cocores, Patel, Gold, & Pottash, 1987; Gittelman et al., 1985; Khantzian, 1983, 1985; Khantzian, Gawin, Kleber, & Riordan, 1984; Weiss & Trokenberg-Hechtman, 1986; Weiss, Pope, & Mirin, 1985) later in life. A follow-up study by Mannuzza, Klein, and Addalli (1991) found that hyperactive boys, compared to their brothers, were significantly more likely as young adults to have pervasive mental illness, multiple *DSM-III* diagnoses, and a more severe form of antisocial disorder.

In 1980, the APA, reflecting this relatively new awareness of the persistence of symptoms into adult life, created a diagnostic category for the disorder in adults, called attention deficit disorder, residual type. This category was subsequently eliminated in the revised edition, *DSM-III-R* (APA, 1987) and replaced with the label undifferentiated attention deficit disorder, with the caveat that further study is warranted to determine the validity of this diagnostic category. Over the years, we have treated many adults with this disorder. Some were parents of ADHD children who were also in treatment. Recognizing similar symptoms in themselves, a few had sampled their child's medication, reporting that it had a calming effect, making them feel more relaxed, more clear-headed, less out of control, and less disorganized. One parent admitted that she had routinely "experimented with speed" in the past and had experienced a similar calming effect—even to the point of falling asleep. Consistent with the reports of others (e.g., Wender, 1987), we have found that ADHD can persist well into adulthood, where it often goes unrecognized and untreated, and not infrequently, misdiagnosed.

■ USEFUL MEDICATIONS

For children, the most widely accepted and validated approach to treatment includes psychomotor stimulant medication, for example, dextroamphetamine, methylphenidate, and magnesium pemoline, in combination with an operant conditioning approach to the management of behavior. The tricyclic antidepressants, for example, desipramine, imipramine, and nortriptyline, as well as newer generation antidepressants, for example, Wellbutrin® (bupropion hydrochloride), have also been found to be effective in some children and adolescents, but to date the psychostimulants remain the drugs of choice (see review by Elia, 1991).

Preliminary findings have also demonstrated that clonidine (Catapres®), primarily used as an antihypertensive agent, may be of some benefit. In a retrospective study of 18 prepubertal boys, ages 6 through 12, with comorbid Attention Deficit Disorder (ADD) and conduct disorder, 61% reportedly had marked improvement with clonidine (Schvehla, Mandoki, & Sumner, 1994). Others have also found clonidine to be beneficial, particularly in the relief of sleep difficulties associated with stimulant pharmacotherapy (see review by Wilens, Biederman, & Spencer, 1994).

For adults, the medications of choice have traditionally been the tricyclic antidepressants. These compounds have been preferred because, unlike the Class

II stimulants, they are rarely associated with abuse and because they are not as stringently regulated by federal and state authorities (Huessy et al., 1979). From our perspective, this regulation is unfortunate as we have typically found the stimulants to be the more effective of the two classes of compounds. In our experience, the main deterrent to prescribing the Class II stimulants has been the strong reluctance on the part of many psychiatrists and physicians who see these adults for treatment. Several have openly admitted that they were reluctant to prescribe them for fear of an unnecessary investigation by the Drug Enforcement Administration.

There is some indication, however, that the appropriateness and effectiveness of stimulant therapy with adults is beginning to be better recognized. As more studies germane to this issue are reported in the literature (e.g., Matochik et al., 1994; Wender, Reimherr, Wood, & Ward, 1985; Yellin, Hopwood, & Greenberg, 1982), physicians and psychiatrists may begin to feel more comfortable using the Class II stimulants with adults. But, as with any scientific finding, it will take some time before such findings become widely accepted, and before adults are routinely given dextroamphetamine or methylphenidate for symptom control.

Other potentially useful medications are: Pondimin® (e.g., see Aman, Kern, McGhee, & Arnold, 1993), Adderall®, and Desoxyn Gradumet®. Pondimin (fenfluramine hydrochloride) is a 5-HT agonist, which has traditionally been used to treat adult obesity. Both Adderall and Desoxyn Gradumet are amphetamine derivatives. Adderall is made up of equivalent amounts of dextroamphetamine saccharate, amphetamine aspartate, dextroamphetamine sulfate, and amphetamine sulfate. Its components have varying dissolution rates, which may make it comparable to long-acting Dexedrine Spansules® in duration of action. Desoxyn Gradumet is methamphetamine in sustained-release form. Methamphetamine is commonly known as a street drug of abuse, and many physicians and psychiatrists may be unwilling to prescribe it for this reason.

There have also been reports of a remission of symptoms in adults treated with the dopamine agonist, bromocriptine, (e.g., Cocores et al., 1987). The efficacy of fluoxetine hydrochloride (Prozac®), a more specific serotonin (5-HT) re-uptake inhibitor, is also being explored (Barrickman, Noyes, Kuperman, Schumacher, & Verda, 1991).

5

The Psychomotor Stimulants

How Do They Work?

■ **NEUROTRANSMITTER SYSTEMS AFFECTED AND SITES OF ACTION**

The medications that have proven to be the most effective in relieving the symptoms of ADHD and that remain the drugs of choice for children, that is, methylphenidate and dextroamphetamine, appear to have their therapeutic effect by increasing the functional levels of a specific class of neurotransmitters known as the monoamines. More specifically, these drugs increase functional, that is, extracellular, concentrations of DA, NE (norepinephrine), and 5-HT in brain. Among other functions, the monoamines are known to underlie important behavioral processes related to activity level and motivation. More specifically, activity in specific DA pathways has been shown to be involved in an organism's tendency to approach objects and places that have previously been associated with the delivery of a primary reward (Carr & White, 1983, 1986; Hiroi & White, 1990; Taylor & Robbins, 1984; Wise, 1987; Wise & Bozarth, 1987; Wise & Rompre, 1989).

   In contrast, activity in specific 5-HT pathways originating in periventricular structures such as the periaqueductal gray (PAG), for example, has been associated with avoidance responding (Stein, Wise, & Belluzzi, 1977; Wise et al., 1973), or the tendency to escape from objects and places that have previously been associated with the delivery of a punishing stimulus. Obviously any complex approach or avoidance responding must be accompanied by a sufficient degree of arousal, that is, the waking state, and there is evidence that NE plays a critical role in behavioral arousal or vigilance (Aston-Jones & Bloom, 1981a, 1981b; Ennis & Aston-Jones, 1986, 1987).

As mentioned previously, the most effective compounds in the treatment of ADHD have effects on all three monoamine systems. The approach or positively reinforcing properties of dextroamphetamine and methylphenidate have traditionally been thought to be directly related to their ability to increase extracellular levels of DA (Kuczenski, 1983) at specific brain sites, particularly the nucleus accumbens (n. accumbens) (Wise & Bozarth, 1987; Wise & Rompre, 1989). This nucleus is of particular interest as it has been implicated recently as a possible locus for the therapeutic response of ADHD children to low doses of methylphenidate (Porrino & Lucignani, 1987) and dextroamphetamine (Porrino, Lucignani, Dow-Edwards, & Sokoloff, 1984).

Further evidence for the involvement of this nucleus in ADHD symptomatology has been provided by the research of Lou and colleagues (Lou, Henriksen, Bruhn, Borner, & Nielsen, 1989). Using xenon 133 inhalation and emission tomography, Lou et al. measured regional cerebral blood flow in a group of ADHD children ($n = 6$) compared to normal controls ($n = 9$). Striatal regions— presumably including the n. accumbens, which forms part of the ventral striatum— were found to be significantly hypoperfused in ADHD children compared to controls. In contrast, occipital, left sensorimotor, and primary auditory regions were hyperperfused, implying a relatively high degree of neuronal activity in primary sensory and sensorimotor regions, as well as a lack of inhibition of sensory perception. Following a dose of methylphenidate (four of the ADHD children were given their previously established therapeutic dose of between 10 to 30 mg), regional blood flow was increased in striatal regions, as well as in posterior periventricular areas of the brain.

Of particular interest is the finding that it was the *right* striatum and not the left that was significantly hypoperfused in this sample of ADHD children. In rats, lesions of the right n. accumbens have been shown to induce a postoperative locomotor hyperactivity, whereas comparable lesions of the left n. accumbens have not (Starkstein, Moran, Bowersox, & Robinson, 1988). In view of its potential involvement in ADHD symptomatology, a brief overview of the connectivity, neurochemistry, and functional significance of the n. accumbens is presented below.

The n. accumbens, also known as the ventral striatum, is located in the basal forebrain of mammals and is richly connected—either directly or indirectly—to limbic structures (e.g., hippocampus, amygdala, septum, medial prefrontal cortex), a sensory relay nucleus (the mediodorsal nucleus of the thalamus), and motor structures, such as the vental pallidum. The extensiveness of these connections is illustrated schematically in Figure 5.1a and b.

For some time now the n. accumbens has been thought of as having a pivotal role as a functional interface between limbic and motor systems—the place where motivational and sensory information are integrated to produce appropriate patterns of motor activity related to goal-directed behavior (Mogenson, 1987; Mogenson, Jones, & Yim, 1980; Mogenson & Yang, 1991; Mogenson, Yang, & Yim, 1988). The n. accumbens forms part of the mesocorticolimbic dopaminergic reward circuitry of the brain that is activated by the delivery of primary rewards such as food and water, by incentive stimuli that predict that reward will be forthcoming (e.g., Phillips, Atkinson, Blackburn, & Blaha, 1993), and by psychoactive substances such as amphetamine and cocaine (Koob, 1992). This pathway originates in the ventral tegmental area (VTA) of the brain, courses through the medial forebrain bundle (MFB), forms rich synaptic connections with the n. accumbens and ventral portions of the striatum, and projects forward into the medial prefrontal cortex (see Figure 5.2).

Despite its predominant dopaminergic innervation, the n. accumbens is not a neurochemically homogeneous structure. Among other neurotransmitter systems represented in this nucleus are norepinephrine (NE) (Allin, Russell, Lamm, & Taljaard, 1988), acetylcholine (ACh) (Clarke & Pert, 1985; Clarke, Pert, & Pert, 1984; Wedzony, Limberger, Spath, Wichmann, & Starke, 1988), gamma-aminobutyric acid (GABA) (Pickel, Towle, Joh, & Chan, 1988), and glutamate (Wu, Brudzynski, & Mogenson, 1993), as well as the neuropeptides, neurotensin (NT) (Schotte & Leysen, 1989), and cholecystokinin (CCK) (Fallon, 1988; Hokfelt, Skirboll, Rehfeld, & Goldstein, 1980).

Furthermore, some dopaminergic neurons of the VTA contain a subpopulation of cells with DA and CCK co-localized, with DA and NT co-localized, and with DA, CCK, and NT co-localized (Hokfelt, Ljungdahl, Terenius, Elde, & Nilsson, 1987). The neuropeptides are stored in the large dense-core vesicles found within the cell body of the neuron, but not in the smaller vesicles found in terminal regions. The effects of the co-release of these neuropeptides with DA in n. accumbens are not completely understood. Direct injections of low doses of CCK into the posterior medial sectors of the n. accumbens have been found to potentiate DA-induced hyperactivity. In contrast, direct injections of CCK into the anterior sectors of the accumbens inhibited DA-induced hyperactivity. These opposing effects on activity level of CCK in posterior medial and anterior sectors of the accumbens are most likely due to an enhancement of DA release via a CCK-A receptor dependent mechanism and an inhibition of DA release via a CCK-B dependent mechanism, respectively (Crawley, 1991, 1992).

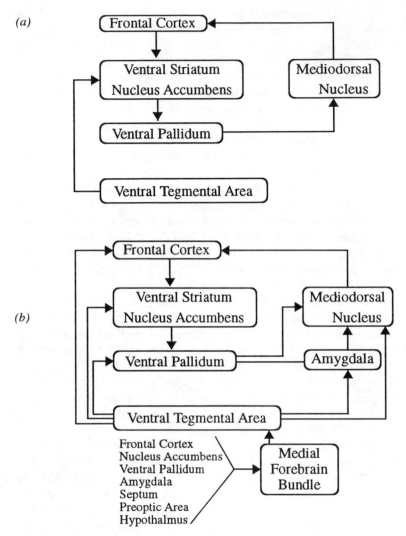

Figure 5.1: Schematic Illustration of Connectivity of Nucleus Accumbens.
(a)Transthalamic circuitry of the "limbic" striatum (ventromedial sector plus n. accumbens). (b) Feedback circuits associated with the ventral tegmental area.
Source: Domesick (1988), p. 23. Reprinted by permission of the *Annals of the New York Academy of Sciences* and V. B. Domesick.

Finally, there is some evidence suggesting that the frequency of stimulation may be a factor in co-release, with low-intensity stimulation of the mesocorticolimbic pathway resulting in the selective release of DA, whereas high-intensity stimula-

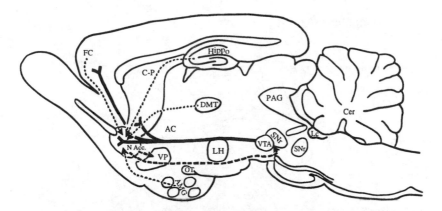

Figure 5.2: Sagittal Rat Brain Section Illustrating Neural Reward Circuitry That Includes a Limbic-Motor Interface. Shown are: limbic afferents to nucleus accumbens (N Acc.) from amygdala (AMG), hippocampus (Hippo), dorsomedial nucleus of the thalamus (DMT), and [medial sectors] of frontal cortex (FC) (dotted lines); efferents from n. accumbens to ventral pallidum (VP) and ventral tegmental area (VTA) (dashes); afferents from VTA to n. accumbens, ventral striatal sectors of the caudate-putamen (C-P), and frontal cortex (solid black lines).

Source: Adapted from G. R. Koob (1992), "Drugs of Abuse: Anatomy, Pharmacology, and Function of Reward Pathways," *Trends in Pharmacological Sciences, 13,* 178.

Note: The dopaminergic (DA) pathway originating in the A10 cell group of the VTA and projecting to the N Acc, ventral striatal sectors of C-P, olfactory tubercle (OT), and FC (projections of the mesocorticolimbic DA system) is thought to form a critical substrate for psychomotor stimulant reward. Other abbreviations: Cerebellum (Cer), periaqueductal gray (PAG), locus coeruleus (Lc), substantia nigra (SNr), lateral hypothalamus (LH).

tion results in co-release of DA with one or both of the neuropeptides. For example, low-frequency stimulation of the mesocorticolimbic pathway resulted in the selective release of DA, but not NT, in rat prefrontal cortex (Bean & Roth, 1991).

The n. accumbens also receives projections from 5-HT neurons originating in the dorsal raphe and the PAG of the midbrain (Li, Rao, & Shi, 1989) (see Figure 5.3).

Concentrations of NE and 5-HT in the n. accumbens are small relative to DA. More specifically, DA/5-HT concentration ratios in the accumbens have been found to range from 2.1 to 18.8, depending on which part of the nucleus is assayed—rostral, medial, or caudal; DA/NE ratios, from 3.9 to 40 (Allin et al., 1988). Given that 5-HT and NE levels are low relative to DA levels in the accumbens, amphetamine- and methylphenidate-induced effects on n. accumbens 5-HT and NE overflow can be expected to be less potent compared to their effects on DA overflow (e.g., see Figure 5.4).

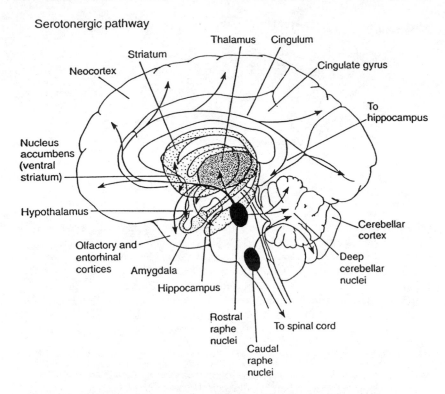

Figure 5.3: Schematic Drawing of Serotonergic (5-HT) Pathways in the Mammalian Brain. Shown is a lateral view of the brain.

Source: Reprinted from E. R. Kandel (1991), "Disorders of Thought: Schizophrenia," in E. R. Kandel, J. H. Schwartz, & T. M. Jessell (Eds.), *Principles of Neural Science* (3rd ed.), 874, with kind permission from E. R. Kandel and Elsevier Science-NL, Sara Burgerhartstraat 25, 1055 KV Amsterdam, The Netherlands.

Note: Although the raphe nuclei form a fairly continuous collection of cell groups close to the midline throughout the brain stem, they are illustrated here in a distinct rostral and caudal group for the sake of simplicity.

Nevertheless, one still has to question the possible functional—behavioral—significance of the simultaneous release of 5-HT, NE, and DA in the n. accumbens in response to these psychomotor stimulants. For example, there is evidence that the amphetamine-induced increase in locomotor activity is enhanced when the brain content of serotonin is lowered (e.g., by midbrain raphe lesions), suggesting that 5-HT release in the n. accumbens might function to dampen the magnitude of behavioral responses to increased levels of extracellular DA (Breese, Cooper, & Mueller, 1974; Lucki & Harvey, 1979; Mabry & Campbell, 1973; Neill, Grant, & Grossman, 1972).

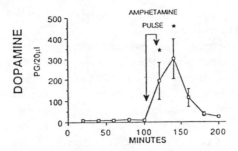

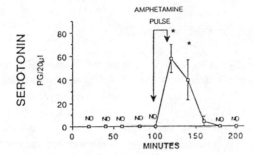

Figure 5.4: Comparison of Amphetamine Effects on Dopamine and Serotonin Release in Nucleus Accumbens. Amphetamine (4 µg) was infused into the n. accumbens via the microdialysis probe for 20 minutes (between the arrows) while microdialysis continued throughout. ND = not detected.

Source: Reprinted from L. Hernandez, F. Lee, & B. G. Hoebel (1987), "Simultaneous Microdialysis and Amphetamine Infusion in the Nucleus Accumbens and Striatum of Freely Moving Rats: Increase in Extracellular Dopamine and Serotonin," *Brain Research Bulletin, 19,* 626, with kind permission from Elsevier Science Inc.

$*p < 0.01$.

In support of this hypothesis, microinjections of 5-HT directly into the accumbens have been demonstrated to decrease locomotor activity (Pijnenburg, Honig, Van der Heyden, & Van Rossum, 1976). This putative inhibitory link between serotonergic activity and dopaminergic function is supported by an extensive body of research (e.g., see Montgomery, Rose, & Herberg, 1991, and references cited therein). As will be discussed more fully in Chapter 9, there is considerable evidence to suggest that the participation of both the reward and punishment systems of the brain can be felt in what would appear at first glance to be purely approach or purely avoidance responding. The complementary and reciprocal nature of these two opposing motivational systems of the brain was originally proposed by Stein (1964).

Understanding how amphetamine and methylphenidate work in the brain to bring about their therapeutic effects is helping to advance our thinking regarding the possible biochemical and neurophysiological underpinnings of ADHD. We can now say with reasonable certainty, for example, that dopaminergic systems are involved, and that the n. accumbens as well as periventricular regions of the brain are among those sites whose function may be "normalized" by these compounds (e.g., see Lou et al., 1989). By integrating the findings from human and animal research across a broad spectrum of disciplines, we will eventually piece together other important clues.

■ CELLULAR MECHANISMS OF ACTION

With respect to understanding how these drugs work on a cellular level, neuroscience researchers continue to learn more as the technology improves. Until very recently, information about the mechanisms of action of dextroamphetamine and methylphenidate was derived primarily from in vitro studies employing postmortem, excised brain tissue. In interpreting the results of these studies, one can only infer indirectly what is happening in the intact, living organism in the synapse where psychoactive compounds exert their therapeutic effects. Although they represented the state of the art at the time, many of the studies investigating monoamine function routinely employed procedures (e.g., the use of physiologically relevant concentrations of ascorbic acid in incubation media) (Hadjiconstantinou & Neff, 1983) that call into question the reliability of some of the information obtained. The problems associated with the use of postmortem tissue preparations, and why the data from these studies should be interpreted with caution, are reviewed elsewhere (e.g., Gonzalez-Mora, Maidment, Guadalupe, & Mas, 1989; Vulto, Sharp, Ungerstedt, & Versteeg, 1988).

With the recent development of more sophisticated in vivo (in the living organism) techniques such as *microdialysis,* researchers are now able to monitor directly neurotransmitter responses to local and systemic applications of clinically important psychotropic compounds in awake, freely moving animals. In this procedure, a small diameter (e.g., 200 uM), semipermeable dialysis membrane—usually of cylindrical shape—is surgically implanted into the brain of an anesthetized animal (see Figure 5.5). The procedure causes minimal discomfort. Once the surgical wounds have healed, the animal is free to move about in its home cage while the experiment is in progress (see Figure 5.6).

About 18 to 24 hours after surgery, the animal is connected to a minipump fitted with a microsyringe containing artificial cerebral spinal fluid (CSF) and

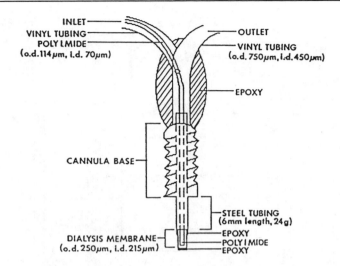

Figure 5.5: Schematic Diagram of a Microdialysis Probe (not drawn to scale).
Dialysis occurs through 2 mm of the exposed regenerated hollow fiber dialysis tubing
(M.W. cutoff = 6000; Spectrum Medical Industries).
Source: Reprinted from S. K. Woods & J. S. Meyer (1991), "Exogenous Tyrosine Potentiates the
Methylphenidate- Induced Increase in Extracellular Dopamine in the Nucleus Accumbens: A Microdialysis
Study," *Brain Research, 560,* 98, with kind permission from Elsevier Science-NL, Sara Burgerhartstraat 25,
1055 KV Amsterdam, The Netherlands.

the drug in question. The drug is then gently delivered to the brain area being
studied through tubing attached to the inlet line of the microdialysis probe. The
drug crosses the membrane of the probe by diffusion. The pores of the membrane
are large enough to allow the passage of small-diameter molecules, such as
neurotransmitters and drugs, and small enough to exclude large-diameter molecules, such as the enzymes that break down neurotransmitters and metabolites.

The traffic between the interior of the dialysis membrane and the brain is
two-way. Neurotransmitters and metabolites present in the extracellular space
of the brain diffuse into the interior compartment of the microdialysis probe and,
through the outlet tubing, are collected in small quantities in vials mounted
outside the animal. Any changes in the levels of these neurotransmitters and their
metabolites in response to drug infusion are then measured by comparing
predrug (baseline) levels to drug and postdrug levels. Alternatively, the compound to be studied can be given systemically, for example, intraperitoneally
(i.p.). Prior to sample collection, a period of time is allowed for the drug to cross
the blood-brain barrier. For more information about this technique, see Westerink, Damsma, Rollema, de Vries, and Horn (1987), and Westerink and de Vries
(1988).

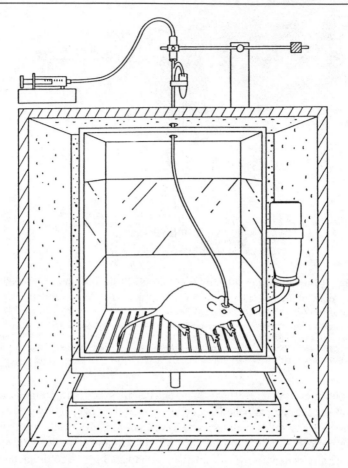

Figure 5.6: Schematic Diagram of a Behavioral Activity Chamber Used in Microdialysis Experiments. The chamber is located in a sound-proof cabinet. Dialysis samples are collected outside of the chamber, remote from the experimental animal. The dialysis probe is attached to the awake animal via a permanently implanted stainless steel guide cannula.

Source: Kuczenski & Segal (1989), p. 2052. Reprinted by permission of the Society for Neuroscience.

Microdialysis studies have shown that dextroamphetamine produces dose-dependent increases in extracellular concentrations of DA in striatum (Kuczenski & Segal, 1989), n. accumbens and dorsal caudate (Carboni, Imperato, Perezzani, & Di Chiara, 1989) (see Figure 5.7a & b), and medial prefrontal cortex (Moghaddam & Bunney, 1989; Moghaddam, Roth, & Bunney, 1990) (see Figure

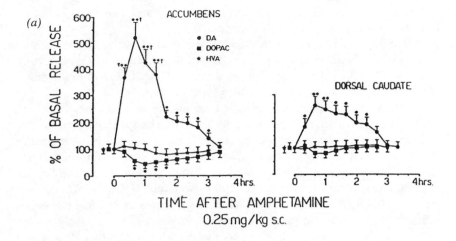

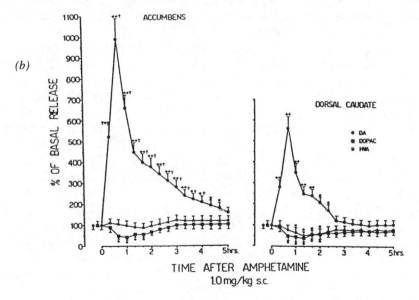

Figure 5.7: Comparison of Dose-Dependent Release of Dopamine (DA) by Amphetamine in Nucleus Accumbens and Dorsal Caudate. Effect of (a) 0.25 mg/kg s.c. Effect of (b) 1.0 mg/kg s.c. of amphetamine on DA and metabolite (DOPAC, HVA) overflow. Results represent means ± SEM of at least five rats (*$p < 0.05$, **$p < 0.001$ with respect to basal values). Note preferential release of DA in n. accumbens versus dorsal caudate (+$p < 0.05$ with respect to corresponding changes in dorsal caudate).

Source: Reprinted from E. Carboni, A. Imperato, L. Perezzani, & G. DiChiara (1989), "Amphetamine, Cocaine, Phencyclidine, and Nomifensine Increase Extracellular Dopamine Concentrations Preferentially in the Nucleus Accumbens of Freely Moving Rats," *Neuroscience, 28,* 655, with kind permission from Elsevier Science, Ltd, The Boulevard, Langford Lane, Kidlington OX 1GB, UK.

5.8). Note the preferential increase in DA overflow in n. accumbens versus dorsal caudate in the Carboni et al. study (Figure 5.7a & b).

Methylphenidate has also been shown to produce dose-dependent increases in extracellular DA in striatum (Butcher, Liptrot, & Aburthnott, 1991; Nomikos, Damsma, Wenkstern, & Fibiger, 1990; Zetterstrom, Sharp, Collin, & Ungerstedt, 1988) (see Figure 5.9), and n. accumbens (Woods & Meyer, 1991).

Although both compounds increase extracellular levels of DA, the manner in which they do so differs. Amphetamine's effects, for example, have been found to be mediated by the DA re-uptake carrier—also called the DA transporter (Parker & Cubeddu, 1988; Schwarz, Uretsky, & Bianchine, 1980)—and to be stimulation- (Westerink, Tuntler, Damsma, Rollema, & de Vries, 1987) and calcium-independent (Nomikos et al., 1990; Westerink, Hofsteede, Tuntler, & de Vries, 1989). The DA transporter functions to recapture DA that has been released into the extracellular space, either through naturally occurring nerve cell activity or through nerve cell activity that has been artificially induced, for example, by the ingestion of a psychoactive compound. Recapture of DA in this manner is one of the ways that the extracellular effects of DA on pre- and postsynaptic cells are terminated.

The extracellular effects of DA are also terminated by degrading enzymes present in the extracellular space and by diffusion away from the site of release; however, in n. accumbens, recent evidence suggests that re-uptake is the predominant mechanism for terminating the extracellular actions of DA (Cass, Zahniser, Flach, & Gerhardt, 1993).

By binding to a site on the DA transporter, amphetamine blocks the recapture of DA from the synapse. This prolongs the effects of DA on the pre- and postsynaptic cell. Moreover, unlike many other re-uptake blockers, which merely block the action of the transporter, amphetamine appears to be a substrate for transport into the interior of the cell (Zaczek, Culp, & De Souza, 1991). Once inside the cell, the amphetamine molecule is thought to be released into the cytoplasm, freeing the binding site on the DA transporter to bind a cytoplasmic DA molecule and to transport it back outside the cell, where it is released into the extracellular space. This model of amphetamine action—*the exchange diffusion model*—was originally suggested by the finding that drugs that block DA re-uptake inhibit amphetamine-stimulated DA release (Fischer & Cho, 1979; Liang & Rutledge, 1982).

Amphetamine may also act within the cell to promote the efflux of DA from storage vesicles into the cytoplasm (Sulzer, Maidment, & Rayport, 1993; Sulzer & Rayport, 1990). This is presumably related to the fact that amphetamine is a weak base with a pK_a of approximately 9.9 (Mack & Bonisch, 1979). As a weak base, the amphetamine molecule tends to pick up a positive charge in acidic environments. And relative to the cytoplasmic compartment of the cell, the

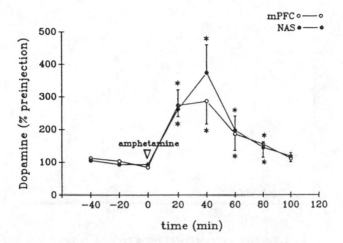

Figure 5.8: Effect of Amphetamine on Dopamine (DA) Overflow in Medial Prefrontal Cortex (mPFC) and Nucleus Accumbens Septi (NAS). Effect of 1 mg/kg i.v. injection of d-amphetamine on extracellular levels of DA. For each time point, means ± SEM ($N = 5$) are expressed as percent of the respective basal DA levels.
Source: B. Moghaddam & B. S. Bunney (1989), "Differential Effect of Cocaine on Extracellular Dopamine Levels in Rat Medial Prefrontal Cortex and Nucleus Accumbens: Comparison to Amphetamine," *Synapse, 4,* 159. Reprinted by permission of John Wiley & Sons, Inc.
*$p < 0.05$.

interior of the storage vesicle is quite acidic. In fact, it is the highly acidic environment of the vesicle interior that keeps DA sequestered inside the vesicle. This is because the positively charged DA molecule does not cross the lipid membrane of the vesicle as easily as the uncharged molecule.

According to Sulzer and coworkers, any uncharged amphetamine molecules within the cytoplasm can presumably gain access to the interior of the vesicle by passive diffusion. Once inside the acidic environment of the vesicle, the amine group on the amphetamine molecule would tend to pick up an electric charge, that is, an H^+ ion. As a consequence, the protonated amphetamine molecule—like the protonated DA molecule—would tend to become sequestered inside the vesicle because its positive charge would not allow it to cross the vesicular membrane as easily as the unprotonated form. Furthermore, a reduction in the concentration of free H^+ inside the vesicle would be expected to reduce the pH gradient across the vesicle membrane, thus promoting the efflux of DA from the vesicle and inhibiting its re-uptake. Increasing the efflux of DA from storage vesicles means that there is more available in the cytoplasm to be carried out of the cell by the DA transporter. The various ways in which amphetamine may

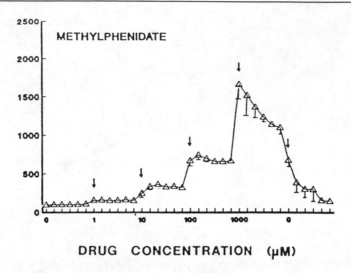

DRUG CONCENTRATION (µM)

Figure 5.9: Effect of Local Application of 1, 10, 100, and 1,000 uM Methylphenidate on DA Overflow in Rat Striatum. Each point represents the mean ± SEM (*N* = 4) percentage change in dialysate DA levels over baseline levels during each 10-minute sampling period. Arrows indicate the first sample after administration of each dose of methylphenidate.

Source: G. G. Nomikos, G. Damsma, D. Wenkstern, & H. C. Fibiger (1990), "In Vivo Characterization of Locally Applied Dopamine Uptake Inhibitors by Striatal Microdialysis," *Synapse, 6,* 109. Reprinted by permission of Wiley-Liss, Inc., a subsidiary of John Wiley & Sons, Inc.

exert its effects are illustrated schematically in Figure 5.10. Seiden, Sabol, and Ricaurte (1993) have speculated that the various mechanisms of amphetamine action may be dose-dependent. For example, at low doses, only exchange diffusion would occur. At higher doses, both exchange diffusion and passive diffusion would occur and so on (see Figure 5.10). This hypothesis remains to be validated.

In contrast to amphetamine, which has effects on both cytoplasmic and vesicular pools of DA, methylphenidate is thought to increase extracellular levels of DA by its actions on the vesicular pools of DA (Chiueh & Moore, 1975; Fuller & Snoddy, 1979). This effect involves a process known as exocytosis (Butcher et al., 1991; Nomikos et al., 1990; Westerink, Tuntler, et al., 1987; Westerink et al., 1989) and is dependent upon the large influx of extracellular calcium (Smith & Augustine, 1988) that accompanies nerve cell firing. When a nerve cell fires, that is, generates an action potential, calcium ions enter the cell through voltage sensitive calcium channels located on the outer cell membrane.

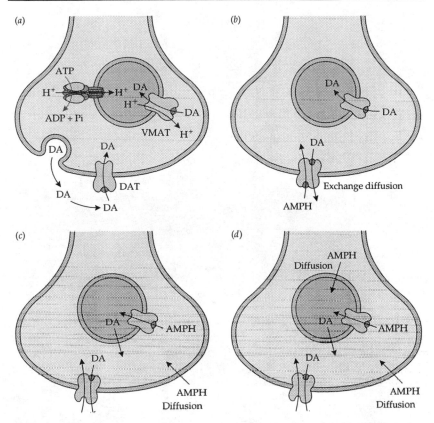

Figure 5.10: The Possible Mechanisms of Amphetamine-Induced Dopamine (DA) Release. (a) Some of the normal processes occurring in a DA nerve terminal, including release of DA via exocytosis, DA uptake into the nerve terminal via the plasma membrane transporter (DAT), and DA uptake into synaptic vesicles via the vesicular monoamine transporter (VMAT). Possible mechanisms of amphetamine action: (b-d) plasma membrane transport-mediated amphetamine uptake coupled to cytoplasmic DA release (exchange diffusion); (c-d) amphetamine entry into the terminal by passive diffusion; (c-d) amphetamine entry into the vesicles mediated by the vesicular transporter and/or passive diffusion.

Source: R. S. Feldman, J. S. Meyer, & L. Quenzer (1996), *Principles of Neuropsychopharmacology*, Sunderland, MA: Sinauer Associates, 554. Adapted from Seiden et al. (1993). Reprinted with permission from Sinauer Associates, Inc. Thanks to Dean Scudder of Sinauer for his assistance in this matter.

Note: Seiden, Sabol, & Ricaurte (1993) have hypothesized that the processes shown in b-d occur in sequential order as the dose of amphetamine is increased; for example, at low doses, only exchange diffusion would take place.

This influx of calcium triggers events resulting in the movement of DA storage vesicles located within the cytoplasm toward the outer membrane of the cell, the

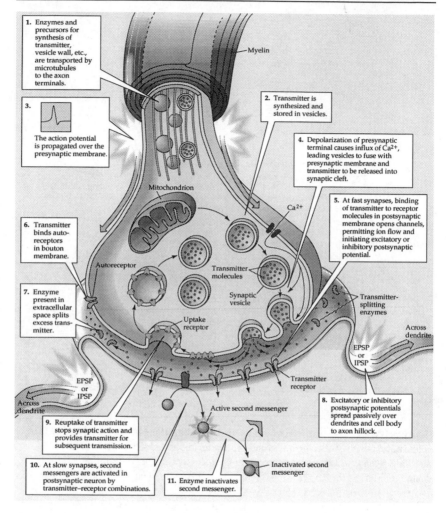

Figure 5.11: Steps in Chemical Neurotransmission.
Source: M. R. Rosenzweig, A. L. Leiman, & S. M. Breedlove (1996), *Biological Psychology,* Sunderland,
MA: Sinauer, 161. Reprinted by permission of Sinauer Associates, Inc.

subsequent fusion of the vesicular membrane with the outer membrane, and the
release of DA into the synapse (see Figure 5.11).

Although we have ample evidence that methylphenidate effects on DA
overflow are exocytosis-mediated, we still do not have a complete understanding
of the underlying molecular basis of this effect. For example, it is unclear how

methylphenidate acts to allow calcium ions into the interior of the cell, given that methylphenidate has been shown to be a potent inhibitor of the firing of DA neurons located in substantia nigra (Shenker, Bergstrom, & Walters, 1990) and probably VTA. Woods and Meyer (1991) have speculated that stimulation of the nicotinic cholinergic receptor, located presynaptically on DA cell terminals, may be involved. This possibility was originally suggested by the work of Shi and colleagues (e.g., Shih, Khachaturian, & Barry, 1974; Shih, Khachaturian, Barry, & Hanin, 1976; Shih, Khachaturian, Barry, & Reisler, 1975; Shih, Khachaturian, & Hanin, 1977), who found nicotinic receptor stimulation to be an important component of methylphenidate effects in the mesencephalic reticular formation. A tentative model of methylphenidate action in the brain—specifically in the n. accumbens—which includes this possibility has been proposed, but to date has not been tested (see Figure 5.12).

In this model, occupation of the nicotinic cholinergic receptor by methylphenidate is thought to open calcium channels, thus allowing for an influx of extracellular calcium in the absence of nerve impulse flow. The rationale and evidence for this model are discussed more fully in Woods (1990), and briefly in Woods and Meyer (1991).

Like amphetamine, methylphenidate also acts by blocking the re-uptake of DA into the cell (Ferris & Tang, 1979; Ferris, Tang, & Maxwell, 1972), presumably by binding to a site on the DA transporter. Unlike amphetamine, however, methylphenidate is not a substrate for transport and therefore is not carried into the interior of the cell. Thus its inhibiting effects on DA re-uptake are presumed to be on the recapture of DA that has been previously released into the synapse via the process of exocytosis.

In addition to its effects on DA, microdialysis studies have shown that amphetamine increases extracellular concentrations of 5-HT in striatum (Hernandez, Lee, & Hoebel, 1987; Kuczenski & Segal, 1989), n. accumbens (Hernandez et al., 1987), and lateral hypothalamus (Parada, Hernandez, Schwartz, & Hoebel, 1988). However, in the study by Kuczenski and Segal (1989), only the higher doses of amphetamine, that is, 2.0 mg/kg and greater, had significant striatal 5-HT releasing effects.

Less is known about the mechanism of action of magnesium pemoline. In vitro, this compound has been shown to increase concentrations of DA via re-uptake inhibition and release, although it is considerably less potent than amphetamine in this respect (Fuller, Perry, Bymaster, & Wong, 1978). And like methylphenidate, pemoline has been shown to inhibit the firing of DA neurons in vitro (Shenker et al., 1990).

All three psychostimulants are reportedly rapidly absorbed following oral administration. Serum blood levels of methylphenidate reportedly peak within 1 to 2 hours, while its half-life ranges from 2 to 4 hours after an oral dose.

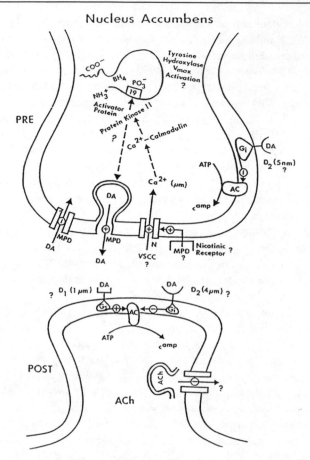

Figure 5.12: Proposed Model of Methylphenidate Action in Nucleus Accumbens.
In this hypothetical model, methylphenidate (MPD) binds to nicotinic receptors
located on the presynaptic (PRE) dopaminergic (DA) terminal. Binding opens N-type
voltage sensitive Ca^{2+} channels (VSCC). Ca^{2+} enters the presynaptic terminal, where
it participates in exocytotic release of DA, and possibly Vmax activation of tyrosine
hydroxylase as well. The rationale for this hypothetical model is explained fully in
Woods (1990) and briefly in Woods & Meyer (1991) and has yet to be validated.
Other well-established MPD actions occurring in the cell: inhibition of DA uptake
into the presynaptic terminal (presumably by binding to a site on the DA transporter).
Abbreviations: D_1, DA receptor; D_2, DA receptor; ATP, adenosine triphosphate; $_c$amp,
cyclic AMP; AC, adenylate cyclase; G_i, inhibitory G protein; G_s, stimulatory G
protein; ACh, acetylcholine; BH_4, tetrahydrobiopterin; 19, serine 19 on the tyrosine
hydroxylase molecule.
Source: Woods (1990).

Note: Minus signs indicate inhibition of a specific cellular process; plus signs indicate facilitation; unknowns
or speculations are indicated by a question mark.

Dextroamphetamine is more slowly absorbed, peaking in 2 to 3 hours, with a half-life of 6.8 hours. Serum concentrations of pemoline reportedly peak around 2.4 hours, with a half-life of from 7 to 7.5 hours (Stevenson & Wolraich, 1989). The other amphetamine compounds, that is, Adderall and Desoxyn Gradumet, have half-lives of 7 to 8 hours and 10 to 12 hours, respectively.

6

ADHD and Monoamine Function

■ **OPENING COMMENTS**

In light of the previous discussion on how the psychomotor stimulants act in the brain to potentially bring about their therapeutic effects, a brief review of some of the evidence for decreased monoamine function in this population is presented below. We begin by acknowledging the early contributions of Paul Wender, widely known in the field for his early theoretical work and ongoing research. On the basis of the favorable response of children and adolescents to the psychomotor stimulants, and in view of what was known at the time about the neurochemical effects of these compounds, Wender (1971, 1975, 1978) hypothesized that ADHD involves a functional underactivity of one or more of the central nervous system monoamines (NE, DA, and/or 5-HT) due to decreased synthesis, release, and/or receptor sensitivity. According to Wender, this functional underactivity led to deficits in both classical and instrumental conditioning—to a diminished sensitivity to reward and punishment.

Since that time, much of the research on the possible underlying neurophysiological basis of ADHD has focused on these important neurochemical systems, with special attention paid to the dopaminergic systems of the brain. In the neurosciences, basic research efforts have been directed at finding a viable animal model (Bareggi et al., 1979a, 1979b; Kohlert & Bloch, 1993; Luthman, Fredriksson, Lewander, Jonsson, & Archer, 1989; Sagvolden et al., 1992; Sagvolden, Metzger, & Sagvolden, 1993), as well as uncovering the exact

70

mechanisms of action of the compounds that are commonly used in treatment, along with their sites of action.

More recently, the early speculations of Wender, especially regarding brain reward systems, have received renewed attention in the ADHD literature—with others (e.g., Haenlein, & Caul, 1987; Levy, 1991; Quay, 1988) giving their own variations on this basic theme. And there is some evidence that the popular model of cognitive attentional deficits may be giving way gradually to the so-called newer motivation deficit model of ADHD (e.g., see comments in Barkley, 1990, pp. 26-27). Barkley's motivational model hypothesizes that ADHD children have developmental deficits—compared to their normal peers—in the areas of rule-governed behavior and responsiveness to consequences. Such deficits result in problems with inhibition and with sustained attention (Barkley, 1990). In a more recent statement of his theoretical position, Barkley (1994) attributes the core features of ADHD to a primary deficit with response inhibition resulting in a hyperresponsivity to immediate stimuli.

■ STUDIES OF MONOAMINE FUNCTION IN HUMAN SUBJECTS

Although human research is limited by obvious ethical considerations, there have been some attempts to document this hypothesized neurochemical dysfunction in ADHD children and adults. For example, Shaywitz, Cohen, and Bowers (1977) found significantly lower levels of the DA metabolite, homovanillic acid (HVA), in the cerebral spinal fluid (CSF) of a clinically homogeneous group ($N = 6$) of ADHD children, as compared with controls ($N = 26$). Both groups had been pretreated with probenecid (100-150 mg/kg, orally), a drug that blocks the removal of acidic monoamine metabolites from CSF. CSF concentrations of 5-hydroxyindolacetic acid (5-HIAA), the principle metabolite of 5-HT, were not significantly different between groups. In a related study, Reimherr, Wender, Ebert, and Wood (1984) found that CSF levels of HVA and 5-HIAA tended to be lower in adults who responded positively to a subsequent trial of methylphenidate therapy, in comparison to nonresponders and controls.

More recently, CSF levels of 5-HIAA and HVA were measured in prepubertal boys, ages 6 through 12, with ADHD (Castellanos, Elia, et al., 1994). The results of this study were in the unexpected direction in that levels of 5-HIAA were positively correlated with the Brown-Goodwin Lifetime History of Aggression scale, and levels of HVA were positively correlated with several measures of hyperactivity. The predictive value of CSF monoamine metabolites still remains to be determined, and it is the subject of ongoing work by Rapoport and colleagues.

In another related and provocative study, plasma levels of seven essential amino acids were measured in a group of children ($N = 28$) meeting *DSM-III*

(APA, 1980) criteria for ADHD (Bornstein et al., 1990). All 28 children were medication-free at the time of testing. Fasting venous blood samples were reportedly taken in the morning, immediately following a period of 48 hours on a low amine diet. Compared to controls ($N = 20$), ADHD children had significantly lower levels of phenylalanine, tyrosine, tryptophan, histidine, and isoleucine. Of particular interest are the findings of lower plasma levels of the aromatic amino acids, tyrosine and tryptophan. These amino acids serve important precursor functions in the synthesis of the monoamines. Specifically, tyrosine serves as the amino acid precursor to DA and NE (see Figure 6.1), and tryptophan, as the precursor to 5-HT (see Figure 6.2).

As an essential amino acid, tryptophan cannot be synthesized by the body, but rather supplies must be replenished from the diet. And although tyrosine can be synthesized in the liver from phenylalanine, the major source of tyrosine is also the diet. Both nutrients belong to a group of large neutral amino acids (LNAAs) that compete for the same saturable uptake carrier into the brain. Research in animals has shown that brain levels of these important nutrients depend upon and fluctuate with plasma levels (Wurtman, 1982; Wurtman, Hefti, & Melamed, 1981).

■ FACTORS INFLUENCING THE TRANSPORT OF MONOAMINE PRECURSORS INTO THE BRAIN

Because of the competition among the LNAAs for the same saturable carrier system, the amount of tyrosine or tryptophan that actually gets into the brain is determined by the ratio of each to the sum of all the other LNAAs in plasma. This carrier system in turn may be controlled by noradrenergic beta-receptors (Eriksson & Carlsson, 1988), in the sense that stimulation of these receptors can increase the transport of LNAAs into the brain. Activation of this noradrenergic system is known to occur during times of stress. Research in humans (e.g., Banderet & Lieberman, 1989; Lieberman & Banderet, 1990) and animals (Brady, Brown, & Thurmond, 1980; Reinstein, Lehnert, & Wurtman, 1985) has shown that supplemental tyrosine can actually reduce the deleterious effects associated with experimentally induced stress (e.g., acute exposure to hypoxia and cold).

Other factors that influence the amount of tyrosine or tryptophan that actually gets transported into the brain are: (a) the ratio of protein to carbohydrate in a particular meal, and (b) insulin secretion. For example, a carbohydrate-rich meal stimulates insulin secretion, which in turn promotes preferentially the uptake of the branched-chain (leucine, isoleucine, valine) versus the aromatic (tyrosine, tryptophan, phenylalanine) LNAAs into skeletal muscle. By reducing the levels of competing amino acids in plasma, insulin secretion actually increases the relative abundance of tyrosine and tryptophan in plasma. This means that more

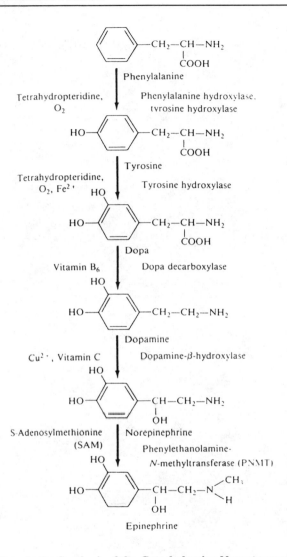

Figure 6.1: Steps in the Synthesis of the Catecholamine Neurotransmitters.
Synthesizing enzymes are shown to the right of the arrows; cofactors (e.g., O_2, Fe_2, vitamin C) and the methyl donor, S-adenosylmethionine (SAM), are shown to the left of the arrows.
Source: R. S. Feldman & L. Quenzer (1984), *Fundamentals of Neuropsychopharmacology*, Sunderland, MA: Sinauer Associates, 167. Reprinted by permission of Sinauer Associates, Inc.

of these important neurotransmitter precursors can be bound by the carrier system and transported into the brain. A protein-rich meal, on the other hand,

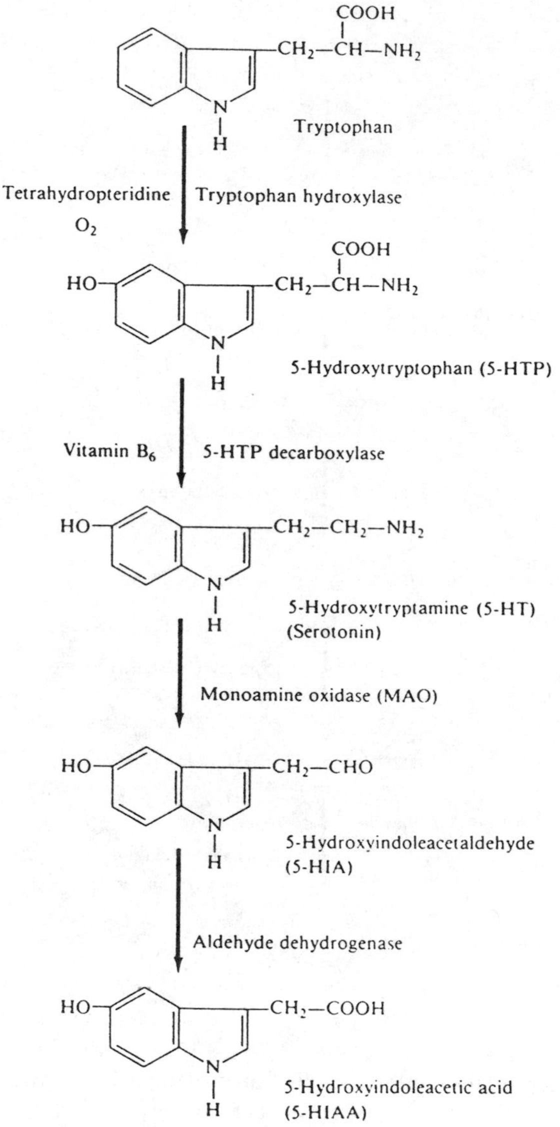

Figure 6.2: Steps in the Synthesis and Catabolism of Serotonin. The synthesizing and catabolizing enzymes involved in the reactions are shown on the right of the arrows; the cofactors (e.g., O_2) are on shown on the left.

Source: R. S. Feldman & L. Quenzer (1984), *Fundamentals of Neuropsychopharmacology,* Sunderland, MA: Sinauer Associates, 213. Reprinted by permission of Sinauer Associates, Inc.

will elevate the levels of all of the LNAAs, thereby effectively reducing the number of tyrosine and tryptophan molecules that can be transported into the brain. The net effect is that less precursor reaches the neurons where DA and 5-HT synthesis takes place.

With respect to 5-HT synthesis, the picture is more complicated than is apparent from the preceding discussion, for there are other plasma components, for example, albumin and nonesterified fatty acids, which influence tryptophan transport into the brain. For a more complete treatment of this and related topics, see Maher (1988), Wurtman (1982), and/or Wurtman et al., (1981).

■ PRECURSOR CONTROL OVER MONOAMINE SYNTHESIS

It has now been established that the synthesis of 5-HT and DA is controlled, in part, by the availability of their respective precursors (Fernstrom, 1983; Fernstrom & Wurtman, 1971, 1974; Maher, 1988; Milner & Wurtman, 1986; Wurtman, 1982). This is because the enzyme that converts tryptophan to 5-HT, that is, tryptophan hydroxylase, and the enzyme that converts tyrosine to DA, that is, tyrosine hydroxylase, are not fully saturated with their amino acid substrate in vivo. Consequently, both enzymes can be more fully saturated when their respective precursor is supplied exogenously—either through nutritional supplement or by manipulation of the diet.

In vivo, tyrosine hydroxylase is estimated to be about 70% to 80% saturated with precursor substrate, compared to 50% for tryptophan hydroxylase (Carlsson & Lindqvist, 1978). Unlike what happens in 5-HT synthesis, however, increasing the supply of tyrosine does not necessarily translate into significant increases in functional (synaptic) concentrations of neurotransmitter. This is because—in contrast to 5-HT biosynthesis—the synthesis of DA and NE is more tightly controlled by other factors, such as end-product inhibition. In other words, under resting, baseline conditions when neurons are relatively quiescent, rising levels of intracellular DA and NE can compete with cofactor, that is, tetrahydrobiopterin, for the same binding site on the tyrosine hydroxylase molecule. By preventing the binding of tetrahydrobiopterin, DA and NE can effectively inhibit their own biosynthesis: thus the origin of the term end-product inhibition.

Nevertheless, some areas of the brain seem to be more readily influenced by increases in tyrosine availability than others. For example, even under baseline conditions, supplemental tyrosine has been shown to induce modest increases in functional levels of DA in striatum and n. accumbens—areas of the brain that, as previously mentioned, have been implicated in the underlying neurophysiology of ADHD. Using the technique of in vivo microdialysis, During, Acworth,

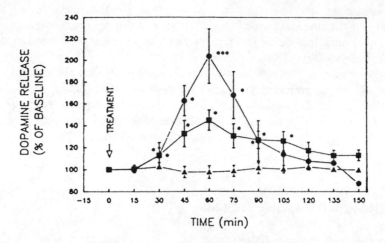

TIME (min)

Figure 6.3: Systemic Tyrosine Enhances Dopamine (DA) Release from Nucleus Accumbens and Corpus Striatum. Concentrations of DA in nucleus accumbens (circles) and corpus striatum (squares) following tyrosine (200 mg/kg i.p.). Data points represent means ± SEM (vertical bars) of four to five animals. Data are also shown for saline controls (triangles). Significantly different from saline controls at *$p < 0.05$; significantly different from striatal concentrations at ***$p < 0.05$.

Source: Reprinted from M. J. During, I. N. Acworth, & R. J. Wurtman (1988), "Effects of Systemic L-Tyrosine on Dopamine Release from Rat Corpus Striatum and Nucleus Accumbens," *Brain Research, 452,* 379, with kind permission from Elsevier Science-NL, Sara Burgerhartstraat 25, 1055 KV Amsterdam, The Netherlands.

and Wurtman (1988) found modest, but significant increases in extracellular levels of DA in striatum and n. accumbens with exogenous tyrosine. Furthermore, because of their higher basal activity level—midbrain DA systems are known to exhibit different basal firing rates and bursting patterns, with neocortical systems having the highest bursting rates (Tam, Elsworth, Bradberry, & Roth, 1990)—the effect of tyrosine was more pronounced in n. accumbens than in striatum. More specifically, exogenous tyrosine resulted in peak increases in DA overflow of 104% over baseline levels, compared to only 45% in striatum (During et al., 1988) (see Figure 6.3).

Woods and Meyer (1991) have also observed modest increases over baseline DA levels in n. accumbens with exogenous tyrosine, confirming the previous findings of During et al. (1988) that even under baseline conditions, exogenous tyrosine can induce modest, yet significant increases in extracellular concentrations of DA.

And when dopaminergic neurons increase their firing frequency over baseline levels, or increase synaptic concentrations of neurotransmitter by a mechanism that does not depend upon nerve cell firing, for example, amphetamine or methylphenidate, there is evidence that tyrosine availability may play an even more significant role in maintaining functional levels of neurotransmitter. For example, Milner and Wurtman (1985) found that when either the intensity or duration of DA nerve cell firing in striatal tissue was increased, more tyrosine was needed in order for DA synthesis to keep pace with release. This effect may have been mediated in part by a stimulation-induced increase in the more activated, more phosphorylated, form of tyrosine hydroxylase within the neuron, and in part by a concomitant decrease in the ability of DA to inhibit its own biosynthesis. Having more tyrosine hydroxylase in the activated form, as well as more available tyrosine, means that more DA can be synthesized within a given period of time.

More recently, Woods and Meyer (1991) showed that when DA neurons were activated pharmacologically by methylphenidate, exogenously supplied tyrosine potentiated the effect of methylphenidate on DA overflow in the n. accumbens (see Figure 6.4).

This effect was not evident immediately, but rather 60 and 80 minutes following the start of the methylphenidate plus tyrosine co-infusion. Moreover the peak increase induced by tyrosine co-infusion came a full 40 minutes after the peak induced by methylphenidate infusion alone. Furthermore, 100 minutes after the start of tyrosine co-infusion, extracellular concentrations of DA were still significantly elevated over baseline levels, whereas in the methylphenidate-alone condition, extracellular concentrations of DA had already returned to baseline. The most parsimonious explanation of these findings is that exogenous tyrosine prevented the depletion of intracellular stores of DA, allowing DA synthesis to compensate for declining functional concentrations brought about by continuous methylphenidate infusion.

■ NUTRITION AND MONOAMINE FUNCTION IN ADHD: A POTENTIALLY FRUITFUL LINE OF STUDY

The previous research findings on precursor availability and monoamine function reinforce our commonsense perception that good nutrition is necessary for adequate brain functioning. Furthermore, taken together with the findings of Bornstein et al. (1990), they raise interesting questions about the relationship between precursor availability and monoaminergic activity in ADHD children. For example, were plasma stores of tyrosine and tryptophan low in ADHD children versus normal controls in the Bornstein et al. study because of poor gastrointestinal absorption or some other factor, such as hepatic first-pass clearance?

Alternatively, were plasma stores low because brain monoaminergic systems were *hypoactive* relative to normal controls? Put another way, are there feedback mechanisms from brain to blood that translate into something along the lines of,

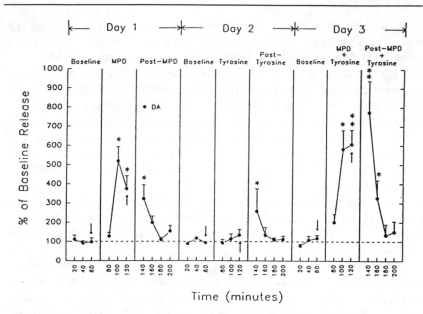

Figure 6.4: Potentiation of the Methylphenidate-Induced Increase in Dopamine
(DA) Overflow in Rat Nucleus Accumbens by Tyrosine. Mean ± SEM ($N = 7$)
percent change in extracellular concentrations of DA during the three successive days
of testing across each treatment (30 µM methylphenidate (MPD), 100 µM tyrosine, or
30 µM MPD plus 100 µM tyrosine), phase (baseline, treatment, posttreatment), and
sampling interval.

Source: Reprinted from S. K. Woods & J. S. Meyer (1991), "Exogenous Tyrosine Potentiates the
Methylphenidate-Induced Increase in Extracellular Dopamine in the Nucleus Accumbens: A Microdialysis
Study," *Brain Research, 560,* 100, with kind permission from Elsevier Science-NL, Sara Burgerhartstraat 25,
1055 KV Amsterdam, The Netherlands.

Note: A repeated measures design was used involving the continuous collection of 20-minute dialysate
samples for a 4-hour period, once a day for 3 consecutive days. Treatments were counterbalanced to control
for possible order effects. Arrows indicate the beginning and ending of a 60-minute period of infusion with
the active compound(s). Note the small, but statistically significant increase in DA induced by tyrosine
alone, which is evident at 140 minutes. *significantly different from baseline at $p < 0.01$; **significantly
different from MPD alone at the corresponding sampling interval at $p < 0.01$.

I don't need more precursor because I'm not working that hard. And if we make
these systems work harder, by activating them pharmacologically with Ritalin
or Dexedrine, for example, should we be concerned about maintaining adequate
levels of these precursor amino acids in the diet? If so, what is the best way to
do that? For example, given that we now know that under certain conditions
(protein plus carbohydrate sufficient to stimulate insulin secretion), the relative
abundance of these precursor amino acids in plasma and ultimately in the brain
can actually be increased (e.g., see Mauron & Wurtman, 1982), should we try
manipulating the ratio of carbohydrate to protein in the diet?

Furthermore, would it be beneficial to give tyrosine supplement simultaneously with Ritalin or Dexedrine to ensure that DA synthesis keeps pace with DA release? These and related questions point to a potentially fruitful line of study. In humans, tyrosine supplement has been shown by some researchers to relieve the symptoms associated with depression (e.g., Gelenberg, Wojcik, Growdon, Sved, & Wurtman, 1980; see also a study by Gibson & Gelenberg, 1983, and other work cited in van Praag & Mendlewicz, 1983). However, as with any compound with psychoactive effects, the dose must be taken into consideration, as large versus small doses of exogenous tyrosine may actually have an inverse effect on the activation of tyrosine hydroxylase, inhibiting (via substrate inhibition of the enzyme) rather than stimulating DA synthesis (e.g., see Badawy & Williams, 1982).

Interestingly, some of the mothers of the ADHD children we see for treatment continue to insist that their child's behavior "gets worse" on "sugar" or "candy." Our tendency has been to dismiss this as popular myth, especially in view of the research indicating no significant relationship between sugar intake and hyperactivity (e.g., see review by Milich, Wolraich, & Lindgren, 1986). However, considering what we now know about the role of carbohydrate and insulin secretion in determining the relative abundance of tyrosine and tryptophan in plasma, and therefore the amount available for transport into the brain, perhaps we as researchers and practitioners should be paying more attention to diet composition as a potentially important aspect of treatment—to be included in a total approach along with pharmacotherapy, psychotherapy, and behavior management.

Work by Chiel and Wurtman (1981) in animals has provided some indirect evidence suggesting that short-term alterations in diet composition may indeed influence motor-activity level. Using the total number of infrared photocell beam interruptions in successive 20-minute periods as their measure of activity, these investigators studied the spontaneous nocturnal activity of rats fed diets in which the ratio of carbohydrate to protein was systematically varied. One group ($N = 20$) received a diet containing 18% protein (casein), 57% carbohydrate (dextrose, sucrose, and dextrin), and 15% vegetable fat; a second group ($N = 20$) received no protein, 75% carbohydrate, and 15% vegetable fat. As the ratio of carbohydrate to protein increased, rats were found to be significantly more continuously active. Moreover, animals eating the 18% protein diet demonstrated a distinctly different pattern of activity during darkness; periods of intense activity were followed by periods of complete quiescence. In contrast the animals fed the no-protein diet were almost continuously active during darkness, with few or no periods of quiescence. No correlation was found between an animal's activity pattern, its body weight, or the fat content of its diet.

Returning to the previously mentioned observation of our mothers, and speaking hypothetically, a snack consisting exclusively of simple carbohydrate, for example, candy, could potentially exacerbate the child's symptoms—at least temorarily—for example, by depleting the child's stores of plasma tyrosine. This is because in the absence of protein, the carbohydrate-induced stimulation of insulin secretion would further stimulate the uptake of all plasma LNAAs, including tyrosine, into skeletal tissue. Although some plasma tyrosine may still be available for transport into the brain, the relative amount transported would not be expected to be as much as that transported following a meal consisting predominantly of carbohydrate, but including some protein. And although natural rewards such as sugar are known to be accompanied by an increase in DA release in the reward systems of the brain (e.g., see Wise, 1987; Wise & Rompre, 1989)—which may indeed make the child feel better for the moment—the sugar-induced stimulation of insulin secretion and the associated reduction in plasma tyrosine may quickly translate into decreased functional concentrations of DA—perhaps below baseline levels—at least until the next well-balanced meal. This is speculation on our part, but we have tried not to dismiss out-of-hand the observations of parents, even when they fly in the face of accepted research findings: that is, there is no significant relationship between sugar intake and the child's behavior.

Alternatively, the surge of insulin secretion that accompanies a snack consisting exclusively of simple sugars could, in a short time, lower blood-sugar levels. In the extreme case, a hypoglycemic reaction could result that is commonly accompanied by unpleasant feelings of irritability. It is not hard to imagine how such internal feelings of irritability may, in turn, translate into a decreased frustration tolerance, thus exacerbating the child's difficulties.

Finally, taken together with the previously cited findings of Wender and coworkers (Reimherr et al., 1984), and Shaywitz et al. (1977) on human subjects, the findings by Bornstein et al. (1990) of lower plasma levels of tyrosine and tryptophan in ADHD children provide us with further evidence in support of an abnormality in DA—and possibly 5-HT—neurochemistry in the brains of ADHD individuals. From our perspective—as detailed in previous chapters—this neurochemical dysfunction affects behavior primarily by the impairment it produces in the reward and punishment systems of the brain. The inadequate functioning of these critical motivational systems leaves the individual with a diminished capacity for imprinting feelings of psychic pain, for example, guilt, remorse, shame, and psychic pleasure—from the pleasant feelings associated with a pair of comfortable slippers to the more profound feelings of joy and euphoria. Assuming that the effects of conditioning are based on a more usual degree of activity in these systems, individuals with ADHD have a more difficult time, relatively speaking, internalizing the lessons of experience; that is, the anticipation of reward or punishment plays little part in motivating ongoing behavior.

Section 3

Brain Reward and Punishment Mechanisms

A Closer Look

■ **INTRODUCTION**

Some of the material in this section is rather technical. For those wishing to skip the bulk of this section, the important conclusions to take with you are:

1. The reward and punishment systems are real physical entities existing in discrete populations of neurons and fiber tracts of the living brain.
2. Research suggests that these critical motivational systems are opposing in nature and reciprocally activated—much like antagonistic spinal reflexes; that is, when one is activated the other is suppressed.
3. Activation of these systems, whether through natural or artificial means, for example, psychoactive compounds, subserves our subjective experience as humans of psychic pain and psychic pleasure.

81

The body of literature on the reward systems of the brain is already extensive and is rapidly expanding. On the other hand, much less research has been conducted on the punishment systems of the brain. We suspect that following the discovery and preliminary characterization of these systems in the 1950s and 1960s, researchers may have become increasingly hesitant to subject animals to punishing stimuli, especially given the development of the animal rights movement. From our perspective, it is certainly preferable to study reward-related phenomena, although as we will see, there is evidence that the impact of both systems can be felt in what would seem—at first glance—to be pure pleasure or pain.

Moreover, in view of the commonality of these systems among all mammals, the possibility that other mammals experience—to varying degrees—analogous feelings of psychic pleasure and psychic pain cannot be overlooked. Anyone who has ever owned a dog would no doubt agree. In his later years, Ivan Pavlov (1928) began to study such "psychical" phenomena in dogs, differentiating among four distinct types, or "nervous systems," and basing his typology on his earlier work on the simple conditioned reflexes. Pavlov's early contributions are discussed in Chapter 3.

7

Brain-Stimulation Reward

■ A PIVOTAL ROLE FOR DOPAMINE

Since the initial discovery by Olds and Milner (1954) that electrical stimulation of certain discrete areas of the brain (especially, the medial forebrain bundle) can serve as a reward, and by Delgado, Roberts, and Miller (1954) that stimulation of different discrete areas (e.g., the periventricular system of the diencephalon and midbrain) can serve as a punishment, researchers have attempted to investigate the neuroanatomical and neurochemical bases of these phenomena, and evidence has accumulated that monoaminergic and possibly cholinergic systems of the brain are critically involved (Gratton & Wise, 1985; Wise, 1980, 1987).

Work by a number of researchers has indicated that DA plays a critical role in brain-stimulation reward (see Wise & Rompre, 1989, for a critical review). The most convincing evidence has been obtained from pharmacological research. Specific DA receptor blockers, for example, decrease responding for medial forebrain bundle (MFB) stimulation in a dose-dependent manner over and above any motor impairment they may induce, and concomitantly produce dose-dependent increases in the intensity of MFB stimulation necessary to sustain even minimal rates of responding—levels that have been shown to be well within the response capacity of the animal even under high doses of drug (Esposito, Faulkner, & Kornetsky, 1979; Fouriezos, Hansson, & Wise, 1978; Schaefer & Michael, 1980; Stellar, Kelley, & Corbett, 1983). DA agonists, on the other hand, have the opposite effect. Systemic amphetamine, for example, has been shown to induce dose-dependent decreases in the intensity of MFB stimulation needed to sustain low rates of responding (Colle & Wise, 1988; Gallistel & Karras, 1984).

Whereas amphetamine is known to affect NE as well as DA release and re-uptake, apparently it is its actions at DA synapses that are responsible for its rewarding properties, as shown by the following findings. First, selective DA receptor blockers (e.g., haloperidol) attenuate the rewarding effect of intravenous amphetamine, whereas selective NE receptor blockers do not (Davis & Smith, 1975; Risner & Jones, 1976; Yokel & Wise, 1976). Second, lesions of noradrenergic systems have no affect on amphetamine self-administration, whereas destruction of dopaminergic nerve terminals in the n. accumbens with 6-OHDA blocks the acquisition and maintenance of amphetamine self-administration, as do 6-OHDA lesions of the DA cell bodies of the ventral tegmental area (VTA) (Lyness, Friedle, & Moore, 1979; Wise, 1987).

■ DOPAMINE RECEPTOR SUBTYPES AND THE REWARD SIGNAL

Although the above studies provide fairly convincing evidence that DA-receptor blockade attenuates the pleasurable consequences of brain stimulation and psychomotor stimulant reward, the specific receptor class involved has yet to be unequivocally identified. With respect to this issue, there have been conflicting reports in the literature. Gallistel and Davis (1983), for example, found the reward-attenuating effect of neuroleptics on MFB stimulation to be highly correlated with their affinity for D_2 and not D_1 receptors.

On the other hand, Nakajima and McKenzie (1986) found that the rewarding impact of MFB stimulation was reduced by systemic SCH 23390, a specific D_1 blocker, but not by sulpiride, a specific D_2 blocker. In a related study, Nakajima (1986) found suppression of operant responding for more natural rewards (food, water) with SCH 23390, but not with sulpiride, suggesting that the differential effects of these dopaminergic antagonists are not limited to brain stimulation reward or psychomotor stimulant reward.

More recently, Kurumiya and Nakajima (1988) examined the involvement of DA-receptor subtypes in the reinforcing effect of ventral tegmental stimulation. Rats were implanted with electrodes in the VTA and with cannulae in either the n. accumbens or the caudate putamen (CPu). Injections of SCH 23390 (5μg) into the n. accumbens ipsilateral to the electrode site completely suppressed responding for VTA stimulation within 20 minutes, but injections into contralateral n. accumbens or ipsilateral CPu were without effect. In contrast, sulpiride (20 μg) had no effect on responding when injected into the n. accumbens, but it did suppress responding to a small but statistically significant degree when injected into the ipsilateral CPu. These results confirm the involvement of D_1 receptors in the n. accumbens in the rewarding effect of VTA stimulation.

Complicating this issue is the evidence suggesting that D_1 and D_2 receptors are functionally linked and may act synergistically to produce their effects (Braun & Chase, 1986; Breese & Mueller, 1985; Seeman, Grigoriadis, & Niznik, 1986; Walters, Bergstrom, Carlson, Chase, & Braun, 1987; White, 1987; White & Wang, 1986). In a series of studies, the results of which are summarized in Walters et al. (1987), the abilities of selective D_1 and D_2 agonists, administered alone and in combination, to induce apomorphine-like changes in the firing rates of globus pallidus neurons and to elicit classical agonist-induced changes in spontaneous motor activity in rats were examined. These investigators consistently found a potentiation of D_2 agonist-induced (e.g., quinpirole; RU 24926) neuronal activity by prior administration of a D_1 selective agonist (e.g., SKF 38393). This increase in single-unit activity was indistinguishable from that observed by the administration of the nonselective DA agonist, apomorphine.

The results of their behavioral studies were consistent with this finding. Quinpirole, for example, produced a significant increase in locomotion, grooming, and sniffing but failed—even at high doses—to induce the intense stereotypical licking, biting, and gnawing that is typically observed with apomorphine. Similarly, SKF 38393 alone significantly increased grooming but elicited no stereotypical behavior. When quinpirole and SKF 3893 were administered simultaneously, however, intense stereotypical licking, biting, and gnawing were observed, along with a concomitant decrease in locomotion, grooming, and sniffing.

Supporting the observations of Walters et al. (1987), White (1987) found evidence for a synergistic relationship between D_1 and D_2 receptors in the control of neuronal activity in the n. accumbens. In his study, iontophoretic application of the D_2 agonist, quinpirole, inhibited the spontaneous firing of n. accumbens neurons; systemic pretreatment with the tyrosine hydroxylase inhibitor, alpha-methyl-para-tyrosine (AMPT), significantly attenuated this effect. Concurrent iontophoretic application of the D_1 agonist SKF 38393 and quinpirole to n. accumbens neurons of AMPT-pretreated animals reinstated the inhibitory effect of quinpirole, even on neurons that were not sensitive to SKF 38393 alone. The results suggest that D_1 receptor stimulation by normally present endogenous levels of DA may play a necessary facilitating role in D_2 receptor-mediated functional responses.

Further complicating this issue is the finding that these two receptor subtypes may have opposite effects on cyclic adenosine 3,5-monophosphate (cAMP) and adenylate cyclase activity; that is, D_1-receptor stimulation enhances cAMP formation, whereas D_2-receptor stimulation inhibits it (Stoof & Kebabian, 1981). cAMP is required for the phosphorylation of protein molecules and is known as a second messenger in the brain. Second messengers act to translate the signal received on the outer surface of the cell membrane by specialized molecules known as receptors into the complex physiological changes that occur on the inside of the cell, resulting in such processes as nerve cell firing and neurotransmitter synthesis.

Finally, molecular subtypes of the D_1 and the D_2 receptor have recently been discovered in the brain (Sibley, 1991; Sokoloff, Giros, Martres, Bouthenet, & Schwartz, 1990; Sunahara et al., 1991; van Tol et al., 1991). Specifically, D_3, D_4, and D_5 receptors have been identified (Sibley & Monsma, 1992). The D_4 receptor is of particular interest, for, as previously mentioned, polymorphic variation in the gene encoding this receptor may contribute to the expression of ADHD symptoms in children (see LaHoste et al., 1996). As our understanding of these novel DA-receptor subtypes increases, previous neurochemical and behavioral data will no doubt have to be reevaluated.

■ KEY ANATOMICAL SITES SUBSERVING BRAIN-STIMULATION REWARD

Anatomically, brain-stimulation reward has been found at specific locations extending from the medial prefrontal cortex to the nucleus of the solitary tract in the hindbrain, and passing through the MFB in the hypothalamus (Phillips, 1984). Given these multiple sites, brain stimulation reward is unlikely to have a single anatomical substrate. Although noradrenergic and dopaminergic systems overlap in many of the areas, giving rise to intracranial self-stimulation behavior in rats, only DA fibers are confined to areas that mediate brain reward, whereas NE fibers extend into other regions (Routtenberg, 1978). Wise (1980) found self-stimulation reward to be uniquely associated with the layer of DA-containing cells in the substantia nigra and the VTA. The occurrence of robust, low-threshold, self-stimulation from DA cells and the lack of occurrence of self-stimulation from bordering areas suggest a unique involvement of DA cells or their afferents in brain-stimulation reward in at least these anatomical sites. As suggested by Wise and Bozarth (1987) whatever the specific anatomical substrate of brain-stimulation reward ultimately turns out to be, it is certain to involve activation of the dopaminergic circuitry of the MFB.

Of the various dopaminergic pathways, the most strongly implicated is the projection from the VTA to the n. accumbens, which passes through the MFB in the lateral hypothalamus (Wise, 1987; Wise & Bozarth, 1984). A diagram of this pathway can be found in Chapter 5 (Figure 5.2). Intracranial self-stimulation of the MFB has been shown to increase extracellular concentrations of the DA metabolites, DOPAC and HVA, in the n. accumbens of rats, as measured by in vivo microdialysis (Nakahara, Ozaki, Miura, Miura, & Nagatsu, 1989).

As previously indicated, microinjections of amphetamine into th
facilitates responding for MFB brain-stimulation reward (Colle & W
Rats will even learn to press a lever for direct injections of amphetamin
the accumbens (Hoebel et al., 1983). And chemically induced lesions of the
accumbens (with 6-OHDA) have been shown to moderately attenuate the
discriminative stimulus properties of amphetamine (Dworkin & Bimie, 1989).

Of relevance here are the previously reported findings of Porrino and coworkers, implicating the n. accumbens as a possible site for the therapeutic response
of ADHD children to d-amphetamine (Porrino, Lucignani, et al., 1984) and
methylphenidate (Porrino & Lucignani, 1987). As previously discussed, these
investigators measured changes in local cerebral glucose utilization (LCGU)
simultaneously in over 30 brain structures in rats following intravenous injections of low and high doses of drug. Whereas a low dose of methylphenidate
(1.25 mg/kg) significantly increased LCGU in n. accumbens, olfactory tubercle,
substantia nigra, frontal cortex, and mediodorsal thalamus, increases in LCGU
under low doses of d-amphetamine (.2 and .5 mg/kg) were confined mainly to
one structure—the n. accumbens. Under high doses of either compound, much
more involvement of the extrapyramidal motor system, neocortex, and limbic
and related structures were observed. Behaviorally, locomotor activity was
enhanced under low doses, whereas stereotypy predominated under high doses.
The similarity in the pattern of LCGU induced by low doses of d-amphetamine
or methylphenidate, as well as the observation that it is typically the lower doses
that are clinically effective, suggested to Porrino and coworkers that the n.
accumbens may be involved in the therapeutic response of ADHD children to
these drugs.

Consistent with this idea, Lou et al. (1989) measured regional cerebral blood
flow distribution in six ADHD children and found significant hypoperfusion in
the right striatum (and presumably ventral striatum, which includes the n.
accumbens). When methylphenidate was administered to four of these children,
blood flow to this region was increased, although the results failed to achieve
statistical significance. Interestingly, low doses of cocaine have been shown to
induce selective increases in glucose utilization in the n. accumbens (Porrino,
Domer, Crane, & Sokoloff, 1988). The similarity in selectivity of structures
(primarily n. accumbens) activated by low doses of amphetamine, methylphenidate, and cocaine raises the possibility that a subpopulation of individuals who
consistently abuse cocaine and amphetamine may be undiagnosed ADHD
individuals attempting to self-medicate.

Khantzian (1985) has also raised the issue of self-medication with respect to
adults addicted to cocaine and heroin and, moreover, has found methylphenidate
useful in the treatment of cocaine dependence (see Khantzian, 1983; Khantzian
et al., 1984). From our perspective, it seems reasonable that the abuse (or use?)
of these stimulants may be accompanied by an increased activation of brain

structures subserving psychic feeling. Such an activation would be expected to result in some relief—if only for the short-term—from distressing psychic symptoms.

■ HYPERPOLARIZATION BLOCK
AND COLLISION STUDIES:
EVIDENCE FOR THE INVOLVEMENT
OF CHOLINERGIC SYSTEMS

Despite the overwhelming evidence for the involvement of the dopaminergic circuitry of the MFB in brain-stimulation reward, there is evidence that dopaminergic fibers in the MFB are not the first to be activated by electrical currents used in brain-stimulation reward experiments (Gratton & Wise, 1985). In fact, the conduction velocities and refractory periods of most MFB fibers have reportedly been shown to be faster than those of the unmyelinated dopaminergic fibers (e.g., Shizgal, Schindler, & Rompre, 1989). Moreover, the reward-relevant depolarizing signal has been shown to travel in a rostral to caudal direction, opposite to the direction of conduction for dopaminergic fibers (Bielajew & Shizgal, 1982, 1986).

The results of collision studies (see Wise & Bozarth, 1984) and hyperpolarization block studies by Shizgal and coworkers (Shizgal, Bielajew, Corbet, Skelton, & Yeomans, 1980; Shizgal, Bielajew, & Kiss, 1980) have provided direct evidence that the MFB (at the level of the lateral hypothalamus) and VTA are bridged by a common set of descending, directly activated, reward-mediating fibers.

Along these lines, Gratton and Wise (1985) have shown that fast-conducting, myelinated, cholinergic fibers with relatively short refractory periods are among the first fibers to be directly activated by rewarding MFB stimulation, and they have proposed that cholinergic (muscarinic) fibers may represent a first stage system in transmitting the reward-relevant signal, with synapses on dopaminergic cell bodies of the VTA serving as the second-stage system. This is supported by evidence showing that VTA infusions of the cholinergic muscarinic agonist carbachol is reinforcing, as measured by the conditioned place preference paradigm (CPP), whereas injections of the muscarinic receptor blocker, atropine sulfate, increases thresholds for MFB self-stimulation (Yeomans, Kofman, & McFarlane, 1985).

Whether more than one first-stage fiber population is involved in carrying the reward-relevant signal has yet to be unequivocally determined. Yeomans and colleagues (Yeomans, 1989; Yeomans et al., 1985; Yeomans, Maidment, & Bunney, 1988; Yeomans, Mercouris, & Ellard, 1985) have found evidence indicating that ascending DA axons or other slow-conducting, higher-threshold, unmyelinated axons of the MFB can contribute about 20% to 50% to the reward signal if stimulation parameters are adjusted to allow for higher currents or longer duration pulses. In all likelihood, both descending and ascending MFB fibers will be found to contribute to the reward-relevant signal, with ascending dopaminergic fibers forming an important anatomical link in a multisynaptic pathway involving the participation of more than one neurotransmitter system.

■ **ENDOGENOUS OPIOIDS AND OTHER NEUROTRANSMITTER SYSTEMS CONTRIBUTE TO THE REWARD SIGNAL**

In addition to the possible contribution of cholinergic systems, endogenous opioids have been found to interact with dopaminergic systems in mediating some portion of brain-stimulation reward (Di Chiara & North, 1992; Schaefer, 1988; Wise, 1989). The sites of this interaction appear to be the VTA and n. accumbens, where direct injections of opioids and opiate compounds, for example, morphine, facilitate responding for brain-stimulation reward (Jenck, Gratton, & Wise, 1987; Rompre & Wise, 1989; West & Wise, 1988; Wise, 1989) and are also rewarding in their own right (Bozarth, 1987; Bozarth & Wise, 1981; Goeders, Lane, & Smith, 1984; Phillips & LePiane, 1980). Self-stimulation of either site can be partially attenuated by the opiate antagonists, naloxone and naltrexone, over and above any motor impairment they can induce (Trujillo, Belluzzi, & Stein, 1986, 1989), whereas the lateral hypothalamus is relatively refractory to the effects of these compounds.

As suggested by Trujillo et al. (1989), the finding that self-stimulation is not completely blocked by opiate antagonists in the VTA or n. accumbens is not surprising because elimination of the opioid component would still allow for the expression of the dopaminergic component of reward.

More recent evidence suggests that the activation of the mesocorticolimbic dopaminergic reward pathway by morphine or heroin is indirect; that is, it is mediated by stimulation of mu-opioid receptors located on GABAergic interneurons in the VTA. Stimulation of these receptors hyperpolarizes GABA interneurons, which results in an inhibition of GABA release. This decreased release of GABA onto DA cells of the VTA in turn increases the firing of DA cells (Di Chiara & North, 1992).

There is also evidence that other neurotransmitter systems may play more of a modulating role in transmitting the reward relevant signal. For example, work by Rompre and Gratton (1993) suggests that activation of neurotensin receptors of the ventromedial tegmental area can potentiate responding for brain-stimulation reward, most probably by enhancing DA neurotransmission.

■ ADDITIONAL ANATOMICAL SITES
IN THIS MULTISYNAPTIC PATHWAY

Logically speaking, likely candidates for additional links in this multisynaptic reward pathway are the major terminal or projection fields of the VTA and n. accumbens, including, among other structures, the ventral pallidum, the dorsomedial nucleus of the thalamus, and the medial prefrontal cortex. For example, the ventral pallidum has recently been shown to participate in opiate- and cocaine-induced reward (Hubner & Koob, 1987), and there is increasing evidence that the medial prefrontal cortex, in addition to serving as an important site for contingent brain-stimulation reward, mediates an important aspect of cocaine- (Goeders, Dworkin, & Smith, 1986; Goeders & Smith, 1983, 1986; Koob, 1992) and amphetamine-induced reward (Koob, 1992; Phillips, Mora, & Rolls, 1981).

Although direct evidence for the involvement of the dorsomedial nucleus of the thalamus in reward has not yet been demonstrated, Porrino, Esposito, et al. (1984) found selective bilateral increases in LCGU in this nucleus during goal-oriented, response-contingent, unilateral self-stimulation of the VTA. This finding extends previous work by a number of researchers suggesting that the dorsomedial nucleus of the thalamus and the prefrontal cortex form a critical functional unit in goal-oriented delayed response tasks (e.g., see Fuster, 1973). Considering the well-documented effects of severing the thalamo-cortical connections to the frontal cortex (frontal lobotomy), and the sensory information (emotion) that is thought to be processed and relayed to the frontal cortex via this nucleus, evidence for its involvement will no doubt be forthcoming, as researchers begin to turn their attention to the thalamic nuclei. Increases in LCGU were also found in other terminal fields of the VTA during response-contingent reward, including the n. accumbens, medial prefrontal cortex, amygdala, hippocampus (CA3), locus coeruleus, dorsal raphe, and lateral septum (Porrino, Esposito, et al., 1984).

Interestingly, a different pattern of selective increases in LCGU was seen during noncontingent (experimenter-administered) stimulation of the VTA. For example, in the medial prefrontal cortex and n. accumbens, significant increases in LCGU were found in the response-contingent group, but not in the experimenter-administered group. During experimenter-administered stimulation of the VTA, increases in LCGU were restricted to the ipsilateral lateral septum, dorsomedial nucleus of the thalamus, and hippocampus (CA3), as well as bilaterally to the dorsal raphe and locus coeruleus. These clear differences in LCGU during contingent versus noncontingent reward were accompanied by clear-cut differences in behavior. The behavior of animals responding in the contingent condition was reported to be highly organized and goal-directed, whereas the behavior of animals in the noncontingent group was disorganized and nondirected (Porrino, Esposito, et al., 1984).

■ A PROMISING NEW TECHNIQUE

In the near future, neuroscientists may use living strains of viruses to trace the movement of the reward signal through the brain. In contrast to more conventional chemical tracers, which stop after reaching their initial destination, living strains of viruses can follow the flow of a nerve impulse from one cell to another for a greater distance and with a greater degree of resolution. This is because living viruses move farther and replicate in every cell along the pathway (Leutwyler, 1996).

8

Conditioned Reward

CONDITIONED PLACE PREFERENCE AND
CONDITIONED REINFORCEMENT PARADIGMS

Attempts to distinguish between conditioned versus primary reward have made use of sensitive conditioned place preference (CPP) and conditioned reinforcement (CR) paradigms. In the CPP paradigm, an animal is conditioned to associate the pleasurable effects of rewarding brain stimulation or drug-induced reward with a particular environment. Then on drug-free or stimulation-free test days, the amount of time spent in the rewarding versus neutral environment is measured. The existence of a preference for the rewarding environment is taken as evidence that the drug or the stimulation had rewarding effects on training days. In this manner, the behavior measured on test days is not a measure of the primary reward *experienced* during training, but rather a measure of the *memory* of that experience, that is, conditioned reward.

Implicit in this paradigm is the assumption that particular stimuli present within the drug environment or the brain stimulation reward environment take on discriminative stimulus properties, forecasting, if you will, the probability that primary reward will be forthcoming.

In the CR paradigm, animals learn a new instrumental response (e.g., bar pressing) solely as a consequence of being reinforced by a stimulus (e.g., a tone or a light) that has previously been associated with the delivery of a primary reward (e.g., food, water, sex). As in the CPP paradigm, the conditioned reward stimulus is effective because it sets up the *expectation* that primary reward will be forthcoming.

■ THE NUCLEUS ACCUMBENS: AN IMPORTANT SUBSTRATE FOR CONDITIONED REWARD

Consistent with the findings of Porrino, Esposito, et al. (1984), who found selective increases in local cerebral glucose utilization (LCGU) in the n. accumbens and medial prefrontal cortex in animals self-stimulating for brain-stimulation reward, the results of CPP and CR experiments provide strong evidence that the n. accumbens serves as an important substrate for conditioned reward (e.g., White, Packard, & Hiroi, 1991). For example, microinjections of d-amphetamine into the n. accumbens (anteroventral regions medial to the anterior commissure were most effective), but not caudate, produced conditioned place preferences (Carr & White, 1983, 1986; Hiroi & White, 1990) and a dose-dependent enhancement of responding for conditioned reinforcers (Kelley & Delfs, 1991a, 1991b; Taylor & Robbins, 1984). Moreover, amphetamine-induced enhancement of responding for conditioned reward can be attenuated by 6-OHDA-induced lesions of the n. accumbens, but not caudate (Robbins & Everitt, 1982; Taylor & Robbins, 1986), providing further evidence that dopaminergic fibers projecting to the n. accumbens are critically involved. Microdialysis studies have demonstrated that amphetamine increases simultaneously extracellular levels of DA in the n. accumbens and medial prefrontal cortex (Moghaddam et al., 1990). As with other types of reward phenomena, more than one brain site no doubt forms the substrate for the amphetamine-induced enhancement of conditioned reward.

More recently, Cador, Taylor, and Robbins (1991) found that DA injections alone into the n. accumbens potentiated responding for conditioned reinforcement. Further evidence for the involvement of this structure in conditioned reward has also been provided by the work of Phillips, Atkinson, Blackburn, and Blaha (1993), who observed significant increases in n. accumbens DA overflow upon the presentation of a conditioned stimulus predictive of food reward. Not only was DA overflow elevated during the presentation of the conditioned stimulus, but it remained elevated during and following consumption of the meal. Similar increases in n. accumbens DA have also been observed during the presentation of cues signaling other types of natural rewards, for example, the incentive olfactory and behavioral cues associated with an estrous female prior to active copulation (Pfaus et al., 1990; Wenkstern, Pfaus, & Fibiger, 1993).

■ THE NUCLEUS ACCUMBENS: WHERE MOTIVATION AND ACTION INTERFACE

It has been suggested that the n. accumbens is the site where the motivational inputs to the brain meet the motor outputs (e.g., Mogenson, 1987; Mogenson et al.,

1980); that is, the n. accumbens is where these systems interface and integrate to convert motivation into action. Anatomical evidence places the n. accumbens strategically between limbic and motor structures. And, as previously indicated, the accumbens receives multiple converging inputs from both cortical and limbic brain structures. Current thinking is that DA release in the accumbens may actually function—in part—to modulate the influence of such inputs.

For example, there is evidence that the *hyperkinetic* response that occurs via stimulation of glutamatergic hippocampal afferents to the n. accumbens, and the *hypomotor* response that occurs via stimulation of glutamatergic amygdala inputs to this nucleus are reversed by n. accumbens DA (Mogenson et al., 1988). These opposite and seemingly complementary effects of n. accumbens DA on behavior are thought to be mediated via stimulation of D_2 receptors located presynaptically on hippocampal and amygdala afferents to the accumbens, for they can be reproduced by D_2 but not D_1 agonists.

According to Mogenson and coworkers (1988), such presynaptic control of multiple converging limbic inputs to the n. accumbens would permit the selective expression of certain behaviors associated with a particular pattern of limbic input, as well as the simultaneous suppression of conflicting or inappropriate behaviors associated with another pattern of limbic input. Thus sexual behavior would be facilitated under certain conditions, while competing consummatory behaviors such as eating or drinking would be suppressed.

■ A CELLULAR ANALOGUE
OF CONDITIONED REWARD

One of the most exciting recent developments in the attempts of neuroscientists to identify the neurophysiological substrate(s) of reward has been the identification by Stein and colleagues (Stein & Belluzzi, 1989; Stein, Xue, & Belluzzi, 1993, 1994) of an apparent cellular analogue of operant conditioning. Using the rat hippocampal slice preparation, these researchers found that a naturally occurring response (i.e., a bursting pattern of firing of individual CA1 neurons of the hippocampus) could be positively reinforced by local, contingent application of DA, cocaine, or the dopamine D_2 agonist N-0437 as the reinforcing substance (see Figure 8.1).

The rewarding effect of DA on CA1 bursting activity was shown to be dose-related and to be constrained to a rather narrow range of doses (see Figure 8.2). More specifically, bursting rates peaked at 1 mM, and fell sharply when this dose was either halved or doubled (Stein et al., 1993). In an earlier study (Belluzzi & Stein, 1987), the reinforcing effect of the DA agonist N-0437 on CA1 bursting was found to be completely eliminated by reinforcement delays of 200ms or greater (see Figure 8.3).

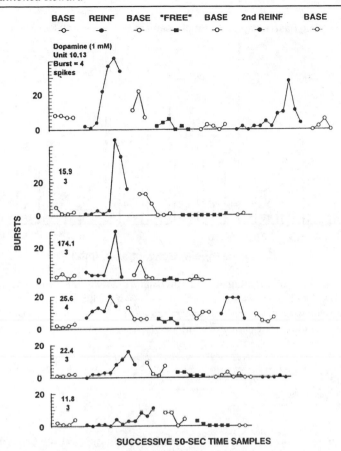

Figure 8.1: Operant Conditioning of CA1 Pyramidal Cells of the Hippocampus by Contingent Application of Dopamine (DA). The bursting activity of the six CA1 pyramidal cells throughout the seven phases of a complete experiment is shown. Each point shows the number of bursts in successive 50-second samples. BASE = baseline or extinction periods, in which bursts have no programmed consequences; REINF = first reinforcement period, in which each burst is followed immediately by a 50-second micropressure injection of 1mM dopamine (DA); FREE = burst-independent DA injections (matched to the three highest numbers of contingent injections per 50 seconds earned in the first reinforcement period). Bursting rates were increased by contingent injections during reinforcement periods but were not increased by a matched number of noncontingent injections during FREE periods. Numbers above the initial baseline period in each plot designate different CA1 units and spike requirements for bursts.

Source: L. Stein, B. G. Xue, & J. D. Belluzzi (1994), "In Vitro Reinforcement of Hippocampal Bursting: A Search for Skinner's Atoms of Behavior," *Journal of the Experimental Analysis of Behavior, 61,* 160. © 1994, by the Society for the Experimental Analysis of Behavior, Inc. Reprinted by permission of the Society and Larry Stein.

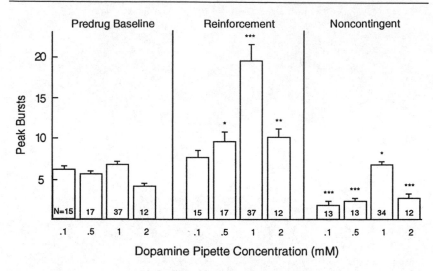

Figure 8.2: Operant Conditioning of CA1 Bursting Activity as a Function of Dopamine (DA) Dose. Eighty-one CA1 pyramidal cells of the hippocampus received operant conditioning training at various concentrations of DA. Bars indicate mean ± SEM peak rates of bursting during baseline, reinforcement, and noncontingent match control phases of the experiment. N = number of cells.

Source: L. Stein, B. G. Xue, & J. D. Belluzzi (1993), "A Cellular Analogue of Operant Conditioning," *Journal of the Experimental Analysis of Behavior, 60,* 47. © 1993, by the Society for the Experimental Analysis of Behavior, Inc. Reprinted by permission of the Society and L. Stein.

Note: Significantly different from baseline at $*p < 0.05$; $**p < 0.01$; $***p < 0.001$.

This finding is consistent with the well-known findings from behavioral studies demonstrating the adverse effect of reinforcement delays on the acquisition of operant behavior. For example, the acquisition of bar-pressing for rewarding electrical stimulation of the MFB has been shown to be completely eliminated by delays of 1 second or more (Black, Belluzzi, & Stein, 1985) (see Figure 8.4). As Stein and coworkers have suggested, the fact that a similar delay-of-reinforcement gradient can be demonstrated on the cellular level suggests that behavioral and cellular reinforcement processes are interrelated.

Furthermore, taken together, the above findings lend support to the hypothesis that positive reinforcement is exerted at the cellular rather than the systems level. That is, it is now thought that positive reinforcement involves a strengthening of the responses of the *relevant individual neurons* within the neuronal system subserving a particular behavior, rather than a strengthening of, or a reorganization of the entire system involved in the response (Stein et al., 1993).

Future research using the hippocampal slice preparation and other models of cellular conditioning should lead to exciting new insights into the cellular

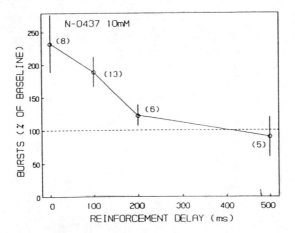

Figure 8.3: Reinforcement Delays Diminish the Effectiveness of Reinforcement on CA1 Bursting Activity. Delay of reinforcement gradient in cellular operant conditioning using the DA agonist N-0437 (10 mM) as the reinforcer. The number of neurons tested at each reinforcement delay is indicated in parentheses. Vertical lines indicate ± SEM. Note that delays exceeding 200 ms largely eliminate the effectiveness of N-0437 reinforcement on CA1 bursting.

Source: L. Stein, B. G. Xue, & J. D. Belluzzi (1993), "A Cellular Analogue of Operant Conditioning," *Journal of the Experimental Analysis of Behavior, 60,* 50. © 1993, by the Society for the Experimental Analysis of Behavior, Inc. Reprinted by permission of the Society and L. Stein. After Belluzzi & Stein, 1987.

mechanisms subserving reinforcement and memory. From a clinical perspective, this line of research may eventually help us to understand, for example, how psychic feeling is complexed with events and behaviors in memory—that is, how events and associated behaviors acquire their meaning. We do know that activation of the hippocampus is necessary for memory consolidation. Given that there are reciprocal connections between the DA reward systems of the brain (e.g., n. accumbens) and CA1 neurons in the hippocampus, it would be interesting to determine, for example, whether activity in this pathway is critically involved. That is, does the consistent, contingent delivery of a rewarding stimulus—in this case, DA—in response to a particular pattern of activity of CA1 cells of the hippocampus function to strengthen the activity of neurons subserving—in part—the memory of an event and its associated behaviors?

Furthermore, when these previously reinforced CA1 hippocampal inputs to the n. accumbens are subsequently activated, does this increase the probability of a particular operant running off to completion because the neurons subserving, in part, the memory of that operant have been strongly imprinted with psychic pleasure (reward) in the past, and therefore are more strongly associated with the probability of rewarding consequences in the future?

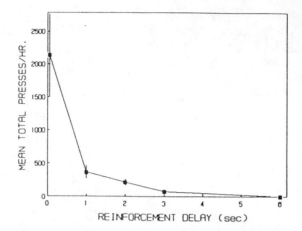

Figure 8.4: Reinforcement Delays of as Little as 1 Second Impede the Acquisition of Self-Stimulation Behavior. Acquisition of lever-pressing behavior for medial forebrain bundle (MFB) stimulation as a function of reinforcement delay. Shown are the total number of lever presses on the first day of training for different groups of rats whose responses were reinforced by MFB stimulation after the indicated delay. Note that a delay of only 1 second produced a rate decrease of about 80%. Compare with the delay-of-reinforcement gradient shown in Figure 8.3.

Source: L. Stein, B. G. Xue, & J. D. Belluzzi (1993), "A Cellular Analogue of Operant Conditioning," *Journal of the Experimental Analysis of Behavior, 60,* 50. © 1993, by the Society for the Experimental Analysis of Behavior, Inc. Reprinted by permission of the Society and L. Stein. After Black et al., 1985.

The answers to these and related questions will no doubt be years in coming, but such research holds the promise of establishing a true science of human behavior. From a clinical perspective, this will give us something real to hang our theories and concepts on. When we use accepted psychological terms such as repression or projection, for example, we may finally be able to point to an associated neurophysiological mechanism subserving such phenomena. Conversely, as we learn more about brain function and behavior, many of our long-standing notions about psychic phenomena will no doubt fall by the wayside.

Finally, Wise (Wise, 1987; Wise & Bozarth, 1987) and others (Glickman & Schiff, 1967) have argued that there is one final common pathway subserving brain-stimulation reward, the rewarding effects induced by natural reinforcers such as food and water, and the pleasurable effects associated with the ingestion of addictive substances such as alcohol or cocaine. It is an endogenous reward pathway involving the reward circuitry of the MFB, which evolved in the service of more natural rewards and has as its final common denominator the elicitation of pursuit or approach behavior (for a review of the evidence for this view, see Wise, 1987, and/or Wise & Bozarth, 1987). Subsequent work by Gratton and Wise (1988) is supportive of this viewpoint; that is, activation of a subpopulation of MFB fibers sustaining both brain-stimulation reward and stimulation-induced feeding were found to have remarkably similar refractory periods, suggesting that common fibers subserve the two behaviors.

9

Punishment Systems, Functional Interactions With Reward Systems

■ **PUNISHMENT SYSTEMS OF THE BRAIN**

In contrast to the reward systems, the punishment systems of the brain have been less well-studied and therefore less well-characterized. Available evidence suggests that serotonergic pathways are involved (Stein et al., 1977; Stein, Wise, & Berger, 1973), as well as periventricular structures such as the dorsal portion of the periaqueductal gray (PAG) (Olds & Olds, 1963). In an early study, Wise et al. (1973) observed suppression of self-stimulation and increased suppression of punished behavior in rats with intraventricular injections of 5-HT and the alpha-noradrenergic antagonist phentolamine, whereas injections of p-chlorophenylalanine (PCPA), a 5-HT synthesis inhibitor, produced increased rates of punished behavior. This latter effect was reversed after intraperitoneal injections of the serotonin precursor, 5-HTP (5-hydroxytryptophan).

Similar to the previously discussed argument by Wise and colleagues regarding endogenous reward (Wise, 1987; Wise & Bozarth, 1987), we may find that there is one common final pathway subserving the punishing effects associated with electrical stimulation of the periventricular structures of the brain, the painful effects of naturally occurring noxious stimuli, and the unpleasant feelings accompanying so-called psychic phenomena such as guilt, anxiety, and shame. Although yet to be fully identified, this putative endogenous punishment system may have evolved in service of more natural punishers and have as its final common denominator the suppression or inhibition of ongoing behavior.

■ FUNCTIONAL INTERACTIONS WITH REWARD SYSTEMS: SOME PRELIMINARY EVIDENCE

As originally suggested by Stein (1964), there is reason to believe that these two opposing and complementary motivational systems of the brain "are mutually inhibitory, like antagonistic spinal reflexes" (p. 115). Moreover, there is evidence that these systems work in concert—that the influence of each may be felt in operant behavior. In the literature, an operant is defined as any behavior that is emitted or generated voluntarily—at least to some degree—by an organism, in contrast to reflexive behavior, which is involuntary. An operant is said to be voluntary in that it is often impossible to determine the specific stimulus that could have elicited it. The primary distinction between the two classes of behavior is largely in terms of the control exerted by the environment. In the case of reflexive behavior, the critical environmental stimuli precede the response and specifically elicit it; in the case of operant behavior, the critical stimuli follow the response and modify its rate of expression. Rewarding stimuli make the behaviors they follow more likely; punishing stimuli make the behaviors they follow less likely.

If reward is withheld or punishment terminated, opposite effects are observed. Operants previously maintained by rewarding consequences tend to be inhibited or extinguished under such conditions; operants maintained by the avoidance or termination of a punishing stimulus tend to be facilitated (see Table 9.1). Further, it is well-established that rewarding stimuli are less effective under the threat of punishment and, likewise, that punishing stimuli become less effective under a background of rewarding stimulation (e.g., see Figure 9.1).

With these basic principles of conditioning in mind, it is possible to extrapolate to a hypothetical situation from everyday life to illustrate Stein's (1964) concepts of joint action and reciprocal inhibition. Suppose, for example, that you have to make an unpleasant phone call. You have been putting it off—anticipating the potential for unpleasantness. Finally, you have a couple of glasses of wine and are relieved to find that the call no longer seems so aversive. You approach the phone and make the call. How can we explain this behavior physiologically? To paraphrase Stein (1964)—after all, how can an anticipated future punishing event—which, by definition, has yet to occur—act on a present operant, decreasing the likelihood of its emission. Moreover, how can we explain

TABLE 9.1 Experimental Situations Resulting From Presentation or Withholding
of Either Reward or Punishment After a Designated Response

Type of stimulus	Presented	Withheld
Rewarding	Reward (facilitation)	Extinction[a] (inhibition)
Punishing	Punishment (inhibition)	Avoidance (facilitation)

Source: L. Stein (1964), "Reciprocal Action of Reward and Punishment Mechanisms," in R. G. Heath (Ed.),
The Role of Pleasure in Behavior, New York: Harper & Row, 121. Reprinted by permission of
Lippincott-Raven Publishers.

Note: Effect on the behavior is given in parentheses.

a. Strictly speaking, this refers to an experimental situation in which the regular presentation of reward is
interrupted each time the response occurs. In the usual extinction situation, reward is withheld altogether.

such a change of heart following a couple of glasses of wine? As previously
discussed, Stein speculated that it is the *expectation* and not the actual delivery
of reward or punishment that directly engages or motivates operant behavior,
and moreover that this expectancy mechanism is a *Pavlovian conditioned reflex*
resulting in the activation of response-facilitating "go" systems in the case of
reward and response-suppressant "stop" (or no-go) systems in the case of
punishment. The actual delivery of reward or punishment serves to maintain or
solidify the expectation.

In the above hypothetical example—following Stein's (1964) reasoning—
because of unpleasant consequences in the past, the thought of making the call
induced a reflexive activation of the punishment systems, stimulating subjective
feelings of an unpleasant nature. Such feelings are inhibitory—decreasing the
probability that the call will be made. However, if we alter the situation by a
pharmacological activation of the pleasure centers of the brain—alcohol, in low
doses, has a well-documented stimulating effect on dopaminergic reward and
motor systems of the brain (e.g., Samson & Harris, 1992)—we would release
the reward and ultimately the motor systems from their previous level of
suppression by punishment systems. Reward systems would enjoy a brief period
of increased activity in this case, thereby increasing the likelihood that the
operant will progress to completion. In other words, the background of pleasurable sensations has, so to speak, taken the sting out of the anticipated aversive-
ness of the phone call—it has reciprocally inhibited the inhibitor.

As illustrated in this hypothetical situation—as in the experimental findings
shown in Figure 9.1—both systems played a part in the final net outcome. From
a commonsense perspective, such an outcome must be subserved by a physiological mechanism that allows for an intimate and interdependent communication between the reward and punishment systems of the brain on the one hand
and between these systems and the motor systems of the brain on the other.

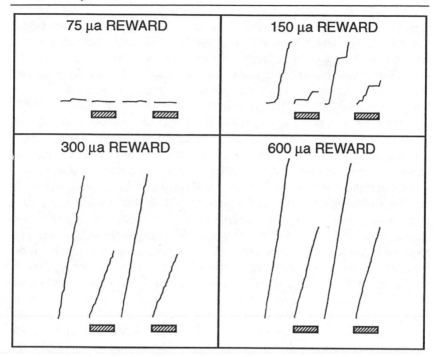

Figure 9.1: Effect of the Simultaneous Delivery of a Punishing Stimulus and a Rewarding Stimulus on Self-Stimulation Behavior. Shown are the cumulative response records from one animal self-stimulating for reward alone (first and third segments of each quadrant), and for both reward and punishment (indicated by black horizontal bar in second and fourth segments of each quadrant). The height of each segment indicates total self-stimulation output in a 5-minute period. Electrode coordinates are in millimeters as follows: anterior (+), or posterior (–) from bregma; lateral from midline; depth from surface of brain.

Source: L. Stein (1964), "Reciprocal Action of Reward and Punishment Mechanisms," in R. G. Heath (Ed.), *The Role of Pleasure in Behavior,* New York: Harper & Row, 120. Reprinted by permission of Lippincott-Raven Publishers.

Findings from a study by Feldman and Quenzer (1984) looking at the effect of fluoxetine versus chlordiazepoxide on punished behavior will further illustrate this point. Fluoxetine is a specific 5-HT re-uptake inhibitor. By inhibiting the re-uptake of 5-HT, fluoxetine potentiates 5-HT effects in the synapse. In contrast, chlordiazepoxide belongs to a class of compounds known as the benzodiazepines, which have inhibitory effects on 5-HT. The benzodiazepines are used to relieve anxiety, a psychically aversive state characterized typically by excessive worry over some impending or anticipated event. The specific antianxiety effects of the benzodiazepines are thought to be mediated by a GABAergic inhibition of 5-HT release (Feldman, Meyer, & Quenzer, 1996). Operant responding in animals treated with the benzodiazepines is atypical; that is, operants previously suppressed by punishing consequences are no longer suppressed to the same degree, but rather response rates tend to increase depending upon the dose, with higher doses having a more pronounced effect.

In their study, Feldman and Quenzer (1984) used a modification of the classic conflict paradigm of Geller and Seifter (1960). In this paradigm, operant responding is reinforced by the delivery of reward, but sometimes the reward is also accompanied by the delivery of a mild punishing stimulus, for example, foot shock. Animals will continue to work for the reward under these conditions, but response rates are lower than rates observed under the reward-only condition.

The specific experimental conditions employed by Feldman and Quenzer (1984) were as follows. In one condition, the bar-pressing behavior of rats was reinforced on a variable interval schedule (VI-40 second) of sweetened milk reward. After 5 minutes on this schedule, a light appeared over the milk dispenser, and the schedule was changed to one of continuous reinforcement (CRF). During the CRF conflict period, each bar press was followed by presentation of the sweetened milk reward, but simultaneously, the animals received a brief (0.5 second) mild foot shock. Under the conflict condition, a complete suppression of the operant would not be anticipated as the background of rewarding conditions; that is, the delivery of the sweetened milk along with the foot shock would be expected to maintain the operant, although at lower levels. These two conditions alternated every 5 minutes for a total of 60 minutes. During test days, experimental conditions remained unchanged except that the animals were given fluoxetine or chlordiazepoxide.

Figure 9.2a depicts the cumulative response record from a single fluoxetine-treated animal. As predicted, baseline response rates were higher during the variable interval (VI) reward-only condition than during the CRF reward-plus-punishment condition, that is, 23.6 versus 8.13 responses per minute, respectively (see Session 1). During Sessions 2 to 5, there was a further suppression of CRF responding induced by fluoxetine, with higher doses having a more pronounced effect. At the highest dose tested (15 mg/kg) there was an almost total suppression of bar pressing in comparison to the control (no drug) condition, that is, 0.7 versus 8.13 responses per minute, respectively.

In the presence of 15 mg/kg fluoxetine, the same intensity shock had become a more powerful deterrent; the animal was no longer willing to work for the

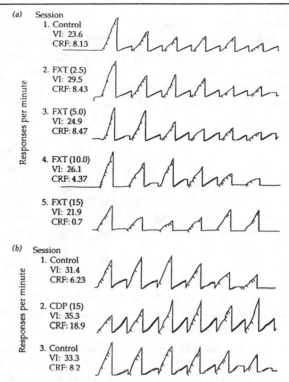

Figure 9.2: Effect of Fluoxetine (FXT) and Chlordiazepoxide (CDP) on Punishment-Induced Behavioral Suppression. (a) FXT, an indirect 5-HT agonist, further decreases responding (dose-dependently) during the reward-plus-punishment CRF schedule. (b) CDP, a 5-HT antagonist, markedly increases responding during the reward-plus-punishment CRF schedule.

Source: R. S. Feldman & L. Quenzer (1984), *Fundamentals of Neuropsychopharmacology,* Sunderland, MA: Sinauer Associates, p. 359. Reprinted by permission of Sinauer Associates, Inc., and R. S. Feldman.

sweetened milk reward under such conditions. Following Stein's (1964) reasoning, the expectation of punishment, established through prior experience, had been heightened by fluoxetine, presumably by increasing 5-HT activity in the synapse. Simultaneously, the expectation of reward had been diminished. The net outcome—an almost total suppression of operant responding—may be said to have been determined by the two systems working in concert. In other words, by potentiating the effectiveness of the punisher, fluoxetine had also diminished the effectiveness of the reward. In this case, punishment avoidance systems almost totally superseded reward approach systems, but clearly both systems determined the final net outcome.

That this effect was specific to the CRF conflict condition and not due to a generalized fluoxetine-induced impairment in responding is indicated by the performance of the animal during the VI schedule; response rates remained relatively unchanged by 15 mg/kg fluoxetine in comparison to baseline, that is, 21.9 versus 23.6, respectively. In other words, fluoxetine by itself is not necessarily aversive or inhibitory; but providing it under a background of aversive stimuli can potentiate, in a dose-related fashion, the inhibitory effects of such stimuli. This explanation is consistent with the idea that, under other conditions, fluoxetine may even facilitate responding, for example, by enhancing the effect of negative feedback to errors made during the acquisition of a chain of responses comprising an operant. In other words, wrong moves in the chain may be more effectively punished and therefore more quickly inhibited thereby decreasing the expectation for punishment; on the other hand, correct moves in the chain would continue to be rewarded. The net effect may be a quicker acquisition of the operant.

This idea is also consistent with the observation that, at least for this animal, lower doses of fluoxetine appeared to have a mild facilitory effect on bar-pressing behavior during the VI (reward only) schedule of reinforcement; that is, VI response rates appeared to be slightly elevated by 2.5, 5.0, and 10.0 mg/kg fluoxetine in comparison to the control (nondrug) condition. How can we explain this effect? It is well-known that animals trained on VI schedules of reinforcement maintain high rates of responding. This appears to be related to the predictability of the timing of the reward; that is, due to past experience, the animals "know" that pressing the bar will eventually result in the delivery of the reward, but they don't know exactly when. In this case, the effects of prior reward persist and appear to maintain responding during times in the interval when reward is not immediately forthcoming. Said another way, the loss of reward associated with not responding is aversive and therefore serves to inhibit the behavior of not responding. The net outcome, again determined by the joint action of both systems, is that responding is maintained at a high rate. Here again we see that punishment mechanisms participated in what would appear, at first glance, to be a pure reward situation.

Figure 9.2b depicts the cumulative response record for a single animal treated with chlordiazepoxide (CDP) (15 mg/kg). As can be seen, CDP was associated with a marked increase in responding during the CRF conflict period, in comparison to the control no-drug session, that is, 18.9 versus 6.23 and 8.2 times per minute, respectively. The animal was now more willing to work for the sweetened milk reward in the presence of the shock. CDP had—so to speak—taken some of the sting out of the punisher, presumably by a GABAergic-mediated enhanced inhibition of 5-HT release. CDP had—in effect—inhibited the inhibitor. Using Stein's (1964) reasoning, the expectation of the punishing consequence, established through prior experience, had been diminished by CDP; reflexively, the expectation of reward was increased. Incentive pursuit or "go" systems rebounded from their previous level of inhibition by punishment suppressant "stop" systems, resulting in the observed increase in bar-pressing behavior. Clearly, both reward and punishment mechanisms participated in the final outcome. This idea of a reciprocal inhibitory relationship between punishment and reward systems receives additional support from the well-documented, mutually inhibitory link between 5-HT activity and dopaminergic function (e.g., see Montgomery et al., 1991, and references cited therein).

■ SUMMARY

Stein (1964) has proposed that operant behavior is directly engaged by the expectation of either reward or punishment. The actual delivery of the rewarding or punishing consequence serves a critical but indirect role, that of maintaining the expectation. Further, the mechanism for expectation is said to be a Pavlovian conditioned reflex, resulting in the activation of pursuit mechanisms in the case of reward or the avoidance of punishment and of avoidance systems in the case of punishment or extinction (loss of reward). Activation of reward systems provides positive feedback and facilitates operant responding; activation of punishment systems provides negative feedback and inhibits it. Furthermore, reward and punishment mechanisms are mutually inhibitory; that is, when one is activated the other is suppressed. The extent to which these systems rebound following inhibition is said to vary directly with the intensity of their previous suppression. Finally, as supported by the data from the above studies, these critical motivational systems are said to work in concert—to feed continuously into motor systems, and to jointly determine the net effect on operant behavior.

Stein's (1964) explanation of operant behavior puts into words (and provides a neural mechanism for) what we already know from a commonsense perspective—that the effects of our prior experience persist and over time begin to take on predictive value. In everyday language, they begin to set us up to expect similar results in the future because of similar outcomes in the past. The predictive value of such effects can be expected to be profound in the case of intense stimulation of these systems and slight in the case of liminal stimulation.

Factors that enhance the predictive value of rewarding or punishing stimuli may arise either from internal or external sources. In the case of intrinsic factors, for example, the threshold for activation in these systems may be low in the sense that liminal stimulation results in their full-blown excitation. In the case of external factors, drugs that increase the activity of these systems may be administered, resulting in some enhanced internal processing ability in association with ongoing activity. Further, the external environment may be favorably altered; that is, factors that promote conditioning can be made a more salient aspect of the individual's daily existence.

In our treatment of individuals with ADHD, we try to improve the functioning of these two complementary and mutually inhibitory motivational systems of the brain with an eye toward promoting the development of expectancy mechanisms and enhancing the predictive value of relevant stimuli.

Section 4

Treatment

Our Perspective and Practice

10

Behavior Management, Psychotherapy

■ OPENING COMMENTS

The concepts and strategies discussed in this and the subsequent sections on treatment represent our perspective on the underlying nature of ADHD, as well as the approaches that we have—through experience—found useful in treatment. Many recommendations reflect accepted practice. As such the reader should expect to see commonalities between our approach and the published work of others. The fact that we have not cited these authorities in this section should not be interpreted as a lack of appreciation for, or a lack of awareness of, the important contributions that others have made. As a point of view endeavor, our emphasis in this work is on our own conceptual thinking and clinical experience. There are, of course, other perspectives. For an excellent description of prevailing theory and standard practice in the field, the reader is referred to such notables as Barkley (1990).

■ THE THERAPIST AS CONSULTANT

In helping parents and others manage the behavior of ADHD children, we have found that our proper position—at least initially—is one of consultant, that is, teacher, adviser, to those people directly involved in the child's care and development on a daily basis. The more these significant caretakers can appreciate and internalize the basic nature of the child's problem as the inadequate functioning of the reward and punishment systems of the brain, the better they will be at managing the child's difficulties.

As previously noted, we view the normal activation of these systems as being essential to the brain's capacity to process and store in memory the feeling component of experience—painful feelings such as guilt and remorse and pleasurable feelings such as contentment and joy. The implications of a dysfunction in this mechanism for the young child are far-reaching. With other sensory modalities intact, the child can process events into memory, but such memories are fundamentally meaningless.

Without a meaningful repertoire of past experience to draw from in evaluating the stimuli of the moment or in predicting the future, the child is adrift in the world of the immediate moment with no rudder to guide its ship. In more technical terms, the mechanism of conditioned expectancy does not develop—there is insufficient, or in the extreme case, no reflexive activation of the reward and punishment systems in association with ongoing activity, and therefore, no ability to anticipate the possible consequences of words or deeds because of similar consequences in the past.

Instead the child's behavior remains more or less random and unpredictable. Further, without an adequate capacity to experience psychic pain and psychic pleasure, there can be no meaningful internalization of abstract concepts such as right and wrong, or good and bad, that is, no internalization of a moral, humanistic conscience; no deep appreciation of the pleasure and pain of others, that is, no capacity for empathy; no true ability to trust in others for such trust is based on the relative certainty of events in the future because such events were contained in the past.

One can imagine the inner world of ADHD children to be a cold and lonely place indeed, for just as they are unable to attach sufficient meaning to events and objects, such children are unable to internalize the psychic feeling associated with others, so that when a significant other leaves their presence, so too do the feelings associated with that person, with only emptiness remaining. Able to retain only the image and words of that person, the child's memories are more like cool black and white photo snapshots rather than warm colorful paintings.

In view of the difficulty that the ADHD child has with the processing of psychic feeling, individual psychotherapy is contraindicated—at least initially. Until the child is able to develop a feeling bond with the therapist, the therapeutic relationship will be tenuous at best. And given the high activity level and distractibility of children with this temperament, getting and sustaining their attention for such work is a fruitless endeavor. Expecting lasting changes from a weekly 50-minute therapy session under these conditions can be likened to bailing out a sinking boat with a teaspoon. On the other hand, if the parents are open to a trial of medication from the beginning, the medication—in the appropriate dose and dose frequency schedule—will lead to immediate improvements in the child's capacity to process psychic feeling. In this case, individual psychotherapy may be incorporated into the early phase of treatment. But initially, the job of the therapist is to consult—to explain the underlying nature of the disorder, the purpose and use of medication, how to manage the child at home and in school—and to support by lending a sympathetic ear and reinforcing the positive efforts of parents and others involved in the child's direct care.

■ THE FOCUS IN THERAPY

When individual psychotherapy becomes a part of treatment, a major function we fulfill is one of facilitator of the attachment of appropriate feeling tone to past and current experiences as they are revealed in therapy. With very young children, whose verbal skills and logical reasoning capacities are still immature, play therapy is used as the primary vehicle for change. Children are engaged by toys or books or board games or by other activities of interest. Within the context of the play activity, therapeutic correction takes place—positive behavior is rewarded and inappropriate behavior discouraged. Any thoughts or feelings or past experiences that the child reveals during therapy are accepted, discussed and, where necessary, reevaluated for meaning. This reevaluation is accomplished by stimulating—in tone of voice and facial expression, the child's feeling brain. Expressions of approval and praise, for example, are used to complex good deeds with good feeling. Similarly, a sense of personal disappointment in the child, as conveyed by tone of voice and facial expression, is used to complex bad deeds with bad feeling.

Once again, the major emphasis in therapy, as well as in the home management program, is on stimulating the child's feeling brain—complexing good behavior with pleasurable feeling and bad behavior with unpleasant feeling. And in this sense, the role of the therapist is very much like that of the parent—to nurture and to enculturate—to help meet the child's need for feeling attention while teaching the child right from wrong, good from bad, appropriate from inappropriate.

With adolescents, the overall focus of therapeutic intervention is broadened, and more emphasis is placed on encouraging their development as independent individuals within society with their own particular talents and abilities to offer. We use a Socratic approach in this regard in order to stimulate the thinking brain. Questions push for fitting answers. Until the "right" answer is found, there is always some degree of discomfort. Moreover, fitting answers are idiosyncratic—only the individual can tell if "the shoe fits." However, until there has been considerable improvement in the brain's capacity to process psychic feeling, the individual will have little sense of what fits—of what it means to follow a suitable path, to have faith in oneself, to find one's real life's work. Rather, there will be heavy reliance on external happenstance and outside authority for direction. This process naturally takes time, for it is dependent upon the maturation of brain function, and long-term treatment is appropriate.

■ KEYS TO SUCCESSFUL MANAGEMENT: IMMEDIACY, CONSISTENCY, AND CONSTANCY

In managing the behavior of the ADHD child—the emphasis is on the use of *immediacy, consistency, and constancy* in as many areas of the child's life as possible—at home, in school, and, if possible, during leisure activities. These three factors facilitate conditioning and thus are crucial to successful management. In one sense, problems managing ADHD children can be viewed as problems in conditioning. Even the use of medication can be appreciated from this perspective. By decreasing the thresholds of activation in the reward and punishment systems of the brain, medication allows the process of conditioning, that is, socialization, to take its normal course. As such it is essential for therapists to have a working knowledge of behavior management techniques so that they can be effectively communicated to parents and other caregivers.

Concepts of immediacy and consistency, although easily described and understood in principle, are not as easily internalized as one might imagine. Like other skills, they need to be practiced and reinforced before they become automatic. The attitude of the therapist toward the parent(s) during this trial-and-error period is crucial. Mistakes and frustrations are inevitable. Patient repetition of the key concepts and an accepting positive attitude strengthen the therapeutic alliance.

Even more difficult to impart and for parents to internalize is the idea of constancy. By constancy we mean an *enduring sameness* in the child's milieu, as well as an *enduring positive attitude* toward the child. For example, the youngster is assured that he or she is a loved and cherished member of the family, that he or she can succeed, and that the parent or surrogate-parent is there to help. A sense of constancy is engendered by assuring the child of a safe, loving, and predictable place in which to grow and develop—a place where the child can enter and feel comfortable. Classic absence of constancy can easily be observed in children who have been shunted from one foster home to another. Each home has its own set of values as to the appropriateness of behavior, leaving the child in a state of bewilderment and confusion about rules of conduct. A close analogy would be to suddenly—overnight—find ourselves in China with no knowledge of local customs and mores.

Significant change in the child's environment is sometimes unavoidable. To minimize negative consequences, parents are cautioned to prepare the child for any major changes within the home, for example, the arrival of a new baby or of permanent guests such as grandparents, the hospitalization of a parent, a pending divorce or separation, a move to a new home or neighborhood. The change should be repeatedly explained to the child, along with probable consequences. Such change can also create a disturbance in parental management that may show up as regressive behavior in the child. At this point, the parents are apt to request an unnecessary increase in medication. Such situations require parental consultation to help the family cope, and to reinforce the need to adhere to the original management plan.

■ SUPPORTING THE PARENTS/ ENCOURAGING A UNITED FRONT

Parents naturally have to assume the primary responsibility with respect to behavior management. Whenever possible, however, the cooperation of the child's teachers is enlisted. Unfortunately, some of our parents have been reluctant to reveal the child's diagnosis for fear of possible negative consequences, for example, stigmatizing of the child, rejection by peers, or preexisting biases on the part of some of the child's teachers, as well as the powers that be with respect to the validity of the diagnosis and/or the need for medication.

To the uninformed, ADHD symptoms are often viewed as purely psychic in origin, implying that the child has some control over their expression, and/or that poor parenting is to blame. When parents are inappropriately blamed for the child's poor behavior, an ongoing antagonism between the school and parents results. The parents, who already feel considerable guilt over the child's problems, can become even more defensive when this occurs, resulting in a total shutdown of communication between the home and the school. When dealing with an unenlightened school system, rather than push against the tide of popular opinion, the child and family are often better served if the diagnosis and need for medication remain a private matter. The child can still make progress within the classroom, and useless confrontations and power struggles between the school and home can be avoided.

Those who have never had to live with an ADHD child have little appreciation of the colossal commitments of time and energy that are required of parents on a daily basis. And because the mother is still the primary caretaker of young children in our culture, a disproportionate share of the management burden typically rests with her. As such it is easy for mother to become "burnt out," particularly if she does not have the support and cooperation of her husband. Because of the division of labor that normally happens within a marriage, father may be preoccupied with his role as breadwinner in the outside world. If he is absent a lot from the home—either physically or psychologically—he may inappropriately blame his wife for being unable to control the child. Indeed, the child may be better behaved around father, either because his attention and feedback take on added import due to their infrequency, or because father is a harsh disciplinarian, and the child is afraid.

For parents to have a complete picture of the child, good communication is essential. Parents need to understand that the lack of a united front within the home will only exacerbate the child's difficulties due, for example, to the obvious failure to provide needed constancy and consistency. In order to persist in their important functions of discipline and enculturation, the parents of these children need much support. We have found many to be insecure in this role, having been made to feel unnecessarily guilty by those who advocate a more permissive approach. Some have been told by school personnel or by relatives that they were "inhibiting their child's creativity" or "freedom of expression." Such approaches appear to serve the needs of the adults who advocate them more than the needs of the child, who is already floundering in a sea of internal impulses and distracting environmental stimuli, and whose self-directing ability is almost nonexistent. Although many parents have told us that they sensed their child's need for more structure and discipline, they were reluctant to adopt a strict approach. When their confidence was reestablished, and the necessary structure and controls were put in place, the child's behavior improved.

■ PERMISSIVE AND DISORGANIZED ENVIRONMENTS EXACERBATE DIFFICULTIES

If we view ADHD symptomatology as the product of a child-environment interaction, a disorganized, unstable home environment can be expected to promote the development of symptoms more readily than one that is more structured and stable. If the parents can learn to become more organized and structured at home, the child with mild symptoms may make gains without medication intervention. If available, home visits by an experienced therapist who is skilled in behavioral intervention strategies, and who can act as another source of support and reinforcement, can be an invaluable part of the process. Having a therapist in the home is particularly helpful when the child is from a single-parent household. Many single parents are mothers whose only source of income is state welfare programs. Because of the pressures they are under, financial and otherwise, these mothers are especially in need of some added support. Moreover, parents with limited finances often have a difficult time getting to an office. Many simply do not have the transportation. By having a professional in the home on a routine basis, there is always a communication link between the office and the home. Many potentially troublesome situations can thus be avoided.

Depending on the maturity of the parent(s), the lack of organization and structure within the home may be difficult to correct. In such cases, medication may ultimately prove to be necessary. However, such parents must be cautioned and reminded that medication alone will not turn their child into a well-adjusted, socialized individual. Although medication can make the child more able to process the feedback of parents, it cannot *substitute* for that feedback. The parents must do that important socialization work themselves. To some degree, the lack of socialization at home may be offset by the feedback and discipline provided by a well-managed school program, or by a grandparent or some other mature adult in the child's milieu who may be willing to step in—taking on a surrogate-parent role.

It is our understanding that because of the difficulty ADHD children have in processing psychic feeling, they may continually press the limits of more permissive environments. If good behavior receives no positive feeling response, children may provoke the parent or teacher with bad behavior. When the limits and rules are clearly spelled out, and immediately and consistently reinforced with appropriate feeling responses, children are better able to settle down to the task at hand.

Later in development, when progress has been made with respect to reason and forethought and self-control has become a more conspicuous aspect of behavior, children can be allowed more freedom. But first, they need to internalize and conform with existing rules and norms of behavior, and it is the job of the adult members of society to teach them. This is the only way children are going to survive in the outside world. Considering the growing lack of morality and traditional values in today's more present-oriented society, one can't help but be concerned for children with these difficulties. Whereas a freer approach is appropriate for children who are already overly sensitive to the socialization process, it is inappropriate for ADHD children, who are much more difficult to condition.

For young children, school represents the first serious encounter with authority outside the home, and it is essential that the adult prevail. Although one may empathize with the teacher who is continually forced to deal with children who view authority as an alien force interfering with self-gratification, a permissive approach in the classroom and elsewhere will only encourage the expression and continuation of symptoms.

■ BEING DIRECT AND EXPLICIT IN COMMUNICATION

Appreciating the high level of distractibility of ADHD children, because of their poor ability to attach relative meaning to stimuli, that is, to habituate, parents and teachers are advised to be very *direct and explicit* in communicating directions and feedback: making eye-to-eye contact, using a clear, distinct voice and simple terms, and if necessary, holding the child's upper arms while speaking. This is often the only way to maintain the child's attention while relating significant information.

The need for *immediacy* and *consistency* in the relaying of feedback cannot be overemphasized. This allows the brain to simultaneously stamp the behavior or event with the appropriate feeling tone, which in turn helps to establish the *expectation* that if a behavior is unacceptable on Monday, for example, it will also be unacceptable on Friday. Should a delay occur, the incident necessitating a feeling input must first be reactivated in the child's mind. Reviewing the event in explicit terms and immediately applying the appropriate feeling tone helps to ensure their simultaneous processing by the brain.

■ UNDERSTANDING THE HYPERFOCUSED CHILD

Paradoxically the same child who is completely unable to focus one minute may become totally absorbed in a particular activity for an extended period. On such occasions, the child and activity appear glued so to speak; the child's attention and concentration are total. This can happen when the activity has greater personal meaning for the child; that is, it is one that he or she enjoys. One can imagine that there is greater ongoing stimulation of the child's reinforcement systems during this time, the significance of which should not be overlooked by those attempting to find ways to motivate the child, especially when the more usual internal state of the child is subliminal stimulation of these essential feedback systems.

When attempting to disengage the child, the parent may be met with a temper tantrum or some other unpleasantness. Once again, the child's reaction can be understood as an inability to attach *relative* importance to events or ongoing stimuli of the moment, as well as to their extreme here-and-now orientation. Unable to deeply appreciate, and therefore to internalize—in a lasting sense—the feeling associated with parental demands, the child persists in having his or her own way. Moreover, despite the fact that there will be opportunities to engage in the preferred activity in the future, the child's *expectancy* of such is missing.

■ TIME-OUT AND RESPONSE COST TECHNIQUES

It has been our experience that children's negative behavior, over time, can result in a growing frustration and little tolerance on the part of the parents, which can provoke an overreaction including the use of harsh physical punishment. Obviously such harshness, whether verbal or physical, needs to be discouraged. Not only is this bad for the child, it is very disturbing for the parent who loses control and then suffers enormous guilt, perhaps even overcompensating for this by subsequently letting the child have his or her own way.

In helping parents deal more appropriately with the child's negative behaviors, we educate and reinforce parents in the use of response-cost and time-out techniques. These procedures are standard in the field, easy to teach, and fairly easy for parents to internalize. Again, keeping in mind the short attention span of ADHD children and their here-and-now orientation, parents are informed that such consequences need to be immediate and short in duration. Time out is limited to 10 to 15 minutes; the loss of a favorite activity, to that particular day.

Moreover, because of the natural tendency of ADHD children to take criticism personally, we encourage parents to consistently and explicitly make the distinction in the child's mind between the unacceptable behavior and the child. In other words, children are unconditionally loved and accepted for who they are; their behavior, however, must conform to the values of the family, as well as to what is considered appropriate and acceptable in the culture in which they live. Again, this is the only way to assure the child's ultimate survival in the colder, less tolerant, and more judgmental outside world. Therefore, during early childhood, conformity is the operative word. Later in development, when the essential rules have been internalized, the real work of individuation can begin.

■ RESTORING THE BALANCE BETWEEN GOOD AND BAD FEELING

Because of the extreme problems these children have with self-control, they are frequently in trouble with peers, parents, and other authority figures. Moreover, because adults tend to expect age-appropriate and socially acceptable behavior from children without giving it the appreciation and attention it deserves, positive behavior often goes unnoticed and unrewarded. This naturally leaves ADHD children with a poor self-image. So it is particularly important that the child receive positive feedback whenever warranted. Also, because the ADHD child may already be overburdened with a negative self-image, parents and teachers are encouraged to package and stow away the negative experiences of each day, thus allowing the child a fresh, clean start the following morning. This is true even when dealing with the potentially more troublesome aggressive and daredevil types of behaviors that children may demonstrate. Many adults respond to this type of behavior as though it were a deliberate act to upset them. On the contrary, ADHD children are at the mercy of their impulses, which continually press for expression.

Just as ADHD children are unable to habituate to external stimuli, they are unable to evaluate the fitness of internal needs and desires, either for satisfaction or expression. Lacking forethought, such children must experience the consequences firsthand. Whereas all young children need direct experience, this is true in the extreme for ADHD children. One particular youngster comes to mind. This child impulsively jumped off a 10-foot embankment in a neighborhood park to "see how it felt." Fortunately, he was not seriously hurt. When he had to be forcefully prevented by his mother and grandmother from jumping from a second-story balcony, and threatened to leap from his parent's moving car to see "if I would die," his parents decided to seek outside help.

Although such daredevil behavior demands immediate corrective attention by the powers that be, the "clean slate" policy holds for this type of impulsive behavior as well. On the other hand, positive experiences are carried over to the next day and beyond by providing opportunities to discuss and relive positive events and behaviors. This reinforces the child's feelings of self-worth and helps to restore the balance between good and bad psychic feeling.

■ **THE EXAGGERATED FEELING APPROACH**

To help facilitate the processing of psychic feeling, parents and teachers are advised to exaggerate the emotional impact of the child's behavior even in academic tasks, for example, by taking personal pride in the child's accomplishments; by taking the child's lack of persistence as a personal letdown. This is accomplished through the use of exaggerated facial expressions, gestures, and feeling tone of voice. This dramatization of feedback is in keeping with the child's extroverted orientation. Generally speaking, ADHD children are very perceptive and wide awake to the things going on around them. They quickly learn to read the moods of others via direct sensory impressions of facial expressions, gestures, and tone of voice; however, this should not be mistaken for the capacity to empathize with or internalize, in a deeper—more lasting— sense, the feelings emanating from others. Rather their empathic responding is more surface and momentary in quality, quickly disappearing when the other person leaves, or when the feeling is no longer openly displayed. The cliché "out of sight, out of mind" aptly describes their perspective.

The purpose of an exaggerated feeling approach is twofold. First, it might help to activate the reinforcement systems of the brain. Second, it has been our understanding that ADHD children have an almost constant need for personal attention as a consequence of the failure of their own reward and punishment systems, leaving them with an intense awareness of an internal emptiness that can only be relieved through the overt expression of feeling from others.

This is apparent in the difficulty these children have in being alone. The youngster may be constantly underfoot, shadowing the parent around the house. No matter how much attention the parent provides, the child presses for more. Many are subject to intense separation distress—possibly the basis for the later development of panic states and agoraphobia. Unable to keep the feelings associated with significant others in mind, the child seeks their continual physical presence, insisting on a show of feeling. For ADHD children, even bad feelings are better than no feelings. If positive feeling attention is not forthcoming, the child may push the parent with bad behavior, as such behavior is very likely to result in an immediate feeling response on the part of the parent.

In terms of feeling attention, ADHD children are never able to have enough. The inner peace and quietude that normal children experience with more usual amounts of feeling attention appear to be rarely experienced by ADHD children. Whereas open demonstrations of affection are important for all children, they are especially important for ADHD children, who have difficulty picking up on the more subtle indicators of positive parental regard.

One youngster comes to mind. This child became extremely restless and irritable after a change in father's job required the family to relocate to another state. His constant crying and inability to be soothed eventually motivated the mother to seek help from the child's pediatrician. Unable to find anything wrong, the pediatrician referred the mother and child to us. Although mother reported that the child was an extremely active baby and toddler (e.g., mother had to use a harness to restrain him in public), he had not been an unhappy, or irritable child. Prior to father's transfer, the toddler had been cared for by the paternal grandmother while the parents were at work. The child's attachment to the grandmother and the unavoidable separation from her were considered a likely cause of the child's distress. When the grandmother was subsequently able to come for an extended stay, the child immediately calmed down.

Observations of grandmother and child together revealed an affectionate woman who freely reinforced positive behavior with lots of physical attention, for example, hugs, kisses, gentle stroking. This was in contrast to the behavior of his parents, who admitted to being overly reserved in the expression of feeling. As a child, mother had been punished for crying. This case illustrates the role of nurture in the expression of ADHD symptomatology and the effectiveness of touch in getting positive feeling across. It also speaks to the importance of constancy in the child's milieu. The absence of the child's grandmother represented a significant change in the child's environment that was not taken into consideration in the etiology of this youngster's difficulties.

The difficulty ADHD children have in being sated may show up in other ways—even in their eating behavior. It is not unusual for a parent to tell us that their child has a voracious appetite—stuffing him- or herself when he or she is obviously well past the point of satiety. A few of these ADHD children have been overweight. We have often wondered if the pleasurable feelings that naturally accompany food reward do not occur in these children to the degree that they occur in normal children. This inability to achieve what we have termed "psychic satiety" may be a factor in their overeating—a possible basis for the later development of an eating disorder. And perhaps the weight loss that can occur as a side effect of the medication is, in part, a natural consequence of an improvement in the brain's capacity to experience the pleasurable effects associated with food reward. Because food is now more satisfying, that is, more rewarding psychically, there is less motivation to overeat. Obviously, research is needed to evaluate the validity of this idea, which is presented here essentially as food for thought (no pun intended).

In helping to meet the child's almost insatiable need for feeling attention, a pet can sometimes be an invaluable ally, providing a ready source of unconditional loyalty and affection. In the case of an older child, who may be forced by circumstances to spend a part of the day alone, for example, after school until the parent comes home from work, we have sometimes suggested to parents that they purchase a dog or cat to keep the child company.

A word of caution regarding the use of an exaggerated feeling approach. Because ADHD individuals have little firsthand knowledge of deeply experienced psychic feeling, and because such feedback is taken personally and processed in the moment, they may be unusually overwhelmed or frightened by its expression in others, even when such expressions are positive in nature. But this depth of feeling is exactly what such children need. Anyone who can provide this type of stimulation will be a natural source of attraction for the child. However, depth of feeling can be conveyed without hitting the child over the head with it, so to speak. Even matter-of-fact understatement can be very effective, depending upon the person using it. Thus a caretaker with the opposite temperament can present something matter-of-factly yet still convey its import because of the natural tendency to attach more meaning to events and behavior. We suspect that the natural warmth and depth of feeling in someone with the opposite temperament helps to offset the natural coolness and lightness of the child. When the two temperaments are together, they are in better balance. Other things being equal, such caretakers will be better at calming the child's restlessness and maintaining the child's focus of attention where it belongs.

■ THE DIFFICULT WORK OF SOCIAL RELATING

The sense of inner emptiness and coldness that ADHD individuals experience when not in the presence of others cannot be overemphasized; for example, one of our adult patients said it made her feel like she "could chew glass." Because of their here-and-now orientation, this state is experienced as if it will last forever. Driven to constant socializing to find some relief from this internal state, ADHD individuals can be very indiscriminate and demanding in behavior, often alienating others in the process.

One of our adult patients, for example, had a network of friends, mental health clinics, and emergency hot-line services that she attempted to mobilize whenever her sense of inner hollowness became too much for her to bear. No matter what time of day or night, or what the circumstances, she would persist until she found someone to meet her need for feeling attention. Although she knew that her demanding and verbally abusive behavior could, as it had in the past, lead to rejection, she could not control herself. From her perspective, feelings of rejection were still better than the emptiness and panic she felt. Temporarily relieved, she could manage by herself for a short while, but then her inner sense of hollowness would return, panic would set in, and the cycle would repeat itself. At these times, her behavior was desperate and driven in quality; lacking an expectancy reflex, she could not appreciate that significant others would be there again for her in the future because they had been there for her in the past.

The inner peace and quietude that she sought could only be provided by the *immediate* feeling attention of others. On many occasions, she would abruptly leave her apartment and wander the streets visiting the coffee shops of the downtown area in search of some casual acquaintance to be with. In this state, she was extremely vulnerable to whomever she happened to end up with, for she felt no real concern for consequences, merely the need to find immediate relief from intense feelings of emptiness. Eventually, this patient agreed to a trial of medication. On Dexedrine, she was able to obtain significant relief from this symptom, and this dangerous panic behavior stopped.

Too often, these ADHD adults are misdiagnosed by the very system they must turn to for help. Several have come to us with an initial diagnosis of borderline personality disorder, for which there is no standard recourse with respect to pharmacotherapy. And it is not unusual for them to be accused of malingering because of the quickness with which their mood can change. Angry and hostile and threatening drastic action one minute, they can easily turn into putty in the hands of someone who is able to meet their need for warmth of feeling. In fact, as long as their immediate need for positive feeling attention is met, they may be quite enjoyable. Free from guilt and uninhibited in behavior, they are often charming and entertaining. Unable to appreciate what may be inferred by others from their behavior, they are apt to be very open and direct in word and deed—often to the delight of those who, at one time or another, may have secretly wanted to behave similarly. Indeed, their spontaneity and ability to be totally absorbed in the immediate moment are qualities many of us desire. However, they are present in ADHD individuals in the extreme, severely limiting their ability to fit comfortably in society.

The give and take of social relating is very difficult work indeed for people with this problem. Unmindful of consequences and impulsive in actions, they may be genuinely surprised to find that they have hurt someone's feelings or committed some significant faux pas. Important social behaviors such as taking turns, sharing the limelight, keeping confidences, maintaining loyalties, and following other unspoken rules of group conduct are very difficult—if not impossible—for them to internalize. It is not unusual for the individual to prefer the company of much younger children, who may be more docile and easier to control, or of a grandparent or other significant adult who may be more tolerant—even laughing at their antics.

Although the need to belong is very great in ADHD individuals, as evidenced by their excessive need for attention, they are often ostracized by more staid, traditional social groups due to their impulsivity and self-centered ways. To meet their need for social contact, older youths and adolescents may develop associations with other social outcasts with similar problems. Such a "group" is typically devoid of loyalty and structure. Its members are quite mobile, moving quickly from one situation or distraction to the next with much verbosity and noise, in search of activities that may offer some temporary relief from their inner sense of hollowness.

Here again, we see the potential for antisocial behavior. Acts that hurt others, for example, bullying, denigrating, and fighting, are assured of an immediate feeling response. Illicitly available street drugs, such as cocaine or speed, may be especially tempting because of the temporary feelings of well-being and euphoria they can induce. One adolescent female put it this way: "Only sex and drugs make me feel alive." The potential for alcohol abuse may exist for similar reasons, exacerbating problems with impulse control. The temptation provided by open booths in department stores may also be hard to resist, as feelings of aloneness may be relieved, to some extent, by appropriating the appealing object. Sometimes items belonging to significant others are taken as mementos in an attempt to keep that person in mind.

Providing these youths with some place to go within the community where their energies can be redirected by strong, warm, caring authority figures into physical sports or some other positive, structured activity is particularly important. The potential that such community-based programs have for preventing future problems will depend upon the strength of the feeling bond between these individuals and the authority in charge. Such authority figures must be carefully chosen for their warmth, sincerity, and strength of character. The toughness of an army drill sergeant is required, but it must be tempered with a genuine warmth of feeling for those in their charge. When parents cannot provide the necessary stimulation that these at-risk youths and adolescents require, community-based programs run by adults with these qualities can serve as an important alternative source—enculturating, setting limits, and providing a consistent, constant milieu that these children can rely on.

11

Pharmacotherapy

■ ASSESSING THE NEED FOR MEDICATION

The need for medication as part of the overall treatment plan is determined by a consideration of the severity of the child's symptoms as assessed by the following: symptom checklists, direct observations of the child at home and in school, and careful questioning of the parents and the child's teachers. If the child is experiencing particular difficulty with respect to impulsivity and other symptoms, the parents are counseled regarding the need for medication. However, we have found that even children with mild symptoms can benefit from medication. Often such children have been able to compensate, to some degree, for their lack of self-control by developing obsessive compulsive behavior as a defense. As medication relieves the need for this and other extremes in compensatory reactions, for example, being afraid to say or do anything, we always discuss the option with parents, even when symptoms appear mild.

■ DETERMINING THE DOSE

Medication trials begin with the lowest possible dose and dose frequency schedule, with periodic increases until the desired therapeutic effect has been achieved—*a continuous and even suppression of symptoms throughout the day and evening hours.* Alternatively, some physicians prefer to use the weight of the child—so many mg of drug per kg of body weight—as a starting point. Either approach is acceptable. But the final therapeutic dose should always be determined on an *individual* basis through a careful and frequent monitoring of symptoms and side effects across the day. Generally speaking, the more severe the symptoms and the heavier the child—other things being equal—the higher the therapeutic dose.

Effective doses of dextroamphetamine are typically half those of methylphenidate; for example, if the child does well on 5 mg of dextroamphetamine, he or she will probably do as well on 10 mg of methylphenidate. But this rule-of-thumb only applies when *one dose* is considered. Because these compounds differ in their duration of action, Ritalin usually has to be given more often during the day than Dexedrine. Failure to take this into consideration can lead to unnecessary suffering on the part of the child due to the potential rebound in symptoms before the next scheduled dose. Furthermore, parents who are repeatedly confronted with such sudden and unwelcome contrasts in behavior may fail to comply with the initial medication trial.

■ **THE DOSE FREQUENCY SCHEDULE**

Dextroamphetamine and methylphenidate are available in short-acting and sustained release (SR) forms. Theoretically, the SR forms of these compounds allow a reduction in the frequency of dosing across the day. In practice, this tends to hold true for Dexedrine Spansules, but not necessarily for Ritalin-SR®. Many children metabolize Ritalin-SR within 2 to 3 hours. Again, if this is not appreciated by the patient's physician, a distressing and unnecessary rebound of symptoms may occur before the next scheduled dose.

Determining the frequency of dosing is just as important as determining the strength of each individual dose. To achieve the desired therapeutic continuous and even suppression of symptoms, it is best not to rely on what the manufacturer reports about the duration of action of these medications. Because metabolic rates vary between individuals, decisions about dose frequency should always be determined empirically. The importance of feedback from those involved in the child's daily care cannot be overemphasized. If parents consistently report that symptoms reappear around lunchtime, and then again around 4 p.m., for example, a three times a day (t.i.d.) dose schedule is indicated.

Careful questioning of the parents, as well as corroborative data from the child's teacher, will help determine the optimal time for a subsequent dose. Taking into consideration individual metabolic rates and the mild tolerance that develops with continued use, we have come to expect durations that are considerably less than what the manufacturer reports, for example, about 5 hours versus 12 hours for the Dexedrine Spansule.

Finally, it is important for parents—as well as school personnel—to understand the importance of giving the medication *consistently* and *on time*. When doses are either missed or given late, the child is made to suffer needlessly. External signs of the disorder return along with the child's inner sense of emptiness, precipitating the cycle of bad behavior and negative feedback all over again. Moreover, anyone observing the child during this period could conclude mistakenly that the medication is ineffective.

■ BRAND NAME VERSUS GENERIC FORMS

Theoretically, brand name drugs and their generic equivalents should be equally effective at equivalent doses. In practice, this tends to be true. However, on occasion, we and others (e.g., Barkley, 1990) have had parents tell us that generic methylphenidate was ineffective. In such cases, it is best to be safe and specify the brand name on the prescription.

■ FOLLOW-UP MEDICATION CHECKS

During the initial titration period, an effort is made to see the child and parent on a weekly or biweekly basis. Once the therapeutic dose has been determined, follow-up medication checks can be scheduled on a less frequent basis, that is, monthly or bimonthly. During the titration period and thereafter, as warranted, parents are asked to monitor their children's symptoms, using one of the commonly available checklists, for example, Conners's Parent Rating Scale (Conners, 1990). If the child is in school, the child's teacher(s) are also asked to complete the companion Conners' Teacher Rating Scale.

■ ASSESSING SIDE EFFECTS

In addition to behavior checklists, parents are asked to make a note of any side effects that appear, using a simple rating scale format (see Table 11.1). Used properly and with proper monitoring by a competent physician, the psycho-stimulants are safe and effective. Potential side effects are minimal, and typically diminish with continued treatment (Barkley, 1990; Barkley, McMurry, Edelbrock, & Robbins, 1990; Dupaul & Barkley, 1990; Golinko, 1984). The most frequently reported are a depressed appetite and difficulty falling asleep.

Sometimes what appears to be a side effect may actually be related to a preexisting condition, or to other factors that have not been taken into consideration. For example, parents often blame the medication when the child has difficulty sleeping. Reluctant to contribute to sleep problems, many pediatricians avoid medicating the child for the evening hours. Careful questioning of the

TABLE 11.1 Side Effects Checklist for Psychomotor Stimulants

Patient: _____ Date of Birth: _____

Today's Date: _____ Baseline: Yes _____ No _____

Medication/Dose/Dose Frequency: _____

Other Medications Taken During This Time: _____

Any Weight Loss During This Period?: Yes _____ No _____

                                      Unsure _____

Instructions: For each of the following possible symptoms, please circle the number which best indicates how often the symptom has been present during the last 5 to 7 days. A score of 0 means that the symptom has not been present; a score of 5 means that the symptom has been present on a daily basis.

Symptom	*Absent*		*Occasionally*		*Continually*	
Sleep disturbances	0	1	2	3	4	5
Decreased appetite	0	1	2	3	4	5
Stomachaches	0	1	2	3	4	5
Nausea	0	1	2	3	4	5
Headaches	0	1	2	3	4	5
Sensitive to noise	0	1	2	3	4	5
Dizziness	0	1	2	3	4	5
Blurred vision	0	1	2	3	4	5
Rapid heart beat	0	1	2	3	4	5
Heart palpitations	0	1	2	3	4	5
Rash/hives	0	1	2	3	4	5
Itchy sensation	0	1	2	3	4	5
Dry mouth	0	1	2	3	4	5
Unpleasant taste	0	1	2	3	4	5
Anxiety	0	1	2	3	4	5
Nightmares	0	1	2	3	4	5
Overly sensitive	0	1	2	3	4	5
Prone to crying	0	1	2	3	4	5
Irritable	0	1	2	3	4	5
Nail biting/picking	0	1	2	3	4	5
Lip licking/biting	0	1	2	3	4	5
Socially withdrawn	0	1	2	3	4	5
Hallucinations	0	1	2	3	4	5
Paranoid feelings	0	1	2	3	4	5
Confusion	0	1	2	3	4	5
Motor/vocal tics	0	1	2	3	4	5

Comments/Concerns: _____

parent, however, may reveal that the child has never slept well. Moreover, by the time bedtime arrives, the individual may have already metabolized the last dose of medication, especially if the last dose was given in the early afternoon. In this case, the difficulty with sleep may be related to the rebound of symptoms that occurs when the effect of the medication has worn off. In such cases, an evening dose may actually be beneficial, maintaining the desired therapeutic calming effect right through until bedtime. In our practice, medicating for the evening hours has become routine unless, of course, sleep difficulties persist. To determine if side effects are truly medication related, a baseline side effects checklist should always be completed before the initial medication trial.

Proneness to crying and tearfulness are also considered to be potential side effects of stimulant therapy. We actually view these symptoms in a slightly different and more positive light. As the child begins to process psychic feeling on a deeper level, external manifestations of guilt and remorse and sadness over past and present transgressions are bound to occur. The before-and-after contrast is often disturbing to the parent, who is used to the previous devil-may-care attitude of the child. We are therefore careful to tell parents to anticipate their appearance, and to reassure them that these newfound feelings should help the child inhibit the associated misdeed in the future.

In the past, there has been some concern that stimulant medications might suppress growth over the long term; however, more recent reports in the literature indicate that this concern has been unwarranted (Dupaul & Barkley, 1990; Golinko, 1984; Klein & Mannuzza, 1988; Mattes & Gittelman, 1983). Our experience is consistent with this view. In our Springfield practice, for example, we routinely measured the heights and weights of the children treated with methylphenidate and dextroamphetamine. Many of these children were part of the Pupil Adjustment Program (see Appendix A) conducted within the Springfield School Department, Springfield, Massachusetts, where Dr. Ploof was the Consulting School Psychiatrist. Children were typically in this program for a minimum of 2 years. Consistent with the previously cited reports of others, we found no evidence of growth suppression as a result of long-term treatment with these compounds.

Potentially more serious side effects, for example, hypertension, tend to be associated with higher dose levels, and adults are more likely than children to experience elevated blood pressure. Obviously, if serious side effects develop, the medication should be stopped. Again, a cautious approach is the governing rule when contraindicating conditions exist, or when side effects develop; however, because the prognosis for the individual with moderate to severe symptoms is so bleak, stimulant medication should still be considered viable for some of these patients. For example, the physician might consider concurrent treatment with an antihypertensive compound (e.g., see Wender, 1986).

Similarly, children with motor tics should not be excluded automatically as candidates for stimulant medication. For example, there is evidence that stimulant medication may produce no worsening of tics in some ADHD children with preexisting Tourette's syndrome (Erenberg, Cruse, & Rothner, 1985). Erenberg and colleagues reviewed the medical histories of children with Tourette's syndrome who had been treated with one or more of the psychostimulants methylphenidate, dextroamphetamine, and pemoline. Of the 39 subjects with preexisting tics, stimulant medication reportedly increased tics in 11, caused no change in 26, and decreased tics in 2.

Unlike dextroamphetamine and methylphenidate, pemoline has been known to cause an impairment in liver functioning in a small percentage of children. Specifically, a chemical hepatitis has been reported in about 3% of children (Dulcan, 1990). As such, patients taking pemoline should have their liver function monitored routinely.

■ COMPLIANCE ISSUES

Naturally, parents must be willing and able to follow through with the recommendation for medication. Any uncertainty about the validity of diagnosis or the need for medication can result in noncompliance. So it is extremely important for parents to understand the purpose and use of medication and to feel comfortable in expressing openly their fears and concerns. Toward this end, the more specific and concrete we have been in describing the nature of the child's problem as well as the rationale for medication, the more successful we have been in overcoming their initial fears. Many parents who were reluctant at first to try medication, ultimately became convinced of its usefulness when they experienced, firsthand, the improvements in their child's behavior, particularly with respect to empathy and self-control.

Not infrequently, one of the parents is found to have similar symptoms. When we have been able to get him or her on medication, the interaction between parent and child improves, and so does the child's behavior. Parents with more pervasive ADHD who remain untreated can present a serious problem with respect to compliance and behavior management. Specifically, their own problems with attention, organization, and impulse control make it difficult to sustain their focus on the child, where it belongs. Furthermore, being predominantly present-oriented, parents with ADHD are unable to appreciate treatment as a process requiring time and patience, with anticipated adjustments in medication and management. When a problem arises they panic, appearing completely unmindful of the established management plan, previous discussions about the purpose and use of the medication, underlying reasons for the child's impulsivity, and so on.

It is during such times that we get a truer picture of the problems confronting the child in the home. Often such parents are involved simultaneously with a number of professionals and emergency services, with differing opinions and approaches. It is easy to see why such a situation may be unworkable. It can take several months or longer of patient understanding, repetition, and persistence to establish a truly working relationship with such parents; in some instances, the desired relationship never develops. In such cases, it may be best to focus on other patients.

Another compliance issue has to do with the time period between the end of school and home arrival. Often this is when the next dose of medication is scheduled. Between school and home, there are many potentially inviting and distracting stimuli. Many of our adolescent patients have gotten into the most difficulty during this time period. Younger children may be vulnerable, as well. To ensure that the next dose is taken on time, we advise parents to consider picking up their child at school. Alternatively, some have elected to meet the child at the bus stop.

■ MEDICATION HOLIDAYS, MEDICATING FOR SCHOOL MANAGEMENT

Finally, there are two practices with respect to medicating children and adolescents that we would like to discourage: (1) medicating exclusively for school management purposes, and (2) medication holidays. The logic of correcting the child's neurochemical deficit for part of a day or for part of a week, or for just so many months of the year, is incomprehensible, yet these practices, although not as common as they used to be, are still in use. Moreover, if one considers the consequences of an on-again, off-again approach to medication from the perspective of the child, its inappropriateness should be apparent. Having a brain that is able to process the positive and negative feedback of others one day, and then is suddenly unable to do so the next, would be extremely confusing for the child. Such an on-again, off-again approach would never be considered for someone suffering from a more traditionally viewed medical disorder, such as hypertension or diabetes, for example. Giving insulin or blood pressure medication on such a basis would be unthinkable—the consequences life-threatening.

In our opinion, the only appropriate reason for a medication holiday is to assess whether medication is still needed. Following a number of years of pharmacotherapy, the possibility exists that medication can be withdrawn without the return of symptoms. In addition, because medication holidays are typically prescribed for weekends and school vacation periods, times when children can especially benefit from the feedback of parents and other family members, the child is not going to be as sensitive to their input. This deprives the parent of the opportunity to instill in the child the family's moral values. The child's "shoulds" and "shouldn'ts," "goods" and "bads" are then learned primarily at school from teachers and peers. Moreover, during medication holidays, the child's problems with self-control and empathy reappear, and parental attempts to apply corrective measures may take on a colossal quality. Frustration builds on the part of both child and parent, the situation escalates, and the cycle of bad behavior and negative feedback returns. Some parents give up in despair, letting the child have his or her own way, and then find it very difficult to reestablish their former control.

12

Adult ADHD

Some Additional Treatment Considerations

■ **OPENING COMMENTS**

Many report that the hyperactive behavior associated with ADHD diminishes during adolescence. The reason for this is unclear. However, although hyperactivity may not be present, problems with empathy, organization, self-control, and concentration may remain, causing impaired functioning occupationally and socially. Moreover, it is not unusual for us to observe a more circumscribed form of hyperactive behavior in the ADHD adult, whose foot may be in continual motion or whose fingers repetitively tap the arm of the chair during a session. We also consider the pressured speech and the constant searching for stimulation that many of these adults exhibit to be a form of hypermotor behavior.

■ **THE PATIENT-THERAPIST BOND**

Although it is best to treat as early in development as possible, there is still hope for the adult whose problem has only recently been diagnosed. Success in treatment depends in large part on the strength of the relationship between therapist and patient. Such adults need an *enduring* positive relationship with a significant authority figure who can guide them through developmental mile-stones that should have been achieved at a younger age. Realistically speaking, the immature behavior of these patients can be expected to continue until their capacities for psychic feeling and forethought can be stimulated to improved functioning via medication and individual therapy. Depending on the severity of symptoms, long-term intervention—of at least 3 to 4 years, and perhaps even longer—may be necessary.

■ THE DIRECT APPROACH

As with ADHD children, our adult patients respond best to a direct approach. Living largely in the immediate moment and tending to be blunt in communi-cation, many have little patience with more subtle, nondirective, insight-oriented approaches, where the emphasis is on symbolism, past experience, and hidden meaning. Generally speaking, such approaches are reserved for later phases of treatment, following observable gains in empathic responding and impulse control. Moreover, considering the chaotic lifestyle of many of these adults, specific, explicit suggestions on how to better organize their daily activities is sorely needed. They may even request help with the specific wording of something, and such help is freely given.

Due to long-standing difficulties with impulse control and empathic respond-ing, the self-image of these adult patients is largely negative. One of our first treatment goals is to foster a sense of self-acceptance. To help alleviate strongly held feelings of being inherently "bad," the idea that their symptoms may be related to a naturally occurring temperament continuum is introduced. We have also found humor to be particularly beneficial. The spontaneous behavior of these patients can be very entertaining. Acceptance and appreciation of this spontaneity as a part of their natural constitutional style helps foster feelings of self-worth and self-acceptance.

■ OUTER VERSUS INNER WORLD FUNCTIONING

Another important treatment goal is to help the individual distinguish between outer and inner world functioning. Because of their natural spontaneity and tendency to live in the moment, where immediate needs must be gratified, individuals with ADHD are not well-suited to outer world functioning. In the colder, more judgmental world of work and social relating, fixed habits of thinking and behavior are expected. And the gratification obtained in this world typically requires large expenditures of energy, released in a well-defined format. Unable to appreciate the necessity of donning appropriate outer world habits, ADHD adults can easily appear as misfits in society.

In the inner, private world of the individual—as represented by the intimate relating of a couple—more freedom of expression is possible. This world can be likened to the Garden of Eden before Adam and Eve learned of evil by eating from the forbidden tree of knowledge. With awareness of evil came shame over their nakedness—both physical and mental. Donning garments—habits of mind and body—helped them cope with their shame. In the inner world, one can be divested of all robes, uniforms, and habits of thought that are the mark of functioning in the outer world. Ideally, this is an open world where love and unconditional acceptance rule, and where gratification can be free and unconditional with the consequent restoration of psychic and physical energies. These and other distinctions between inner and outer world functioning are frequently discussed and reinforced during therapy sessions.

The difficulty that these patients have with outer world functioning may be extreme, as illustrated by the following case. A 43-year-old female came to us with an number of different diagnoses, including bipolar affective disorder, borderline personality disorder, antisocial personality disorder, and dysthymia. As an adolescent, she was frequently in trouble with authorities for truancy, shoplifting, and indecent exposure. As an adult, she had much difficulty keeping jobs due to continuing problems with authority and with the many rules and standards of behavior and dress associated with the workplace. She eventually "dropped out" of mainstream society, and for several years—before an accident required a significant change in lifestyle—she and her significant other and a few of their friends lived on the periphery of society—literally. They built wooden structures on a secluded piece of land and supported themselves by growing their own vegetables and by various odd jobs that brought in a cash income. These structures had no running water and no indoor bathroom facilities. She and her significant other had been saving money to buy land and build their own home. When the relationship fell apart, intense feelings of panic and emptiness and her genuine suffering over the loss of this significant relationship motivated her first attempt to get help—initially with so-called alternative types of treatments. A year later, a serious injury forced a complete change in lifestyle—moving back into mainstream society, where she had felt and still felt completely alienated. After numerous unsuccessful attempts, over a 3-year period, to get the appropriate help at various mental health clinics, she finally found relief with stimulant pharmacotherapy. Pharmacotherapy, in turn, has helped her to benefit from individual therapy.

Five years later, she is still being seen for monthly follow-up and support. Her maintenance dose of Dexedrine, established about 10 months into treatment, continues to be 20 mg q.i.d., with the option of taking an additional nighttime dose if necessary. Gains in impulse control continue, and she is now able to tolerate being alone. And although she still has difficulty with outer world rules and norms of behavior, she finds she is better able to navigate in this world.

In helping the individual cope with the demands of the outer world, we foster the internalization of one simple governing rule of behavior—a kind of humanistic superego to which the individual can refer. It is explicitly stated to the patient as follows: "Any behavior is OK as long as it does not harm you or anyone else." Expecting these patients to internalize other lengthy lists of "thou shalt nots" is unrealistic.

■ PHARMACOTHERAPY

During the initial phase of therapy, the option of medication is presented and its purpose explained. From our perspective, the class II psychostimulants are the medications of choice as long as their use can be responsibly controlled. If there is a fear of abuse, a trial of pemoline or of one of the tricyclic antidepressants, for example, imipramine or desipramine, is a reasonable alternative. Although the potential for abuse is often raised as an issue—usually by those who have no direct experience treating this population—we have never had an adult patient abuse their stimulant medication. On the contrary, patients whose symptoms are relieved by Ritalin or Dexedrine are better able to attach appropriate meaning to their actions and to consider the potential consequences. This makes appropriate social behavior more rather than less likely. Consistent with the reports of others (Wender, 1981, 1987), our adult patients report inner feelings of calm and well-being in response to the class II psychostimulants rather than euphoria.

Before the medication trial, the potential side effects are discussed, as well as the expected benefits. Patients are told, for example, to anticipate a lessening of panic related to being alone. If medication is refused, the door is always left open for a trial in the future. If symptoms are severe and medication is refused, the prognosis is likely to be poor, largely because the patient will have difficulty developing a feeling bond and therefore a lasting relationship with the therapist.

On the other hand, some of our adult patients have reported an apparent "spontaneous" lessening of symptoms in their 40s and 50s without medication intervention. Our current thinking on this is as follows: Persistent repeated stimulation of the feeling brain over a prolonged period of time may have resulted in some improved capacity to process psychic pain and psychic pleasure, resulting in gains in impulse control, social relating, and foresight.

One important consideration in deciding whether to prescribe Ritalin or Dexedrine for symptom control has to do with dose frequency. As with ADHD children, the therapeutic effects of Ritalin only last for a short time, typically 2 to 3 hours. And during periods of increased stress, the drug may be metabolized within an even shorter time frame. This means that frequent dosing across the day is required to maintain the desired even and continuous suppression of symptoms. During the initial titration period, patients often have a difficult time tolerating the intermittent return of symptoms before the next scheduled dose (see also Wender et al., 1985). Impulse control problems are exacerbated during this time and may lead to actions that the individual later regrets. Feelings of irritability are also common, and similarly may lead to negative acts and consequences before the next scheduled dose.

Patients liken this up-and-down aspect of Ritalin therapy to a roller-coaster ride and moreover, frequently describe rebound symptoms as more intense than baseline symptomatology. This can lead to problems with compliance, and even a decision to stop the medication altogether. Although this rebound effect can be relieved by increasing the frequency of dosing, we often find it more efficacious to start the patient on Dexedrine or the longer-acting Dexedrine Spansule. This reduces the frequency of doses, diminishes the possibility that patient will forget to take one or more of their doses, and most important, eliminates the distressing rebound of symptoms associated with Ritalin.

Another aspect of adult pharmacotherapy that is worthy of mention is the increase in the severity of symptoms experienced by some females prior to menstruation. This can precipitate a regression to previous levels of functioning. Things can easily get out of hand during this time, causing a snowballing effect if problems are not resolved. Although some patients begin to anticipate this increase in difficulty, and may even try to take compensatory measures to avoid it, the increase in inner suffering that they experience is unnecessary. It can be avoided by giving an additional dose of medication for the few days preceding menstruation. This association with premenstrual fluid retention and increased ADHD symptomatology has also been observed by Huessy et al. (1979), who found that symptoms could be relieved by the temporary use of a diuretic.

In response to stimulant pharmacotherapy, adult patients begin to attach more meaning to their experiences—past as well as present. Consequently, we frequently see the increased sadness and tearfulness that we see in ADHD children taking these medications. As past misdeeds are brought up and reevaluated in therapy, newfound feelings of guilt and remorse are to be expected. Once again, these psychically painful feelings can be understood as a natural consequence of activating the feeling brain, and they should be viewed as a positive development—facilitating, for example, the development of a moral, humanistic superego. Moreover, it is through this process that past events can be transformed into meaningful memories, events complexed with the appropriate feeling tone. We help patients cope with these newfound feelings by explaining why this is happening and reassuring them that these new painful memories will help them avoid similar unpleasantnesses in the future.

Adults taking Dexedrine or Ritalin report that they feel calmer, more focused, more clear-headed. In the words of one patient, "the background noise is less . . .

I can grab onto a thought now and make it stand out from all the other sound tracks racing through my brain." Similarly, many patients find that they have an easier time letting go of an idea or thought—in essence, to stop perseverating. Some even describe a "slowing down" in their thinking. Again, these improvements are seen as a natural consequence of activating the feeling brain and the consequent attachment of *relative* importance to internal thoughts. Feelings have weight—they can be light and buoy us up, or heavy and weigh us down. The heavier the feeling, the less movement is possible. This is obvious in the depressed patient, who can't seem to "do" anything. On medication, even the simpler aspects of daily living take on greater meaning, and with this comes an overall decrease in general activity level. One adult patient who had previously complained of not being able to sit still long enough to get through a newspaper or magazine article expressed a newfound pleasure in being able to settle in for the night with a book she had been trying to read for months. This same adult, whose therapeutic dose of Dexedrine was established at 15 mg q.i.d., recently reported the following: "I used to think that I was a compassionate person. I realize now that I only acted that way—I never really felt it. I feel it inside now—I feel connected to others." Feelings are the glue that binds us to others. When that glue is missing, we feel alienated, cold, and alone—even when we are surrounded by others.

■ ENLISTING THE COOPERATION OF SIGNIFICANT OTHERS

Adults with more extreme symptoms, including a history of sociopathic behavior, can be expected to take longer to rehabilitate, even with medication. Although medication can stimulate the feeling brain to improved functioning, an extended period of time is needed to counter the individual's past reinforcement history and the immediate influences of their present environment—many of which may continue to be negative. Moreover, with adults, it is impossible to effect a total approach to treatment, as you can with children. Adults (and this applies to older adolescents as well) are much more mobile, and significant authority figures, for example, parents, teachers, and coaches, are much less likely to be a part of the picture.

On the other hand, if spouses or significant others are available, their help may be enlisted. The more this individual understands about the nature of the problem and the reason for the medication, the more his or her energies can be freed—from a defensive posture—to help with the treatment process. In particular, we try to explain why feeling attention is so important, and why immediate and direct feedback is desirable. Spouses can have considerable difficulty with this, as they are often of the opposite temperament—preferring subtlety over directness and withdrawal rather than confrontation. Acceptance of the natural temperament of the spouse is important; however, we do caution that it is best to deal with problems as they arise. Failure to do so can lead to a buildup of strong emotion with an eventual explosion occurring.

■ KEEPING IN MIND THE
INDIVIDUAL'S LEVEL OF MATURITY

Ever present during treatment is the idea that we are dealing with an individual whose feeling and thinking (forethought) capacities have never matured. Even though the individual may have the outward appearance of an adult, he or she is basically stuck at a very immature level of development—both emotionally and socially. When such adults have children of their own, the situation can be particularly precarious as you essentially have a child raising a child. Persistent and consistent stimulation of the feeling brain over a protracted period of time—through medication and the positive and negative feedback of significant others—is needed to help such individuals mature.

Such increases in depth of psychic feeling lie at the basis of the improvements these patients make in treatment. Without such increases, patients will continue to have difficulty evaluating the *fitness* of their actions with respect to all aspects of their life—the selection of friends, of a marriage partner, of a suitable career, of what clothes to wear, of what environment to approach or flee from.

The following patient comes to mind. This patient had been raped repeatedly as an adolescent and young adult. Psychosocial history revealed that she had left home at the age of 18 to travel alone across the United States, Europe, and the Middle East. During this time, she repeatedly placed herself in dangerous situations—hitchhiking and bicycling alone in desolate country despite having been assaulted in similar situations in the past. Unable to sense that she was in dangerous territory, she had gone alone into some of the most unsavory parts of town. She finally decided to return home after being raped by five "friends" in Beirut. Her colossal lack of judgment with respect to going to Beirut can be better appreciated when you learn that this woman is Jewish.

This case is a extreme example of the degree to which ADHD individuals can be unaware of where they are. They can appear to live in a sort of stuporous state, wondering aimlessly through the outside world, oblivious of the potential dangers and pitfalls that await them. We have questioned the extent to which the visual spatial problems that commonly accompany this disorder may be related to this appearance of disorientation. Some of our adults complain of not being able to read a map and admit openly that they frequently get lost when trying to follow directions. They are often unaware of where they are not only with respect to the ambiance of a particular emotional environment, but also in terms of their position in space.

There is one final point that we would like to address. For teaching purposes, it is frequently necessary to describe extreme examples of symptomatology in order to make a point. In order for the diagnosis to be made, such extremes in behavior need not be present. Many who have sought our help have presented with much milder symptoms. For example, some ADHD adults may do very well until they experience the loss of a significant other who had functioned in more of a surrogate parent role and whose emotional warmth had provided significant relief from inner feelings of emptiness. Although there may be genuine suffering over the loss of that relationship, the distinguishing characteristic is the extreme panic they now feel at finding themselves alone.

13

Long-Term
Stimulant Medication

*Enduring Changes
in Neuronal Function?*

■ **OPENING COMMENTS**

After 3 or 4 years of a positive response to medication, it may be time to assess whether pharmacotherapy is still needed. Patients who demonstrate enduring changes in behavior following the cessation of drug treatment are of particular interest because of the questions they raise regarding the possible cellular/ neurochemical basis of this effect. Logically speaking, lasting changes in behavior must be accompanied by lasting changes in brain function.

One way of approaching this question is to ask what the consequences might be for the cell as a result of long-term exposure to medication, specifically to dextroamphetamine or methylphenidate.

■ **SHORT-TERM EFFECTS: INCREASES IN
SYNAPTIC LEVELS OF NEUROTRANSMITTER
AND TYROSINE HYDROXYLASE ACTIVITY**

The immediate effect of these compounds is to increase extracellular concentrations of DA and other important neurotransmitters (e.g., 5-HT) at specific brain

141

ACCUMBENS   V. STRIATUM

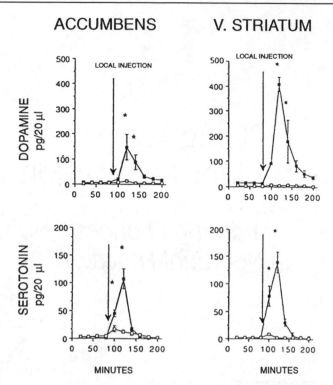

Figure 13.1: Amphetamine Increases Simultaneously Dopamine (DA) and Serotonin (5-HT) Overflow in Rat N. Accumbens and Striatum. Mean ±SEM ($N = 5$) levels of neurotransmitter recovered in 20-minute dialysate samples from the n. accumbens and ventral striatum following local injection of 4 µg d-amphetamine (filled squares) or saline (open squares). Arrows indicate the time of the injection.

Source: Reprinted from L. Hernandez, F. Lee, & B. G. Hoebel (1987), "Simultaneous Microdialysis and Amphetamine Infusion in the Nucleus Accumbens and Striatum of Freely Moving Rats: Increase in Extracellular Dopamine and Serotonin," *Brain Research Bulletin, 19,* 625, with kind permission from Elsevier Science Inc. and B. G. Hoebel.

*Significantly different from predrug levels at $p < 0.01$.

sites such as n. accumbens (Woods & Meyer, 1991; see Figure 5.10) and striatum (Hernandez et al., 1987; see Figure 13.1).

As previously discussed, these structures are of particular interest because they have been implicated as possible substrates for the therapeutic response of ADHD children to these stimulants (Lou et al., 1989; Porrino & Lucignani, 1987). Following a single dose of either compound, extracellular concentrations of DA in striatum and n. accumbens return to pre-drug baseline levels.

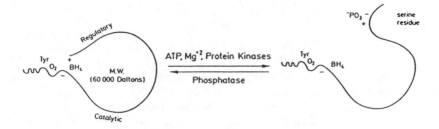

Figure 13.2: Phosphorylation of the Tyrosine Hydroxylase Molecule. The incorporation of phosphate groups into the regulatory domain of the enzyme molecule is thought to change its conformation from a more constrained form into one that renders the anionic site of co-factor binding (on catalytic domain) more accessible. Binding of co-factor (tetrahydrobiopterin) is necessary for synthesis of the catecholamines. Abbreviations: Tyr (tyrosine), O_2 (oxygen), BH_4 (tetrahydrobiopterin).

Source: After Masserano et al. (1989), p. 447. Reprinted by permission.

There is also evidence that a single dose of amphetamine (Schwarz et al., 1980), and possibly methylphenidate (see argument for this in Woods, 1990), can induce rapid increases in the activity of tyrosine hydroxylase, the rate-limiting enzyme catalyzing the synthesis of DA (see Figure 6.1 for a review of the pathway for DA biosynthesis).

This amphetamine-induced increase in tyrosine hydroxylase activity has been found to be dependent upon the second messenger, calcium (Schwarz, Uretsky, & Bianchine, 1980) and is highly correlated with the incorporation of phosphate groups into the enzyme molecule (Masserano, Vulliet, Tank, & Weiner, 1989; Zigmond, Schwarzschild, & Rittenhouse, 1989). Phosphorylation of tyrosine hydroxylase in this manner is thought to change its conformation from a more constrained form into one in which the anionic site of cofactor (tetrahydrobiopterin) binding is made more accessible (see Figure 13.2). Increasing the activity of tyrosine hydroxylase in response to markedly increased functional demands is thought to be the way in which neurons accelerate their synthesis of DA to replace stores diminished by secretion.

The type of activation of the enzyme produced by dextroamphetamine and other treatments that increase extracellular concentrations of DA in the brain, for example, electrical stimulation, high K^+, increases the velocity (Vmax) of the reaction without changing the affinity of the enzyme for tyrosine or for tetrahydrobiopterin and without reducing the effect of end-product inhibition (El Mestikawy, Glowinski, & Hamon, 1983; El Mestikawy & Hamon, 1985;

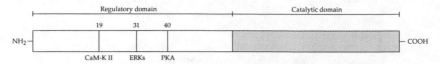

Figure 13.3: Major Phosphorylation Sites on the Regulatory Domain of the Tyrosine Hydroxylase Molecule. Tyrosine hydroxylase possesses several specific serine residues on the regulatory domain of the molecule that are subject to phosphorylation. Shown are three major serine sites of phosphorylation, along with the enzyme(s) that participate in the reaction. Phosphorylation of serine 19 by calcium-calmodulin-dependent protein kinase II in the presence of an activator protein leads to a Vmax activation of the enzyme with no change in the affinity of tyrosine hydroxylase for cofactor. Abbreviations: CaM-K II (calcium-calmodulin-dependent protein kinase II), ERKs (extracellular signal-regulated protein kinases), PKA (cAMP-dependent protein kinase A).

Source: R. S. Feldman, J. S. Meyer, & L. Quenzer (1996), *Principles of Neuropsychopharmacology,* Sunderland, MA: Sinauer Associates, p. 285. Reprinted with permission from Sinauer Associates, Inc. Thanks to Dean Scudder of Sinauer for his assistance in this matter.

Haycock, 1987; Haycock & Haycock, 1991; Masserano et al., 1989; Schwarz et al., 1980). The activation occurs quickly, within 15 seconds, and remains relatively constant in the presence of these types of treatments (Haycock, 1987).

Recent work has demonstrated that this Vmax-type of activation of tyrosine hydroxylase is dependent on the presence of an activator protein (Atkinson, Richtand, Schworer, Kuczenski, & Soderling, 1987; Yamauchi & Fujisawa, 1981; Yamauchi, Nakata, & Fujisawa, 1981) and requires that a specific serine residue (serine 19) on the regulatory domain of the enzyme molecule be previously phosphorylated by calcium-calmodulin-dependent protein kinase II (Masserano et al., 1989; Yamauchi & Fujisawa, 1981) (see Figure 13.3). It differs from the Km-type of activation of the enzyme that occurs in response to DA antagonists such as haloperidol. In contrast to Vmax activation, Km activation is dependent on the second messenger cyclic AMP and is characterized by an increase in the affinity of the enzyme for its cofactor, tetrahyrobiopterin (El Mestikawy el al., 1983; El Mestikawy & Hamon, 1985).

The cascade of intracellular events leading to the Vmax activation of the enzyme begins with a large influx of extracellular calcium—presumably through voltage-sensitive calcium channels, as a consequence of membrane depolarization—and apparently reflects the mobilization of a preexisting pool of inactive enzyme, which is then converted into the activated, more phosphorylated, form. Having more enzyme in the activated form means more DA can be synthesized by the cell in a given period of time. Again, short-term activation of the enzyme in this manner allows the neuron, to some degree, to accelerate its synthesis of DA to replace DA lost by secretion into the extracellular space.

■ LONG-TERM EFFECTS:
INCREASES IN TYROSINE HYDROXYLASE
GENE TRANSCRIPTION?

The long-term effects of amphetamine and other stimulants (e.g., nicotine) on the functional activity of tyrosine hydroxylase within the neuron are just beginning to be studied. Preliminary evidence from the peripheral nervous system indicates that certain adrenergic cells respond to long-term activation by increasing the rate of transcription of the tyrosine hydroxylase gene (Masserano et al., 1989). Prolonged stimulation of the chromaffin cells of the adrenal medulla, for example, leads to an increase in the number of tyrosine hydroxylase molecules within these cells, an effect that is prevented when the afferent input to these cells is severed. This increase in enzyme levels can also be prevented by nicotinic receptor blockers and by inhibitors of RNA and protein synthesis. Available evidence now suggests that it was brought about by prolonged occupation of nicotinic receptors by acetylcholine released from presynaptic nerve terminals (Masserano et al., 1989).

This trans-synaptic induction of tyrosine hydroxylase has also been observed in superior cervical ganglia (Zigmond, 1985). Here increases in the levels of tyrosine hydroxylase, brought about by prolonged stimulation of preganglionic fibers, were accompanied by parallel increases in enzyme activity that persisted long after the source of stimulation was removed and that varied directly with both the duration and the frequency of the stimulus (Zigmond, 1985). Similar to the effect observed in adrenal chromaffin cells, the increase in tyrosine hydroxylase activity could be blocked by nicotinic antagonists, but not by adrenergic or muscarinic antagonists. In the peripheral nervous system, then, CA cells not only can respond to markedly increased functional demands by activating preexisting stores of tyrosine hydroxylase, an immediate effect, but they also can even—over time—increase their levels of this enzyme by increasing the expression of the tyrosine hydroxylase gene.

Whether CA cells of the brain respond in a similar manner as a consequence of prolonged stimulation is not fully known. Some adrenergic cells appear to do so. In the locus coeruleus, for example, tyrosine hydroxylase expression, reflected by changes in enzyme activity, immunoreactivity, and messenger RNA levels, is increased in NE cells as a result of chronic cold stress (Richard et al., 1988). With the development of new molecular techniques, for example, in situ hybridization and cloned DNA probes, researchers will soon be able to provide us with more direct answers to this question.

From our perspective, it would be important to determine if psychoactive compounds such as dextroamphetamine can influence the transcription of this gene in brain structures (e.g., n. accumbens) that have been implicated in the therapeutic effects of these compounds. At the time of this writing, however, the critical studies have not been done. We do know that in animals, long-term exposure to amphetamine can lead to an enduring enhancement in DA release both in vitro (Wilcox, Robinson, & Becker, 1986) and in vivo (Robinson, Jurson, Bennett, & Bentgen, 1988). This enhancement is observable long after the cessation of drug treatment and is accompanied by functional changes in behavior in response to subsequent drug exposure (Robinson et al., 1988).

This effect of amphetamine is thought to be similar to the amphetamine hypersensitivity that develops in some individuals who consistently abuse this compound. Such individuals may present with a drug-induced psychotic condition indistinguishable from paranoid schizophrenia. Although the amphetamine-induced psychosis usually dissipates after the person stops taking the drug, re-exposure to a relatively low dose can precipitate a psychotic episode in former addicts who have been abstinent for months or even years (Sato, 1986; Sato, Chen, Akiyama, & Otsuki, 1983). Indirect evidence from living animals suggests that amphetamine supersensitivity may be explained at least in part by both short- and long-term effects on tyrosine hydroxylase.

For example, Robinson et al. (1988) treated rats with escalating doses of amphetamine (1 to 10 mg/kg) for a period of 6 weeks; control animals received saline. Fifteen to 21 days after the last injection, animals were implanted with microdialysis probes in the ventral striatum, that is, the n. accumbens and olfactory tubercle, and given a challenge injection of 2 mg/kg amphetamine. Samples were collected from awake, freely moving animals every 20 minutes for a total of 200 minutes. Amphetamine challenge significantly increased extracellular concentrations of DA and DOPAC (3,4-dihydroxyphenylacetic acid) in the ventral striatum in both groups, but did so to a significantly greater degree in the amphetamine-pretreated group (see Figure 13.4). Moreover, in response to this challenge, amphetamine-pretreated animals developed the intense focused stereotyped behavior, that is, supersensitivity, typically observed with higher doses of amphetamine, whereas saline pretreated animals did not (see Figure 13.5).

After ruling out other potential explanations for their findings, such as decreased amphetamine metabolism, Robinson et al. (1988) concluded that somehow amphetamine gets better at releasing DA after a long period of drug exposure, although they could not specify the molecular basis of this effect. An alternative explanation is that there is actually more DA to be released. The finding that DOPAC levels were higher in amphetamine-pretreated animals in response to the challenge injection at all points in time, including baseline, is of

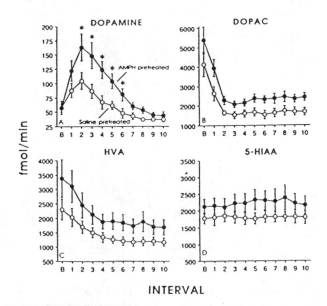

INTERVAL

Figure 13.4: Effect of Amphetamine Pretreatment on Dopamine (DA) Overflow in Ventral Striatum (Nucleus Accumbens) Following a Challenge Injection of Amphetamine. The mean ± SEM extracellular fluid concentrations of DA, dihydroxyphenylacetic acid (DOPAC), homovanillic acid (HVA), and 5-hydroxyindoleacetic acid (5-HIAA) in ventral striatum before (B) and after (20-minute intervals, 1-10) a challenge injection of 2.0 mg/kg amphetamine in rats that were pretreated with either amphetamine (closed circles) or saline (open circles). Amphetamine challenge produced a significantly greater increase in extracellular concentrations of DA in the amphetamine-pretreated versus saline-pretreated animals at $^*p < 0.05$.

Source: Reprinted from T. E. Robinson, P. A. Jurson, J. A. Bennett, & K. M. Bentgen (1988), "Persistent Sensitization of Dopamine Neurotransmission in Ventral Striatum (Nucleus Accumbens) Produced by Prior Experience with (+)-Amphetamine: A Microdialysis Study in Freely Moving Rats," *Brain Research, 462,* 216, with kind permission of Elsevier Science-NL, Sara Burgerhartstraat 25, 1055 KV Amsterdam, The Netherlands.

particular interest because increases in DOPAC are thought to reflect enhanced DA biosynthesis. Because amphetamine challenge can be expected to lead to the rapid Vmax activation of existing pools of inactive enzyme equally in the acutely injected and in the amphetamine-pretreated group, the differential effect of the amphetamine challenge on experienced animals suggests that there may have actually been more endogenous enzyme available to be activated. The finding that extracellular concentrations of DOPAC were higher in the amphetamine-pretreated group, even before the amphetamine challenge, is consistent with this interpretation.

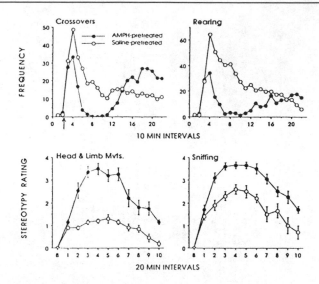

Figure 13.5: Effect of Amphetamine Pretreatment on Behavior Before and After a Challenge Dose of Amphetamine. The challenge dose of amphetamine (2 mg/kg) was given 15-21 days after the last pretreatment injection of saline (open circles) or amphetamine (closed circles). The frequency of crossovers (locomotion from one side of the cage to the other) and rearing was cumulated over 10-minute intervals. Sterotypy ratings (head & limb movements; sniffing) were obtained once during each 20-minute interval. B = the average values obtained during baseline. The arrow in the upper left panel indicates when the amphetamine (AMPH) challenge injection was given. Amphetamine pretreated animals differed significantly from saline pretreated animals on all behavioral measures.

Source: Reprinted from T. E. Robinson, P. A. Jurson, J. A. Bennett, & K. M. Bentgen (1988), "Persistent Sensitization of Dopamine Neurotransmission in Ventral Striatum (Nucleus Accumbens) Produced by Prior Experience with (+)-Amphetamine: A Microdialysis Study in Freely Moving Rats," *Brain Research, 462,* 215, with kind permission of Elsevier Science-NL, Sara Burgerhartstraat 25, 1055 KV Amsterdam, The Netherlands.

■ **UNLOCKING THE CELL'S ACQUIRED POTENTIAL?**

It may be, then, that enduring functional changes in endogenous DA synthesis brought about by long-term amphetamine exposure may not be apparent until some demand is placed on the organism, either as a result of interacting with the environment, through the organism's own internal activity or, as in this case, as a consequence of a subsequent exposure to amphetamine. In other words, homeostatic mechanisms may work to keep extracellular levels within some "normal" resting range, even though enduring changes may have occurred in the amount of DA that the cell can synthesize and mobilize. One would not expect to "see" these changes until the cell was called upon to rise to the occasion so to speak. Any number of different "demand" stimuli (e.g., stress, ingestion of a psychoactive compound, the sight of a sexually receptive mate) could function to unlock the cell's acquired potential.

This idea is consistent with what one group of researchers found in hippo-campus, where chronic exposure (28 days) to a relatively low dose of nicotine (0.8 mg/kg s.c.) significantly increased CA biosynthesis as measured by DOPA (3,4-dihydroxyphenylalanine) accumulation, which was not apparent until the animals were challenged with a subsequent dose of nicotine (Joseph, Peters, Prior, Mitchell, Brazell, & Gray, 1990). Of course, this finding could be explained by an enduring effect of chronic nicotine on the activation of preex-isting enzyme alone; however, if this were the case, one would have expected to see significantly elevated DOPA in chronically treated animals in comparison to saline controls, even in the absence of the acute challenge, but this was not the case. DOPA levels in both groups were the same. Furthermore, DOPA levels in the chronically treated group were significantly elevated over the acutely treated group in response to the same challenge dose of nicotine, that is, 0.8 mg/kg. Again, it is possible that there was actually more enzyme available to be activated in the chronically treated group.

Interestingly, Castaneda, Becker, and Robinson (1988) found that long-term amphetamine exposure enhanced the release of DA from striatal tissue slices evoked either by high potassium or electrical stimulation. In other words, a subsequent application of drug was not necessary in order to see the biochemical effects of previous long-term exposure. Again, their finding suggests that increased levels of enzyme may have already been present within the cell. And due to the synergistic action of both short-term (phosphorylation activation of the enzyme molecule) and long-term effects (increased levels of enzyme avail-able for activation) on tyrosine hydoxylase, DA release was enhanced.

An enduring effect on tyrosine hydroxylase activity is one potential way in which amphetamine may modify the functioning of the cell to produce lasting changes in behavior. There are others. For example, there is evidence that long-term amphetamine use changes the dopaminergic innervation of the striatum (Ellison, Eison, Huberman, & Daniel, 1978).

The above discussion on tyrosine hydroxylase activity was presented essen-tially as food for thought for, as previously stated, any enduring drug-induced changes in behavior that persist following the cessation of drug treatment must, of course, be accompanied by enduring changes in brain function. The more we understand about how the psychomotor stimulants act at the molecular level to modify the long-term functioning of the cell, the closer we will be to a real understanding of how they produce their enduring therapeutic effects.

Closing Thoughts

When we looked beyond the surface behavior of the ADHD individual, we invariably found a profound hunger for the warmth of human feeling—for the nourishment that is as essential to emotional growth and well-being as food is to physical growth and well-being. Having a limited capacity to experience psychic pain and psychic pleasure and a poorly developed expectancy reflex, these individuals are at risk for the development of more troublesome forms of antisocial behavior, including the abuse of affect-inducing drugs (e.g., cocaine, heroin, methamphetamine, alcohol). Although the ADHD individual may be able to obtain some relief from symptoms due to activation of the reward systems of the brain by these drugs, such self-medication is done without rational medical control and can quickly go to extremes, either in drug overdose or social behavior.

Our challenge as professionals is to help society understand this dysfunction so that ways may be found to provide this necessary nourishment before these more difficult problems develop. With respect to afflicted adolescents and adults who may have already developed this pattern, the need to protect society must be tempered with a compassion and empathy for their suffering. These are individuals whose inner emotional life, relatively speaking, is cold and empty—individuals who are dependent upon others to an extreme to provide the warmth of feeling and behavioral control that they cannot provide for themselves. When this stimulation is not forthcoming, they may seek more extreme ways of awakening the feeling brain. Acutely aware of their own lack of self-control, many behave in ways that force others to apply the necessary brakes. Some adult repeat offenders, for example, openly admitted to us that they intentionally committed crimes so that they could be imprisoned. For these individuals, jail is a haven from the confusing and difficult work of adjusting to a society whose rules and standards of behavior they can neither appreciate nor internalize. Considering the ongoing ineffectiveness of prison rehabilitation, one must stop to wonder what percentage of inmates are currently afflicted with this disorder. Among repeat offenders, this percentage must be high indeed, for these are individuals who do not learn from past experience, and much less from punitive threats, which may actually provoke bad behavior. Theirs is an immediate world, and authority figures must be continually present to control and direct their behavior.

Although they may have matured in their outward physical appearance, ADHD adolescents and adults are fundamentally children who are stuck at an early stage of their emotional and social development. If they have been able to internalize a social conscience at all, it is apt to be authoritarian rather than humanistic in nature. More often than not, their social relating is amoral in quality, for the essence of morality is human feeling. Finding more effective ways of identifying and treating these individuals is as important for the overall well-being of our society as it is for the overall well-being of the individual.

Appendix A:
The Pupil
Adjustment Program

A Report Submitted to
the Springfield School Department
Springfield, Massachusetts
in May 1970

■ **I. INTRODUCTION**

From September 1966 to June 1967, the Springfield School Department referred 195 pupils for psychiatric evaluation. Of these referrals, 55% were found to have a condition characterized by impulsive, unrestrained behavior, hyperactivity, distractibility, defiance to authority, opposition, short attention span, low motivation to achieve, and an inability to play well with peers. These symptoms interfere with normal learning. The majority of these children were in need of some type of individual programming.

At that time, there were only two Pupil Adjustment classes in the school system, that is, special classes set aside for the management of emotionally disturbed children. These two classes, instituted in 1958, were limited to a teacher-pupil ratio of 1 to 10. The teachers met weekly with the consulting child psychiatrist, who determined which pupils would be placed in the Pupil Adjustment classes and which pupils were ready to return to regular classes.

Recognizing the growing enormity of the problem, the Bureau of Pupil Services authorized the consulting child psychiatrist and the pupil adjustment counselor to work exclusively with the Pupil Adjustment classes in order that they might develop a comprehensive corrective program that would be workable within the school context. The number of classes was increased to six. The teacher-pupil ratio was decreased to one teacher per eight children. A master teacher was added, and the adjustment counselor was directed to work as a psychiatric assistant, specifically with the parents of the children in the program, that is, the home situation.

As a fuller understanding of the child's problem evolved, it became apparent that it was a product of a child-environment interaction, and that its correction would entail a comprehensive program involving both home and school for a prolonged period of time—at least 2 years per child. The corrective experience, which will be elaborated upon later, was based on:

1. *Constancy*—a firm, positive and enduring attitude maintained toward the child
2. *Consistency*—a congruent structure throughout the program, in school and at home
3. *Immediacy*—of teacher and parental responses to the child's behavior, both in time and proximity

Such a milieu for the child could be effected only through the two most significant and pervasive relationships in their current lives—with parents and with teachers.

The following is an outline of the program as it has developed in order to meet the need-requirements of this particular type of child:

1. Referral: The child is referred following a psychodiagnostic and/or psychiatric study indicating the need for a special program.
2. Intake: (a) The developmental history of the child is taken from the parents, and the parents are evaluated as to their workability and cooperativeness. (b) The child is tested to obtain a baseline for the evaluation of future progress. A parental checklist is also obtained for a profile of the child at home.
3. Parental Involvement: Periodic consultations with the psychiatric assistant or the program psychiatrist, or both, are arranged, which the parents must agree to attend. Consultations are also arranged for emergency situations.

4. Other agencies are involved where indicated, for example, Division of Child Guidance, Probation, et cetera.

5. Weekly observations of classes are made by the consulting child psychiatrist, the psychiatric assistant, and the master teacher.

6. Pupils are evaluated periodically (academic, psychological, and social).

7. Medication is administered when indicated.

8. An individualized curriculum is established for each child.

9. Weekly staff meetings include the consulting child psychiatrist, the psychiatric assistant, and the master teacher.

10. In-service Training: (a) Biweekly meetings are held with teacher groups and the consulting child psychiatrist, and individual meetings are held between teachers and the consulting child psychiatrist, and (b) monthly full-staff in-service meetings are conducted.

11. Transition programs are worked out for each pupil's return to regular classes.

12. Follow-up programming ensures the child's adjustment and evaluates the effectiveness of the program.

13. Data descriptive of the child population are accumulated to gain a further understanding of the problem and to evaluate the progress and effectiveness of the approaches used.

■ **II. PROGRAM OVERVIEW**

The program, as it has evolved, has been a reflection of the gradual unfolding of the the child's problem, through observations of the child and the study of their history and environment, as well as the application of principles of research developed in the fields of neurophysiology, psychology, and pharmacology. We feel that it is of fundamental importance to realize that the program, from its inception, has been an organic part of the school system. It is not a program set apart, but rather the Pupil Adjustment Program functions within the matrix of the school complex. The significance of this fact for the pupil and for school personnel cannot be overstated, for in this way the children continue to be an integral part of their community. Their return to regular class and school is anticipated, and their transition there is thus facilitated.

As a consequence of viewing the problem as a child-environment interaction, the program has had, of necessity, a double focus—one directed to the child and the other directed to the management of the environment as represented by teachers and parents.

A presentation of the dynamic formulation of the child's problem is included below to give a better understanding of the rationale of the program as it has developed.

The symptomatology presented by the disorder may be grouped in clusters of three related to: (1) self-centeredness, (2) authority, and (3) time. We will see how these areas of disturbance are related to an impaired capacity for imprinting feelings of psychic pain and psychic pleasure.

Cluster 1: Self-centeredness. In this category are selfishness, lack of consideration for others, inability to maintain lasting relationships or loyalty to other individuals or groups, lack of ability to empathize with others or their situations, a marked persistence in obtaining immediate gratification, impulsive actions, irresponsibility, and most usually, an attractive surface charm.

Cluster 2: Authority. In this category, the individual is constantly in conflict with authority as represented by parents, teachers, policemen, and other authority figures or by accepted social values, or even when expressed in terms of the rules of a game. Rules or norms of behavior of any kind cannot be understood by such children; thus the group setting offers no place for them, and they are left without a social niche and with a sense of alienation that may lead to aggressive behavior. An inability to comprehend and appreciate authority leaves these children with a concept of authority as an interfering agent in their quests for self-satisfaction; therefore, they frequently react to authority with oppositional behavior or a passive-aggressive stance. Frequent confrontations with authority figures and repeated rejection from peers leaves this type of individual with a poor self-image.

Cluster 3: Time. The children we are describing live only in the present. They have no ties to the past or expectations of the future. Having no past, they cannot profit from experience. Having no future, they cannot direct or channel their energies into goal-rewarding behavior. Living only in the present, they are robbed both of anticipatory rewards and of anticipatory anxieties. Being bound to the present, they respond only to the immediate impulses impinging from within or the immediate stimuli impinging from without. They are predominately impulse-driven and stimuli-bound. Having no past, they feel no guilt or remorse. It is therefore, easy to see why they may be charming and lovable.

Those aspects of living that require an appreciation of the sequence of time play no part in these children's lives. Being bound as they are, they live a horizontal surface-type of existence, constantly shifting and changing from moment to moment, depending upon the stimuli and impulses presented to them. They can view other people only in terms of their own immediate needs, and they persist in having their way, regardless of the feelings of others. Authority is viewed as a strange and alien incomprehensible force, causing them momentary discomfort as it interferes with their efforts to obtain immediate relief from the pressures of their own impulses. Rewards and punishments are soon forgotten, playing no part as motivating forces in their behavior. Even further, their inability to relate to the past deprives them of their cultural heritage, and thus they become aliens in the culture in which they were born.

Certain studies and theoretical formulations may assist us, at least in part, in relating a neurophysiological mechanism to the development of an appreciation of time sequences and, therefore, to a fuller conceptualization of time in its three dimensions of past, present, and future. Here we are referring to the research of Olds and Milner (1954) and Delgado et al. (1954) in discovering the reward and punishment systems of the brain and to the theoretical speculations of Stein (1964) regarding the concept of expectancy. The research of Olds and Milner clearly demonstrated the existence of a positive reinforcement system (feelings of psychic pleasure) of the brain which, when stimulated, results in a return to the behavior that produced the stimulation. Working at the same time, Delgado et al. (1954) discovered the existence of a negative reinforcement system (feelings of psychic pain) which when stimulated, results in an aversion to the behavior that produced the stimulation.

With these systems in mind, Stein (1964) postulated that operant behavior was repeated or avoided because of the *expectancy* of either reward (psychic pleasure) or punishment (psychic pain). The concept of expectancy can exist only if there is some associated memory from the past. He theorized, therefore, that the mechanism of expectation is a Pavlovian conditioned reflex, which results in the activation of the positive or the negative reinforcement systems. For example, by repeated consistent stimulation of the reward system in response to a specific behavior, we reinforce that behavior by associating it with a pleasant or pleasurable feeling tone, which is stored together with the behavior in memory. To obtain again the delicious feeling of reward, the organism will repeat the associated behavior. Consistent repeated stimulation of the negative rein- forcement area will result in the storage of unpleasant or painful feeling associations along with the behavior that elicited them. This type of behavior will tend to be avoided. Accepting this formulation, it is clearly seen how future time (expectancy) and past time (stored memory complex of behavior and associated feeling) are brought into play in the behavior of an individual.

Assuming, however, that this mechanism is not functioning properly and that for some unknown reason the thresholds of the reward and punishment systems are extremely high, we would have a situation where the usual degree of intensity of stimulation of the reinforcement centers would have little effect. Conse- quently, Pavlovian conditioning would not occur—there would be no storage of the feelings associated with events, and therefore, no expectancy either of rewards or punishments. Such a condition could well account for the symptoms manifested in the individual with this disorder.

Certain difficulties would also arise if, in the normal functioning of the reward and punishment systems, the reinforcing stimuli were inconsistent or delayed, that is, the same behavior being positively reinforced in one instance and negatively reinforced in another, or in instances of negative behavior, the corrective measure coming some time after the behavior had occurred.

With the above research and theoretical formulations in mind, one of the areas of research undertaken in this program was a study of parental approaches to such children. The most frequently revealed attitude was *permissiveness*. Parents who vacillate in their approach to their children are unable to provide the children with consistent and constant feedback as to the appropriateness or inappropriateness of their behavior. Parents who are unable to or who do not interfere with the behavior of their children do not provide the necessary quality of immediacy of either positive or negative feedback.

In view of our understanding of the problems presented by the disorder, its correction requires a total program of constancy, consistency, and immediacy. Such a milieu is essential to the correction of the existing symptoms and provides for the development of a healthy character within the educational context, as well as within the child's home environment.

Realizing the level of sophistication of the parents who could benefit from the program, the criteria for the acceptance of parents have been realistically defined. We demand only that: (1) both parents recognize the existence of a problem, (2) both willingly assume some degree of responsibility for its resolution, and (3) at least one parent attends the scheduled meetings. The intake part of the program has been delayed when both parents have not been able to attend because of the importance of the initial interview in the evaluation process. On occasion, other significant figures in the child's life, for example, a grandparent, are solicited to participate in the program, as are the workers of other agencies.

Prior to referral to a Pupil Adjustment Class, children have been examined through psychodiagnostic and/or psychiatric testing and study. If they have not already been administered the Weschler Intelligence Scale for Children (WISC), they will have completed it by the time they enter class. During the period of the evaluation of their parents, the referred child will also be given the Organic Integrity Test, the Bender Gestalt, and the Draw-A-Person. A more intense battery of tests is now being considered, which is to include the Porteus Maze and instruments related to social intelligence (for example, the Expressions Test), as well as screening for perceptual impairments. The purpose of this testing is: (1) to establish a program for the child, and (2) to provide a baseline from which future progress may be determined.

The child's age at the time of referral is a primary consideration in admitting children into the program, as is the degree of workability and cooperativeness of the parents. In our experience, the age of the child has become a deciding factor because: (1) it can be anticipated that the child will be in the program for at least 2 years, (2) returning the child to an elementary school regular class, where there is a greater degree of containment, is preferable to entering a junior high setting, which has a greater degree of mobility, and (3) the earlier the problem is identified and treated, the more successful is its resolution. We are therefore increasingly focusing our attention on younger children—preferably under 10 years of age.

■ **III. THE HOME PROGRAM**

The parents of children who have been accepted into the program agree to meet with the psychiatrist and/or with the psychiatric assistant, who is under the psychiatrist's direction, at monthly intervals or more frequently as the situation dictates. The child's problem, as it exists in the present, is the focal point of these meetings. The parents are informed of the child's present status, and they are reinforced in their roles.

More specifically, attempts are made to establish the authority of the mother and to assist her in developing a constant and consistent approach to the child through the dynamic of *immediate* positive or negative reinforcement of the child's behavior. Fathers are also expected to be an integral part of the program. We have frequently observed that due to the lack of maternal authority, fathers have been forced to assume a strict disciplinary attitude toward their youngsters. A situation such as this usually results in: (1) delayed reinforcement of the child's behavior, and (2) the continuation of an infantile-dependent attitude toward mother. By reversing the previously established roles of the parents, by making mother more authoritative and assisting father in establishing a more warm and positive relationship with the child, there are opportunities for more immediate reinforcement of the child's behavior and more appropriate responses in the interaction of the father and the child. Finally, attempts are made to relieve parental guilt by focusing on the *child's problem,* the *child's temperament,* and the *child's needs.* In this way, we remove the stigma of the "bad parent" and release these parental energies for coping with here-and-now situations.

When a child becomes disruptive and unmanageable in school, the psychiatric assistant is notified. He immediately contacts the parents and schedules a meeting. Parental and school controls are thus reinforced. In cases of persistent disruption, a child may be excluded for 1 or 2 days. The parent is then more forcefully confronted with the child's problem, while the child, who much prefers attending school to remaining at home, becomes more aware of what is acceptable.

A large number of parents have responded well to this simple, direct approach. According to their own statements, they have been aware of their children's need for more discipline but were afraid to be authoritarian because of previous misconceptions regarding parenthood. When their self-confidence has been reestablished, they have been able to respond in a healthy parental manner.

■ IV. THE CLASS PROGRAM

The other most significant relationship in which the children are involved and through which the correction of their problem could be effected is that with the teacher.

Through the evaluation of the social, academic, intellectual, and cultural strengths and weaknesses of the children, the teacher is provided with a level of expectation for the construction of a realistic model for each child. This model is used to develop an individualized program for each child, which is administered by the teacher with enduring constancy, consistency, and immediate reinforcement.

In class, children are taught to be more organized in their thinking and actions through the medium of the learning process. An awareness of the necessity for postponing immediate gratification for a realistically determined future goal (set by the teacher) is a part of this process. Children are assured that they can achieve, can produce, have potential, and are worthy of help, and that someone is there to help them. A benevolent cycle is thus set into motion. By helping children to develop goals and plans within the framework of the model and by appropriately reinforcing their learning behavior in various areas, for example, academic, social, cultural, a reconstruction of their attitudes toward self and others can occur.

Cognizant of the fact that the primary objective of the class program is to return children to regular class, the curriculum is as closely equated with that of regular classes as possible. The regular classroom behavioral expectations and atmosphere are maintained in terms of rules of conduct, schedules, and so on. For students who are particularly deficient in phonics, reading, spelling, arithmetic, and penmanship, the classroom curriculum may be almost entirely limited to these core areas. For others, it is possible to include the entire spectrum of the required curriculum. All students participate in music, physical education, and art. With some students, it is necessary at the outset to provide one-to-one tutoring in all major content areas.

In view of the immediacy of the child's needs, both in time and distance, *proximity* is an essential part of the reinforcement process. Here we are referring to the closeness of the teacher to the children—standing behind or beside them, leaning over them, touching their arm or shoulder while giving the appropriate feedback.

Because such children are lacking in impulse control and are easily distracted, they demand a highly structured, well-organized classroom. Immediate close containment of the children in a tightly structured situation—carrels are ideal for this purpose—is the first order of business, in order to reduce movement in the classroom and to assist the teacher in establishing control. The teacher can then move in immediately to reinforce the behavior of the children. As inner control is manifested in the children's conduct, movement is allowed.

Finally, in view of the very poor psychosexual identity of these children, room assignments are made according to sex. This allows for the development of their sociosexual image with much less confusion than when boys and girls are put together in the same class.

■ V. MEDICATION

In selective cases, medication—dextroamphetamine or methylphenidate—is employed as part of the child's program. This is because these medications have been demonstrated to lower the thresholds of reinforcement in the brain (Stein, 1968), and because they have been proven effective in the management of childhood hyperkinesis (Connors, Eisenberg, & Barcai, 1967).

Before medication is administered, children are observed in the classroom, with particular note made of their distractibility, attention span, hyperactivity, oppositional behavior, and empathic response. If a child is found to be experiencing difficulties in these areas, medication is started on the lowest possible dose. Further adjustments are made based on teacher observations of the child in the classroom and parent observations of the child at home, until the minimum effective dose is established. The minimum effective dose range for dextroamphetamine has been found to be from 5 to 25 mg twice a day, and for methylphenidate, from 20 mg to 60 mg twice a day.

■ VI. THE INTRA-STAFF PROGRAM

The ongoing progress of the children is evaluated through a variety of methods. Bimonthly teacher reports are submitted to the psychiatrist, giving a profile of the academic progress and social development of each youngster. In addition, biweekly brief comments on each child are submitted by the teacher with note of particular problems that arise in the classroom. Weekly observations of the children in their classrooms by the psychiatrist give an opportunity for the demonstration of the specific problems reported.

The psychiatric assistant, in his rounds to the classes, inquires into the behavior of each child whose parents he plans to see in the near future. At this time, the teacher is able to bring into his or her discussion any other child who

is having difficulty and whose parents may have to be seen earlier than scheduled. In this way, communication between home and school is further facilitated.

The master teacher closely supervises the in-class program, working directly
with the teachers on curriculum and periodically sitting in to observe class
procedures and pupil progress. The master teacher also discusses problems and
their possible resolutions with the principals in whose schools the classes are
maintained. The transition of each pupil back to regular class is also programmed
by the master teacher.

Individual teachers meet with the psychiatrist once a month. These meetings
allow each teacher to discuss the problems of their individual class. In addition,
teachers meet as a group biweekly with the psychiatrist, the psychiatric assistant,
and the master teacher. At these meetings, all problems relative to the program
are discussed, for example, transportation of the children, classroom management, specific problems related to the relationship of the classes with the rest of
the schools in which the classes are housed, school policies, program policies,
and so on. These group meetings allow for mutual support among teachers and
a group identity.

Parent-teacher conferences are held as scheduled and as emergencies arise.
At these meetings the usual topics discussed are the child's academic progress,
his strengths and weaknesses, his social level of maturity and so forth.

There is thus an organized communications system between and among those
who affect the child's progress both directly and indirectly. Each member of the
program has a well-defined role, and the cohesiveness of the program is
maintained through information channels and informative exchanges at meetings. The parents are able to meet with all of those who deal with their children.

■ VII. THE TRANSITION PROGRAM

The transition from a Pupil Adjustment Class to a regular class is a process that
begins with a child spending part of a school day or an entire day in a regular
classroom that is in the same building as the child's special class. By the time
children enter into this transition phase, they are able to control their impulses,
and their attention span has increased. They are able to work with less supervision, and their behavior has been stabilized—this improved level of functioning
having been maintained for a minimum of 3 months. During the transition
period, should children experience any difficulty, they may return to special class
full-time to reestablish controls. The cooperation of the transition class teachers
has been found to be essential to the successful adjustment of pupils through
this testy transitional phase. This period may last up to 5 months before the child
is successfully integrated back into regular class. Medication is continued when
indicated through the transition phase and following the return to regular class.

Prior to the child's return, the master teacher prepares the regular class teacher and school principal for the pupil's acceptance. This is frequently a delicate part of the process because there exist preconceptions and misconceptions regarding these children. Resolutions must be found before the child can settle into regular class. Discussions are held with respect to the child's academic and social maturity. Assurances are given that there will be follow-up with both parents and child.

After the child is returned to regular class, the master teacher makes periodic visits to the school. When difficulties occur, he is often able to resolve the situation through consultation with the school principal, the child's teacher, and the child. When problems persist, the parents' help is solicited through the psychiatric assistant. Although informed and consulted in these situations, the psychiatrist enters only when medication adjustments are needed or when the problem persists.

■ VIII. RESULTS OF THE PROGRAM

Since the beginning of the 1967 to 1968 school year, a total of 42 children have left the Pupil Adjustment Classes. The disposition of these 42 children is as follows: 2 children were removed because of a change of residence, 1 child was placed in a training school and will return upon his release, 8 children are in transition status at the present time, and 31 children have returned to regular class or to general auxiliary class for the retarded.

Of the 31 children who were returned to regular class, 50% have experienced some difficulty. Two thirds of these problems have been resolved as of this writing, leaving 5 children still in need of assistance. It should be noted that these 5 children were returned to junior high school, where there is greater freedom and mobility. In focusing on younger children, a greater period of time is allowed in a contained elementary classroom situation, resulting in greater stability prior to entering the freer atmosphere of a secondary school.

■ IX. RECOMMENDATIONS

Recommendations for an extension of this program into the summer months have been made. The need for such cannot be overstated, either in the cost to the school department or in terms of an investment in the continued progress of the pupils.

It has been the experience of those who are involved in the program that the restructuring of classes and the reinstitution of classroom controls in the beginning of each school year is a lengthy process. Unnecessary delays are experienced in the establishment of normal school routines and in pupil progress.

During the summer, when the program is not in operation, the children are, in most cases, without medication or controls. This means, simply, a return of those symptoms for which they were referred initially. The parents are without guidance or support. All around, gains are lost.

As the program is resumed in the fall, each child must be reevaluated. Parents must be interviewed again. It can be difficult to get parents back into the program after a school year of good controls followed by a summer during which the child has been unmanageable, or in some cases, arrested for some unlawful acting-out.

Once again, medication must be reinstated and readjusted for optimal effectiveness. This is accomplished through both scheduled meetings and almost daily contact with the home by telephone.

Although a child's return to regular class may have been anticipated for the new school year, his or her return is often delayed into the winter months because of the hiatus in academic and psychosocial growth. Thus waiting lists gather names, and administrative pressures increase as the pupils of last year undergo reevaluation before any new candidates can be seen.

■ X. A STUDY OF THE CHILDREN CURRENTLY IN THE PROGRAM

As the program developed, it became essential to compile certain data regarding the children who were being serviced. The reasons for this were: (1) to better understand the child's immediate problem in order that responses to it would be appropriate, (2) to be able to accurately evaluate the child's progress, (3) to investigate factors that might be related to causation, both in the child and in the environment, (4) to test the relevance of these factors, (5) to maintain an objective (scientific) attitude toward the child's problem, thus allowing for greater effectiveness in coping with the situation, and (6) to add relevant information to the common body of knowledge concerning this disorder.

Developmental and psychosocial history data were obtained through an interview/questionnaire technique that allowed for parental elaborations of each question, thus enriching the content and quality of their response. For example, in response to questions on weaning, the age at which the child was weaned became an important consideration only after a fuller description of the process by the parent, for example, "He threw the bottle away," or "I boiled the nipple." Parents also filled out a behavior rating scale developed by the program staff. In addition, data were obtained on the children's reading and math achievement (Gray Oral), as well as on their intellectual level of functioning

(WISC). As mentioned previously, a more comprehensive battery of psychological tests is being developed, the findings of which will be included in subsequent reports.

Teacher descriptions of the child in the classroom were also compiled. These anecdotal reports have been found to be one of the most valuable tools in helping to establish the diagnosis.

1. Description of the Child in the Classroom

The following is a composite picture of the child, taken directly from the referral application written by the regular classroom teacher with supplemental reports from the school principal. As seen by the classroom teacher and the school principal, the referred child has confronted the teacher, regardless of grade level, intellectual potential, chronological age or gender, with the following disruptive behaviors. "She hums and sings, or beats on her desk with her fingers until she has the attention of the entire class. During class discussions she answers for others, depriving them of a chance to recite." Class routines are disrupted by such individualistic behaviors with the attention of the teacher and the class drawn to "constant talking" in a "very loud voice," which is often colored with "vulgar language."

Restlessness is always a reason for the referral of this type of child. "He causes constant interruptions in the classroom by annoying children, moving aimlessly about the room, pushing his desk and chair about, squirming and bobbing up and down when he is in his chair, talking out and calling names."

Another child will "not stay in her seat. She follows the teacher around the room, staying close behind her. If she is specifically told to sit, she will carry her chair behind her as she goes here and there in the room. Other times she walks her desk and chair wherever she wants to go." Restlessness is not always confined to the classroom, for without warning, the child will leave the room and "wander" around the building, the school grounds, and the neighboring area or return home. If there are relatives who attend the same school, they may be visited in their classrooms.

Words such as *always, constantly, continually,* and *perpetually* are commonly used in the descriptions of these children. The child:

is always wandering around the room

is constantly out of her seat

perpetually strives for attention and delights in being in trouble

is always out of his seat—needing more freedom of movement due to extreme, uncontrollable restlessness

must be continually encouraged to work at all

constantly puts his coat on, threatens to go home, and runs out of the room, going to
　　his sister's room on the second floor of the building

talks constantly

constantly tries to interrupt the class

is in perpetual motion

The following is a report filed by one teacher on a child she had just referred
to the program:

> N—— is a difficult child for me to understand and to help, as his moods are
> varied and unpredictable. He may respond to one form of approach one day and
> be infuriated by or be indifferent to the same approach another day. He is
> determined to keep your attention focused on him. He seems to be aware of his
> problems but lacks the control needed to correct or help himself. I feel the others
> have suffered through his gains. He has had longer periods of conformity. For
> example, after Christmas recess, he needed no correction for 2 full days. He did
> not accomplish much work but did have his behavior under a degree of control.
> The class was able to go along without interruption—a novelty with N——
> present.

Teachers' attempts at correction elicit a "negative attitude," call forth "defiance," "arguments," "rudeness," "impertinence," "disrespect" and forms of
retaliation such as "dumping contents of desk on the floor," or the use of "foul
language," or the child "feels that he is being treated unfairly and sulks," "pouts
and cries," or "when reprimanded for any misbehavior, appears genuinely
surprised, either not realizing or not remembering what he did," or the child "has
tantrums—crying, yelling, sulking and crying innocence, shoving furniture,
throwing books, and becoming very rude," or "blames others for things he has
done." Chaos reigns with this type of child in the classroom and elsewhere in
the school building.

Other school authorities and rules regarding school citizenship are either
ignored or defied.

> Complete defiance of authority and disrespect for adults and rules demand continued
> 　　supervision and more than reasonable attention.
> Refuses to follow set rules for safety and even talks back to safety officials.
> Obeys none of the school rules for safety or good citizenship.
> Is untrustworthy.
> Puts own name on other children's lunchboxes and lies.

The school lavatory is often the scene of water fights, plumbing mishaps, assaults,
and so on, providing an "escape" from classroom routines and structure.

Descriptive words such as *self-centered, disruptive,* and *aggressive* are typically part of the profile and indicate characteristics that preclude successful peer relationships. Teachers frequently report that this type of child is unable to compete.

> He shows little or no desire to participate in class activity. Although he is quite physical in his playing with children smaller than he, he tries to drift off by himself when his class is having physical education. He avoids all competitive games here at school.

> He annoys his classmates—kicking and pushing them, bringing them to tears.

> He gets into trouble with his playmates because he doesn't share and because he always wants his own way.

> He is not popular with his classmates as he frequently pushes to be first.

> He cannot accept being part of the group unless he is the center of attention.

> When children are working at their seats, he wanders up and down, leaning over their desks and disturbing them.

> His behavior is weakening the spirit of several children in the classroom.

> He has very few friends—his classmates are very disgusted with him because he is so disturbing.

Teachers have also reported that they have been positively affected, paradoxically, by some of the children whom they have referred. For example, one teacher listed on her referral sheet 16 complaints about the child's behavior including restlessness, distractibility, refusal to attempt work assignments, destruction of other children's materials, oppositional behavior toward her, and aggressive behavior toward peers. But in the closing lines of her report she stated: "S—— is a lovable child." There were many such references to the "cute" and "lovable" ways of the children and to their ability to "charm" and "talk his way out of" difficult situations.

2. Description of the Child at Home

Although the parents may be somewhat defensive initially in describing their child, the behavioral picture obtained from them is usually as valuable as the teacher's reports in establishing the diagnosis. The following describes, in composite form, such children at home.

He seems to need constant reminding to finish chores.

She's not happy if she's not in trouble.

He's the biggest liar you'll meet.

He's lazy and easy-going, but playful.

He's miserable when you tell him no.

He'll mind, if he wants to.

She's no problem—if you spoil her.

He doesn't mind doing things—when he feels like it.

She has a big heart but she's not loving.

You can't reason with him.

He argues with everyone at home. I can't do anything with him—nothing I do works.

He can't remember from one minute to the next.

He's spoiled rotten, but sometimes he's sweet as pie.

He can't sit still except for television and even then he still wiggles.

The above descriptions of children by their parents are consistent with what the teacher sees at school—distractibility, restlessness, acting out, and opposition to authority. Many times these children are regarded as "cute" and "lovable," but they are also "unreachable" and "nonconforming." The child may "wander" about the neighborhood, accumulating a number of acquaintances and objects, but he rarely forms close attachments, even with his toys, leaving them strewn about. Moreover, he freely uses others' belongings without asking permission.

And because he is unable to retain the direction given to him, he requires more supervision than his siblings. Finally, parents have frequently reported (and this has also been observed by program staff) that the child relates better to either older or younger children than to his own peer group.

The psychiatric evaluation and the psychodiagnostic instruments administered prior to referral have consistently indicated a character disorder of such magnitude as to require special intervention.

3. Age, Race, and Gender Data

There are 41 males and 6 females in the program. Seventeen children are black, and 30 are white. Ages range from 6 years to 13 years. The average age is 10 years and 0 months. One year ago, the average age was 10 years and 8 months—an indication of earlier detection and referral. It is anticipated that this trend will continue, for the earlier treatment is begun, the better the prognosis.

4. Intelligence

Full-scale WISC scores ranged from 60 to 120. Eighty percent of the children tested in the normal range of intelligence or above. The lower scores of the remaining 20% may be more a reflection of their problems than a true indication of their potential. Verbal IQ scores ranged from 50 to 120; performance IQ scores ranged from 60 to 130. Verbal scores were depressed relative to performance scores, with only 65% of the children scoring 90 points or above on the verbal subtest as compared to 80% on the performance subtest.

5. Reading Achievement

Reading achievement as measured by the Gray Oral ranged from pre-primer levels up to the eighth grade. The average level of reading retardation was 3 years. This was calculated by taking the expected reading level for each child and subtracting the actual reading level and dividing by the total number of children in the study.

6. Medical History

Of the 47 children in the study, the past medical history of 41 is known. Of these 41, 65% have had no serious medical problems. Five percent of these children have petite mal epilepsy, and, as indicated below, 30% have experienced some medical problems in the past, but with no known sequelae. With the exception of the two children with epilepsy, the medical examinations at the time of admission to the program were normal.

1. drank paint thinner ($n = 1$)
2. fell from third-floor window ($n = 2$)
3. convulsions in infancy ($n = 2$)
4. rheumatic fever ($n = 1$)
5. dehydration in infancy ($n = 1$)
6. scarlet fever ($n = 1$)
7. concussion ($n = 3$)
8. high fevers in infancy ($n = 2$)

Emphasis has been placed on the possibility of some type of birth trauma, causing a minimal type of brain dysfunction that may cause behavioral disorders or learning problems. The only remarkable finding with respect to deliveries was the high incidence of normal births, with only six mothers reporting that their children needed some type of extra neonatal care as a result of the birthing process. The birth weights of these children ranged from 5 lbs 0 oz to 9 lbs 6 oz, with 64% of the children weighing between 6 and 8 lbs.

7. Grade in Which Problem Appeared

A review of the teachers' progress notes and report cards to the parents revealed that 80% of the 47 children in the program were experiencing behavioral difficulties by the end of the first grade, and 95% by the end of the second grade. Fifty percent were having difficulty in kindergarten.

This type of problem may not be apparent in the preschool home environment, which too often has allowed the child to govern his or her own behavior or which has buffered the child from the demands of society. Upon entering the classroom, however, where certain behaviors are demanded by both teacher and peers, such children soon find themselves alienated and unable to function adequately.

8. Temperament of the Child

In view of the high level of activity of these children, inquiries were made of the mother relative to the temperament of the child as indicated by pre- and postnatal movements and excitability. Of the 35 mothers who were able to provide this information, 25, or 71%, described their child as hyperactive in utero. Eight mothers said prenatal movements were "normal" and one that the fetus was "quiet." Fifty-four percent of these 35 mothers described their child as excitable and restless in infancy. Eight described their infant as "normal" with respect to these characteristics, and 8 responded that their infant was "quiet."

The continued high activity level of these children could be a reflection of a catering (permissive) environment in which the child's needs were either being continually tended to by an anticipating mother, or in which parental attempts at discipline and control were either lacking or inconsistent. Further data strongly indicate that these children were brought up in a permissive milieu. For example, 71% of mothers reported that their child was weaned by the age of 1. The majority of children gave the bottle up themselves. Attempts made by the mother to remove the responsibility for the child's weaning from herself were accomplished by telling the child that "Santa Claus took it," "The kitty took it," and so on. One mother said that she boiled the nipple of the bottle so that it became ineffective, causing the child to give it up in frustration. With these methods of relating to the child, mothers avoided the positive disciplinary function of mothering by not confronting the child with their role of authority—a role they were later unable to establish. Over 50% of these children had been fed on demand rather than on schedule.

Only 62% of mothers reported that their children were toilet trained by the age of 3, the expected age for completion of this training in our culture. Further, when mothers were asked how they trained the child, the most common response was "he trained himself." Other responses revealed that the child was trained by a grandparent or an "exasperated" father. Toilet training is among the first serious confrontations between the temperament of the child and the authority of the mother. The resolution of this conflict may be one of the determining factors in the mother-as-authority-child relationship of later years. These and subsequent findings of the study suggest that the child becomes dominant in the mother-child relationship.

According to a behavior checklist completed by parents, the majority of children in the program are made up of those who: (1) need much supervision, (2) are easily distracted, (3) often persist in having their own way, (4) often need reminding, (5) frequently have cute and lovable ways, (6) often do not pay attention, (7) often make friends easily, (8) rarely follow rules, (9) are almost never shy with adults, (10) can only sometimes be left alone without worry, and (11) are only sometimes quiet.

The overall picture presented is one of cute, lovable, and very active children who are not shy with adults and pay little mind to authority or rules. These children are strong-willed, insisting on having their own way and persistent in getting what they want, regardless of the feelings of others. They are able to make friends easily because of their lack of shyness and their surface appeal. They are easily distracted and sufficiently impulsive to warrant almost constant supervision.

The foregoing depicts such a child as a package of self-centered energy, presented to an unsuspecting mother at birth for her to enculturate, that is, to bring the child through the development of inner controls, positive direction of energies, the appreciation of social niceties, the internalization of socially appropriate behavior, and the learning of responses to parental expectations and demands.

9. Position of the Child in the Family Relative to Other Siblings

Information was available on 44 of the 47 children studied. Excluding the five families with only 1 child, the ratio of odd-numbered birth-order positions (29) to even-numbered positions (10) is almost three to one. Birth order as a contributing factor will continue to be investigated. The construct we are considering at this time is that a child with the temperament previously described, having entered into a family constellation where siblings are already paired, obtains the position of an only child, that is, he or she has no sibling to pair with. Thus, for awhile at least, he or she is the center of the family's attention and is subject to permissive or overly catering attitudes on the part of significant adults and possibly, even older siblings.

10. A Study of the Mother in Relation to the Child

Mothers' ages at the time of the birth of the child ranged from 15 to 44 years. Twenty-two, or 50%, of the 40 mothers who provided this information were between the ages of 15 and 24. Thirteen mothers, or 33%, were between the ages of 30 and 34, and 3 mothers were 35 years of age or older.

Only 25% of mothers had completed high school. Fourteen percent had a college education or better.

Eighty-seven percent of the 47 mothers were the natural mothers of the children. Only five of the children were living with foster mothers, and only one child was living with a stepmother. The fact that more of these children have not been given over to other parent surrogates or residential treatment centers to socialize may be indicative of the strength of the mother-child relationship, especially if one keeps in mind that such children experience great difficulty in relating to authority figures and that they are extremely difficult to tolerate for extended periods of time unless treated with massive amounts of attention, which they seek, or with indifference.

Only seven mothers were working at the time of the study; 40 mothers were at home.

Seventy percent of the natural mothers stated that they wanted the pregnancy, 24% expressed an attitude of resignation, and 6% expressed definite negative feelings about it.

Fifty-two percent of natural mothers admitted to having had emotional problems during their pregnancy and later following the birth of their child. The majority of problems were described as situational in nature, for example, marital problems, conflicts with in-laws, and so on. Fifty-seven percent of the mothers were incapacitated to some degree during the child's infancy due to either emotional problems or physical illness—the child's early environment being, therefore, unstable and inconsistent.

The presence of the mother in the home is an unknown fact in six cases. Four of the 47 mothers worked at some time in the child's infancy, and 4 other mothers were not close to the child in early infancy because of illness. Children in the latter situation were cared for by grandparents and older siblings. Thirty one mothers reported that they were at home during the entire infancy period.

The overwhelming maternal attitude toward discipline was one of *permissiveness*, with 39 of 41 mothers openly admitting that they had "spoiled" the child. Only 2 mothers said discipline was "normal," while none of the mothers reported that discipline was strict. A few stated that the child was spoiled by others, such as grandparents, baby-sitters, and so on. Although no attempt was made to specifically determine—in terms of statistics—the role of maternal attitude toward discipline in the development of the child's problems, mothers did appear to fall into certain identifiable categories. One of these, the *buffer* mother, hovered around the child satisfying needs immediately and directly, almost keeping the child in-utero, so to speak. Another, the *laissez-faire* mother, displayed the attitude that children will in some way, through the efforts of nature or on their own initiative, learn the skills required to care for themselves and to socially channel their energies. She appears surprised and frustrated when she discovers that her child does not measure up to peers. The third, the *rational* mother, assumes that her child's mind is already a logically thinking and morally conforming instrument at birth. She deals with his or her behavior through long-winded explanations on a "mature, intellectual" level.

11. A Study of the Father in Relation to the Child

Attempts were made to include fathers in the study in order to determine their relevance to the problem.

Fathers' ages ranged from 20 to 60. The average age of the fathers at the time of the study was 28.

Forty-five percent of the 31 fathers whose educational history was known reported that they had completed high school. Ten percent of fathers reportedly had a college education or better.

At the time of admission to the program, 23 children, or 49%, had their natural fathers in the home. Eleven children, or 24%, had no father figure in the home. Eight children had stepfathers, and 5 children had foster fathers.

Forty percent of the 42 fathers who were interviewed about their involvement in the home during the child's early developmental years reported being absent from the home during this time. An additional 19% reported being present but indifferent to the child. These percentages are indicative of some degree of family instability during the child's early years. The effect of this on the mother-child relationship would be twofold. One, without supportive assistance from fathers, mothers might become overwhelmed by the responsibilities of their role and become inadequate in executing its functions. Two, without a husband to relate to, they might transfer their attentions to the child, investing the child with too much of their energies. Such an investment would grossly affect their functions as a mother, particularly the functions of discipline and enculturation, fearing the child's rejection. Either condition could well lead to the fixation of the child at an infantile level of development, at least socially.

12. Summary

Attempts were made to study this behavior disorder from two dimensions: (1) the temperament of the child, and (2) the influence of the environment as represented by the home and, in particular, the mother.

Many characteristics of these children, for example, high activity level, attention seeking, self-centeredness with persistence when it comes to getting what they want but distractibility when performing at the request of authority— in short, strong-willed children bound to themselves and the immediate moment, appeared to be present from birth, with indications that those features related to hyperactivity might have been present in utero.

The child's environment, as represented by mother or mother-surrogate, was either catering or indifferent with resultant permissiveness and lack of enculturation.

A review of the information revealed by this study has pressed us to form the following construct, which has become the rationale of our approach to the problem. The lack of sufficient cultural and social demands on children of this temperament resulted in an inadequate stimulation of certain areas of the brain (fronto-limbic system) that are related to the development of empathy, motivation, behavioral organization, and planning. These areas are stimulated to improved functioning through the administration of specific stimulant medications in combination with a behavior management approach to therapy.

To effect desired results in treatment, a total program involving the home and the school and medication over an extended period of time, that is, a minimum of 2 to 3 years, is required. With a total approach of this type, this behavior disorder can be corrected within the community without the need for residential placement.

Appendix B:
Some Important
Information for Parents and
Teachers of ADHD Children

A Handout for Parents and Teachers

■ **PART 1: UNDERSTANDING ADHD**

Available research and our own clinical experience with individuals with ADHD have led us to the following conclusions about the nature of the disorder and how best to correct it. Attention deficit disorder—with or without hyperactivity—is a biochemical dysfunction affecting primarily the reward and punishment motivational systems of the brain, or what we have come to refer to as *the feeling brain*. Activation of these brain systems leads to internal feelings of psychic pain (e.g., guilt, remorse, shame), in the case of punishment, and to internal feelings of psychic pleasure (e.g., contentment, happiness, joy), in the case of reward.

By experiencing the rewarding and punishing consequences of their behavior over time, normal children eventually learn—without much difficulty—to *anticipate* these consequences *without* having to experience them directly. This

174

is especially true when parents have been *consistent* in their approach to discipline. Put simply, children begin to *expect* that "bad" behavior will be associated with an inner bad feeling and "good" behavior with an inner good feeling.

In time, this *direct experience* of psychic pain and psychic pleasure arising from the consequences of their actions helps children to check their inner impulses—either in word or deed—for their suitability or acceptability *before* they are expressed in behavior. To avoid the unpleasant feelings associated with past punishment, the "bad" behavior is now inhibited; to experience once again the delicious feeling of reward, the "good" behavior is repeated. Gradually the child's behavior becomes more appropriate, as well as more organized and goal-directed in nature. The child is better able to attend to the important things and to ignore the meaningless distractions. Tasks can be completed and the family—and classroom—rules of conduct can be internalized. The pleasurable feeling of reward can now be experienced more often, rather than the aversive feeling of punishment. The child develops a predominantly positive self-image, largely because his or her "good" behavior has been strongly and consistently imprinted with positive psychic feeling in the past.

The development of this type of organized, goal-directed behavior is a *slow, gradual process*—a part of the normal growth and socialization process that begins early in childhood with parental attempts to enculturate their children, that is, to teach them about the rules of appropriate social conduct. This is a very important lesson for children to learn, for in order to survive and function independently in the outside world, children must know what the rules are and have internalized them. But in order for this aspect of development to proceed normally, the *neurophysiological machinery* that is responsible for processing psychic feeling must be functioning normally.

Children with ADHD have much difficulty in this regard because they can't process feelings of psychic pain and psychic pleasure adequately. In comparison to other children, their processing is more *surface* or superficial in quality. This is why rewards and punishments, that is, discipline, have little or no *lasting* effect on their behavior, and why such children keep making the same mistakes over and over again, despite negative consequences in the past. It's no wonder why exasperated parents often report, "I've tried everything—nothing works!" Before abstract concepts such as good and bad, right and wrong, appropriate and inappropriate, can have any *real and lasting* meaning, they must be stamped—by the feeling brain—with sufficient psychic feeling. Adequate feelings of guilt, or remorse, or shame over past misdeeds, for example, must be associated with these misdeeds in memory in order for children to learn to inhibit that "bad" behavior in the future. If the child can *internalize* to a sufficient degree the bad feelings associated with his or her misbehavior, they can then draw upon these painful feeling memories to help them behave appropriately in the future. Similarly,

sufficient feelings of pleasure associated with "good" behavior will help motivate a return to that "good" behavior in the future, once again because the child can
now *anticipate* those pleasant feelings *without* having to experience them directly.

The actual delivery of reward and punishment eventually takes on a more
mature function in the older, more experienced child—that of reinforcing and
maintaining their expectations for the future. Moreover, children who can
anticipate are better able to *wait*—to delay the gratification of immediate needs
and wants. This is because sufficient and consistent activation of the feeling brain
over time is related to the development of a more meaningful—longitudinal—
conceptualization of time. In other words, instead of living for the here and now,
where needs and wants must be immediately satisfied, there is a true appreciation
for past and future time. The child can trust in the future now because his or her
needs and wants were satisfied in the past.

When the feeling brain is working normally, discipline is easier. The child is
better able to internalize, over time, parental, classroom, and cultural expectations for appropriate social behavior. Eventually, the youngster can be trusted to
behave properly even in the parent's—or the teacher's—absence. But when
events and behaviors carry with them only superficial meaning, then the child
truly can't distinguish right from wrong, appropriate from inappropriate, good
from bad, necessitating continual supervision by parents and teachers and others
in authority. Although the ADHD child may be able to retain such abstract words
in memory, the words are of little use in helping them control their impulses and
change their behavior for the better. Instead, such words remain meaningless
abstract concepts, playing little part as motivators in their behavior. Moreover,
when there is little meaning attached to events, objects, and people, such children
are unable to settle down to work. Instead they will be continually pressed to
orient to the things happening around them in repetitive and fruitless attempts
to check them out for familiarity and meaning. It is easy to see why such children
are so distractible.

Paradoxically, these same distractible children can, on occasion, get totally
absorbed in an activity. At these times their attention and concentration appear
total, and the parent or teacher may find it extremely difficult to disengage them.
This typically happens when the activity is one that has more meaning for the
child, that is, it is one that he or she enjoys. One can imagine that there is a more
intense background activation of the feeling brain during these times. And when
activities or events have more personal meaning, it is much easier to ignore—to
tune out—extraneous stimuli. This difficulty disengaging may also show up in
the form of perseveration, or the inability to stop a repetitive activity. Many
parents have complained that their children are "very forgetful" except when it
comes to something they want, or to something promised by the parent. This
perseveration or persistence in getting what they want can be better understood
when considering the extreme here-and-now orientation of ADHD children.

Theirs is a now-or-never and a now-and-always perspective. To children locked in the present moment, future time is meaningless; putting something on the back burner, an impossibility.

We also view sufficient activation of the feeling brain as necessary to the development of an adequate feeling bond with others. This feeling bond is the basis for *empathy*—the ability to experience another's joys and sorrows as if they were our own. Because of the difficulty ADHD children have in processing psychic feeling, they have trouble empathizing with the feelings of others, causing them considerable difficulty when it comes to social relating. Their often described self-centered ways can be better appreciated in this context. Unless there is *obvious* evidence of suffering, for example, the ADHD child may not realize that another person is in pain. Having little ability to participate deeply in the feelings of others, such children may persist in having their own way despite the feelings of others, for in order to be considerate of the feelings of others, children must be sufficiently mindful of their own past psychically painful and pleasurable experiences.

This diminished ability to experience inner feelings of psychic pleasure and psychic pain also results in the ADHD child feeling cold and empty inside, relatively speaking. Consequently *being alone is often hard for them to tolerate.* Many parents report that their child is continually under foot, seeking their constant, undivided attention. The reason for this can be better appreciated when one considers this sense of inner coldness, for when the parent or significant other leaves the child's presence, so too do the feelings associated with that person. This is one of the reasons that ADHD children do better with one-to-one attention, especially if the adult in charge has a natural warmth.

In addition, because good behavior often goes unnoticed and therefore unrewarded, these children will frequently push the parent or teacher with bad behavior, because bad behavior is very likely to result in an immediate *feeling response* on the part of the adult. To children whose inner life is cold and empty, feeling bad is better than not feeling. This need for constant attention, as well as the children's frequent misbehavior, can be understood as the children's attempt to activate their own feeling brain. Unfortunately, because the children's persistent bad behavior typically results in much negative feedback from parents, teachers, and others, they are left with an unbalanced image of themselves as bad.

■ PART 2: TREATMENT

The Use and Purpose of Medication

For most children with ADHD, medication is a routine part of treatment. In view of the nature of the child's difficulties as previously conceptualized, it is essential to improve brain function so that rewards (psychic pleasure) and punishments (psychic pain) can be processed more deeply. This is typically accomplished by giving one of the central nervous system stimulants, for example, Ritalin or Dexedrine. Distinguishing right from wrong, good from bad, will thus be easier for the ADHD child because these abstract words will now carry more meaning. And generally speaking, this will be true for other aspects of the child's life as well, that is, the events and activities that they participate in, their belongings, and their relationships with others will take on more meaning.

Having a more meaningful past to draw upon will help ADHD children make better decisions about future actions. The give and take of social relating will come easier because they will be better at picking up the feelings emanating from others and using this information to modify their responses. Moreover, being able to experience psychic feeling on a deeper level will help calm and comfort such children, for they will be better able to internalize the feelings associated with significant others—to keep the parent, teacher, or grandparent *with them,* so to speak, even when the adult is physically absent.

Medication Dose and Dose Frequency Schedule

As with other medications, the therapeutic effects of Ritalin and Dexedrine are *dose-related.* If the child is not on the proper dose—and this must be determined *individually* for each child—symptoms of the disorder will not diminish. Generally speaking, a child with mild symptoms will require a lower dose than one whose symptoms are extreme. Determining the therapeutic dose takes time and is known as the *titration* period. The physician involved will typically start off by giving the lowest dose possible. Gradually the dose will be increased until the expected positive benefits are seen. Objective feedback from parents and teachers as well as others involved in the child's direct care will help the physician determine the therapeutic dose.

During the initial titration period, the child and parent are seen on a biweekly or more frequent basis. Alternatively, the parent and physician may agree to maintain contact by phone during the first week or two of the initial medication trial. Ideally, a face-to-face office visit is preferable, for it allows the physician to experience firsthand what the parent is reporting. Once the therapeutic dose has been established, monthly follow-up is usually sufficient. These regularly scheduled visits will ensure that there is adequate communication between the parents and the physician about the child's progress and response to medication.

Another decision that the physician will make relates to the *frequency of dosing* during the day. This decision is just as important as determining what dose works best. Once again, decisions about dose frequency should be determined on an individual basis because, among other factors, the therapeutic effect of the medication may not last as long as what the manufacturer reports. For example, we have found that many children metabolize even the sustained release (or long-acting) form of Ritalin within a very short period of time, for example, within 2 to 3 hours. In effect, this means that the child's brain will be working normally for a brief period of 2 to 3 hours, and then all the distressing symptoms will reappear. The reappearance of symptoms indicates that a second dose of medication is needed. To achieve the desired therapeutic effect, that is, *a continuous and even suppression of symptoms throughout the entire day,* some children require three or four or even five doses of Ritalin across the day. A serious problem arises when this is not understood by those involved in the child's treatment. For example, the parent or teacher or other professional may wrongly conclude that the medication is not working—especially if they observe the child during the rebound of symptoms that occurs when the effect of the medication has worn off. To determine the frequency of dosing, children should be watched closely during the day, with careful attention paid to how long after a particular dose is given do the symptoms begin to reappear. This information should then be shared with the child's physician so that the frequency of dosing can be adjusted accordingly.

And because the duration of action of Ritalin is typically much shorter than the duration of action of Dexedrine (the Spansule or long-acting form of Dexedrine can last from 5 to 6 hours and sometimes longer), we often recommend that the child be given Dexedrine Spansules rather than Ritalin. This cuts down on the frequency of dosing, which means that children can get through at least their morning classes before a second dose is needed. This also helps to assure that children will not miss one or more doses of medication, or be late in getting the next dose. When subsequent doses of medication are either missed or given late, children are made to *suffer needlessly.* The inner feelings of emptiness return, along with all of the other distressing symptoms. If your child's pediatrician or psychiatrist does not understand these important aspects of medicating ADHD children, find one who does.

As children grow and/or put on weight, the dose of medication will typically have to be adjusted upward. This is to be expected and is a routine aspect of treatment. If the child who has been responding well to a particular dose of medication suddenly begins to have more difficulty controlling his or her impulses, attending to the task, calming down, empathizing with others, and so on, the parents should contact the physician. Sometimes this increase in symptoms is related to environmental factors—as when a parent has been under stress and has not been as available to the child as usual. In this case, all that may be needed is for the parent(s) to return to the original management plan; but more often than not, it is an indication that the dose of medication has to be adjusted upward.

Finally, with proper medical monitoring by a competent physician, these medications are safe and effective. Parents and teachers can take comfort in knowing that both Dexedrine and Ritalin have been in use of a long time and have been subjected to rigorous scientific study and testing. Dexedrine, for example, was first used for the treatment of ADHD in the 1930s, although the disorder was called hyperkinesis at that time.

Potential Side Effects

Potential side effects of these medications are minimal and are typically dose-related. The most commonly reported are a depressed appetite and difficulty falling asleep. As with any medication, side effects have to be balanced against therapeutic effects. Easy-to-use side effects checklists are available and can be completed periodically as a routine aspect of treatment. Sometimes what appears to be a side effect of the medication may be related to a preexisting condition. For example, it is common for parents to report that children are having difficulty sleeping—especially when medication is first begun. When we question parents further, however, many reveal that their child had rarely slept through the night, or that the child had never required as much sleep as his or her siblings. To rule out preexisting factors, the physician should ask you to fill out a side effects checklist *before* your child is given a trial of one of the stimulant medications. This baseline checklist can then be used in determining if a subsequent symptom is really a side effect of the medication or related to a preexisting condition.

With respect to sleep difficulties, we have found that some children benefit from a nighttime dose of their stimulant medication. Our current thinking on this is as follows: By the time bedtime arrives, the child has already metabolized the last dose of medication, which in most instances has been given mid to late afternoon. What appears to be a side effect of the medication, then, may actually be related to the rebound of symptoms that occurs when the therapeutic effects of the drug have worn off. If this is so, then another dose of medication may actually help the child sleep. Although more trials are needed before we conclude definitively that this should become a routine practice, our preliminary findings in this direction are encouraging. If sleep continues to be a problem, the physician may suggest the use of a medication called clonidine (Catapres). Given at or near bedtime, clonidine has been found to be an effective method of inducing sleep.

Behavior Management

A second and critical part of treatment is for the parents—and the school—to adopt a *consistent* and *united* approach to the child with respect to behavior management. Now that the child is better able to process the rewarding and punishing consequences of his or her behavior, the important work of learning right from wrong, good from bad, acceptable from unacceptable, can begin in earnest. And it is the parents' as well as the teachers' job to ensure that the child's brain is stimulated appropriately in this regard. Toward this end, it is crucial that feeling consequences be applied *immediately*. If this important feedback is delayed, for example, as when mother waits for father to get home to discipline the child, the negative consequences may come at a time when the child is behaving appropriately—the misdeed long forgotten. This means that the now-good behavior of the child will be associated in memory with bad feeling consequences, leaving the child confused about good and bad, right and wrong, acceptable and unacceptable. If this important feeling feedback has to be delayed in time—and this is not a good idea—the offending event must first be reactivated in the child's mind immediately before the child receives the negative consequences. Questioning the child about what happened and why will help to reactivate the event in the child's mind.

Similarly, if the same behavior is rewarded one day and punished the next, children will be confused, leaving them in doubt—once again—as to what is expected. *Consistency* is a very important aspect of a child's behavior management plan—parents and teachers should decide what the rules are, communicate them to the child, and then *stick to them*. If a particular behavior is unacceptable one day, it should not be OK the next.

In addition, because children with this disorder are already overburdened with a poor self-image, it is very important that their positive behavior be *noticed* so that it can receive the rewarding feeling attention it is due. To help children internalize the good feeling associated with reward, we recommend the use of *touch* to go along with your positive words, for example, a hug, a pat on the back, a kiss on the cheek. This important rewarding feedback will help to restore the balance between the child's inner good and bad feelings, and the child's self-image will begin to change for the better. The child will begin to have more confidence that he or she is valued and has the ability to succeed. Unfortunately, the use of appropriate positive touch by teachers is now being discouraged and, in some schools, prohibited altogether. This extreme position, no doubt a defensive reaction to widely publicized incidents of inappropriate conduct by some, has made our classrooms a much colder place to be. This is particularly unfortunate for ADHD children, whose inner state is already on the cool to cold side with respect to psychic feeling. As one ADHD child put it: "I feel like I'm on an island with no one around me. I feel like I need all my teacher's attention all the time." This profound description of the inner life of this ADHD child illustrates the lack of connectedness that many of these children experience, even when surrounded by others, for psychic feeling is the glue that binds us to others.

Finally, because children with this problem live largely in the world of the *immediate moment,* negative feeling consequences should be of *short duration,* that is, limited to 10 to 15 minutes of time out, or in the case of a more serious transgression of the rules, to a response-cost type of approach, where the child is denied participation in an activity that he or she enjoys for that particular day.

We have also found that *exaggerating* the impact of the child's behavior in terms of how it makes the parent or teacher feel—for instance, personally disappointed, hurt, saddened—is very useful in helping the child's brain process feeling consequences. However, once the offending incident is over, a *clean slate* approach is used—all talk related to the event is dropped, and the child is assured once again that he or she is an accepted and loved member of the family, or classroom.

■ PART 3: CONCLUSIONS

Becoming an Informed Parent

Those who have never had to cope with the problems presented by ADHD children on a day-to-day basis have little knowledge of the colossal commitment of parental time and energy that is involved. Many times there is virtually no appreciation of the children's basic temperament on the part of the unenlightened, with the result that the parents—and especially mother—are frequently chastised for being unable to control the child. And if father is too absorbed with his role in the outside world to listen to or to accept what his wife tells him about how difficult it is to manage the child, he soon joins in the chorus. This results in mother feeling overwhelmed and totally to blame for the child's difficulties, as well as alienated from those uninformed professionals who also communicate, either directly or indirectly, that she is to blame. Whereas this is not meant to negate the important role that the environment plays in the expression of symptoms, parental energies must be freed up from a defensive posture to focus on the child's difficulties.

Parents can find relief from unnecessary guilt by becoming more informed. There are many good popular books on the market today, as well as opportunities to join parent support groups offered by organizations such as Children and Adults with Attention Deficit Disorders (CHADD). CHADD frequently has professional speakers at meetings who can address your questions about medication and treatment. Your time and energies will be better spent in this direction rather than on finding fault, either with yourself or your mate. Your mate may be feeling just as frustrated and as burdened with guilt as you do. Similarly, your child's teacher(s) may be frustrated and lacking in good information.

Educate yourselves and then take the necessary corrective steps. Take an objective look at the things you can control, especially with respect to the home environment, and modify those things that need modifying. All children need and can benefit from a structured, predictable, and stable home environment, but the need for such in ADHD children is extreme. In view of the nature of the child's problem, changes may be needed in one or more of these critical areas.

Allow yourselves time to make the necessary changes and to make mistakes. Above all, work together as a unit for your child's best interest. As educated parents, you will be in a better position to advocate for your child, to help other adults respond in more constructive ways, and to evaluate any outside professional help provided.

With respect to dealing with the closed-minded and the unenlightened, precious time and energies can be wasted, so don't become overly invested in this type of struggle. Finally, as you come to appreciate this disorder as an interaction between your child's basic temperament and the stimulation forthcoming from the environment (as represented by you, your child's teachers, and other significant adults involved in your child's care), you will be freer to go about fulfilling your healthy parental functions with more confidence and objectivity.

A *Final Word to Teachers*

Before we conclude, we would like to respond to those teachers who have expressed concern at the apparent increase in the number of children in their classrooms with this disorder. Many have wondered whether this increase was based on "something real" or whether the diagnosis was being overutilized. Our response has been to discuss our thinking on the role played by the environment in the expression of symptoms.

As previously indicated, we view ADHD as an interaction between the fundamental temperament of the child and the stimulation forthcoming from the environment—as represented by parents and teachers, as well as the cultural milieu into which the child is born. In this instance, we are referring to the possible contribution of certain aspects of our cultural heritage. Specifically, in the 1960s, American culture began to move away from more conservative traditional values toward the values of the be-here-now pop hippie culture. Our cultural climate at the time was obviously ready for some movement in this direction, but unfortunately, the pendulum swung—not to the middle where the outcome would have been more balanced—but to the opposite extreme.

In the 1960s, a generation of young individuals grew up embracing the new "radical" ideas of this hippie subculture. Many "dropped out" of mainstream society, lived for the moment, had "free" sex, did "their own thing," and experimented with marijuana and other affect-inducing and mind-altering drugs. Whereas this new, more permissive be-here-now, don't-worry-about-tomorrow attitude may have been genuinely liberating to individuals who were already overly cautious, quiet, and inhibited by nature, it was, in retrospect, detrimental for those individuals who were their polar opposites. Allowing children who are already uninhibited and extroverted by nature to "do their own thing" may be easier for the moment, but, as the parents of such children can attest, the long-term consequences can be disastrous. More specifically, the development of important brain processes related to self-control, empathy, behavioral organization, and forethought can be significantly delayed and, in extreme cases, may never show up in behavior. From our perspective, the resulting shift in values that occurred in the 1960s and that eventually found its way into our school systems, our academic institutions, our homes, and the mores of established society, resulted in a lack of sufficient social and cultural demands on those children who were, by nature, more extroverted and uninhibited.

In retrospect, this new permissiveness appears to have put subsequent generations of children with this temperament at greater risk for the development of symptoms that we label ADHD. Considering the continuing crisis in American values, it is no wonder that many continue to express alarm at the apparent rise in the incidence of children and adolescents in our society with impulse control problems and an apparent lack of compassion for others. In contrast, consider the low incidence of ADHD-like symptoms in cultures like Japan, for example, where traditional family and cultural values are more strongly embraced.

Long-Term Prognosis

Treatment for ADHD is long-term; however, with a total approach to treatment, the prognosis for the child's future is very good—especially if treatment is begun early. Moreover, after several years of medication, children can be given a trial period without medication to see if the gains in behavior remain. If symptoms return, this is an indication that medication is still needed. This does not necessarily mean, however, that children will need medication for the rest of their lives. Over the course of 25 years, we have treated numerous children with this disorder. After several years of pharmacotherapy, many have been able to stop taking their medication with no return of symptoms. We have done much thinking about why this is so. Research on the basis of Ritalin's effect in brain has provided us with some important clues, suggesting that the observed changes in behavior may be supported by lasting changes in brain function.

References

Allin, R., Russell, V. A., Lamm, M. C. L., & Taljaard, J. J. F. (1988). Regional distribution of monoamines in the nucleus accumbens of the rat. *Neurochemical Research, 13,* 937-942.

Amado, H., & Lustman, P. J. (1982). Attention deficit disorders persisting in adulthood: A review. *Comprehensive Psychiatry, 23,* 300-314.

Aman, M. G., Kern, R. A., McGhee, D. E., & Arnold, L. E. (1993). Fenfluramine and methylphenidate in children with mental retardation and ADHD: Clinical and side-effects. *Journal of the American Academy of Child and Adolescent Psychiatry, 32,* 851-859.

American Psychiatric Association. (1968). *Diagnostic and statistical manual of mental disorders* (2nd ed.). Washington, DC: Author.

American Psychiatric Association. (1980). *Diagnostic and statistical manual of mental disorders* (3rd ed.). Washington, DC: Author.

American Psychiatric Association. (1987). *Diagnostic and statistical manual of mental disorders* (3rd ed., rev.). Washington, DC: Author.

American Psychiatric Association. (1994). *Diagnostic and statistical manual of mental disorders* (4th ed.). Washington, DC: Author.

Arnold, F. E., Kirilcuk, V., Corson, S. A., & Corson, E. (1973). Levoamphetamine and dextroamphetamine: Differential effect on aggression and hyperkinesis in children and dogs. *American Journal of Psychiatry, 130,* 165-170.

Aston-Jones, G., & Bloom, F. E. (1981a). Activity of norepinephrine-containing locus coeruleus neurons in behaving rats anticipates fluctuations in the sleep-waking cycle. *Journal of Neuroscience, 8,* 876-886.

Aston-Jones, G., & Bloom, F. E. (1981b). Norepinephrine-containing locus coeruleus neurons in behaving rats exhibit pronounced responses to non-noxious environmental stimuli. *Journal of Neuroscience, 8,* 887-900.

Atkinson, J., Richtand, N., Schworer, C., Kuczenski, R., & Soderling, T. (1987). Phosphorylation of purified rat striatal tyrosine hydroxylase by Ca^{2+}/calmodulin-dependent protein kinase II: Effect of an activator protein. *Journal of Neurochemistry, 49,* 1241-1249.

Badawy, A. A. B., & Williams, D. L. (1982). Enhancement of rat brain catecholamine synthesis by administration of small doses of tyrosine and evidence for substrate inhibition of tyrosine hydroxylase activity by large doses of the amino acid. *Biochemical Journal, 206,* 165-168.

Baker, H., Joh, T. H., & Reis, D. J. (1980). Genetic control of the number of midbrain dopaminergic neurons in inbred strains of mice: Relationship to size and neuronal density of the striatum. *Proceedings of the National Academy of Sciences, 77,* 4369-4373.

Baker, H., Joh, T. H., & Reis, D. J. (1982). Time appearance during development of differences in nigrostriatal tyrosine hydroxylase activity in two inbred mouse strains. *Developmental Brain Research, 4,* 157-165.

Baker, H., Joh, T. H., Ruggiero, D. A., & Reis, D. J. (1983). Variations in number of dopamine neurons and tyrosine hydroxylase activity in hypothalamus of two mouse strains. *The Journal of Neuroscience, 3,* 832-843.

Baker, H., Kawano, T., Margolis, F. L., & Joh, T. H. (1983). Transneuronal regulation of tyrosine hydroxylase expression in olfactory bulb of mouse and rat. *The Journal of Neuroscience, 3,* 69-78.

Baker, H., & Reis, D. J. (1986). Developmental mechanisms which may account for strain differences in the number of dopamine neurons in the midbrain. In C. Shagass, R. C. Josiassen, W. H. Bridger, K. J. Weiss, D. Stoff, & G. M. Simpson (Eds.), *Proceedings of the IVth World Congress of Biological Psychiatry* held from September 8th through 13th, 1985 in Philadelphia, Pennsylvania, *Developments in psychiatry* (Vol. 7, pp. 28-30). New York: Elsevier.

Baker, H., Sved, A. F., Tucker, L. W., Alden, S. M., & Reis, D. J. (1985). Strain differences in pituitary prolactin content: Relationship to number of hypothalamic dopamine neurons. *Brain Research, 385,* 16-26.

Banderet, L. E., & Lieberman, H. R. (1989). Treatment with tyrosine, a neurotransmitter precursor, reduces environmental stress in humans. *Brain Research Bulletin, 22,* 759-762.

Bannon, M. J., & Roth, R. H. (1983). Pharmacology of mesocortical dopamine neurons. *Pharmacological Reviews, 35,* 53-68.

Bareggi, S. R., Becker, R. E., Ginsburg, B. E., & Genovese, E. (1979a). Neurochemical investigation of an endogenous model of the "hyperkinetic syndrome" in a hybrid dog. *Life Sciences, 24,* 481-488.

Bareggi, S. R., Becker, R. E., Ginsburg, B. E., & Genovese, E. (1979b). Paradoxical effect of amphetamine in an endogenous model of the hyperkinetic syndrome in a hybrid dog: Correlation with amphetamine and p-hydroxyamphetamine blood levels. *Psychopharmacology, 62,* 217-224.

Barkley, R. A. (1990). *Attention deficit hyperactivity disorder: A handbook for diagnosis and treatment.* New York: Guilford.

Barkley, R. A. (1994). Impaired delayed responding: A unified theory of attention-deficit hyperactivity disorder. In D. K. Routh (Ed.), *Disruptive behavior disorders in childhood: Essays honoring Herbert C. Quay* (pp. 12-57). New York: Plenum.

Barkley, R. A., Fischer, M., Edelbrock, C. S., & Smallish, L. (1990). The adolescent outcome of hyperactive children diagnosed by research criteria: I. An 8-year prospective follow-up study. *Journal of the American Academy of Child and Adolescent Psychiatry, 29,* 546-557.

Barkley, R. A., Grodzinsky, G., & DuPaul, G. J. (1992). Frontal lobe functions in attention deficit disorder with and without hyperactivity: A review and research report. *Journal of Abnormal Child Psychology, 20,* 163-188.

Barkley, R. A., McMurray, M. B., Edelbrock, C. S., & Robbins, K. (1990). Side effects of methylphenidate in children with attention deficit hyperactivity disorder: A systemic, placebo-controlled evaluation. *Pediatrics, 86,* 184-192.

Barrickman, L., Noyes, R., Kuperman, S., Schumacher, E., & Verda, M. (1991). Treatment of ADHD with fluoxetine: A preliminary trial. *Journal of the American Academy of Child and Adolescent Psychiatry, 30,* 762-767.

Bean, A. J., & Roth, R. H. (1991). Extracellular dopamine and neurotensin in rat prefrontal cortex in vivo: Effects of median forebrain bundle stimulation frequency, stimulation pattern, and dopamine autoreceptors. *Journal of Neuroscience, 11,* 2694-2702.

Bellak, L. (1977). Psychiatric states in adults with minimal brain dysfunction. *Psychiatric Annals, 7,* 58-74.

Bellak, L. (1979). Psychiatric aspects of minimal brain dysfunction in adults: Their ego function assessment. In L. Bellak (Ed.), *Psychiatric aspects of minimal brain dysfunction in adults* (pp. 73-101). New York: Grune & Stratton.

Belluzzi, J. D., & Stein, L. (1987). Operant conditioning of hippocampal CA1 neurons required immediately-contingent activation of dopamine D2 receptors. *Society for Neuroscience Abstracts, 13,* 834.

Benjamin, J., Li, L., Patterson, C., Greenberg, B. D., Murphy, D. L., & Hamer, D. H. (1996). Population and familial association between the D4 dopamine receptor gene and measures of novelty seeking. *Nature Genetics, 12,* 81-84.

Bernardini, G. L., Gu, X., & German, D. C. (1991). Nucleus A10 dopaminergic neurons in inbred mouse strains: Firing rate and autoreceptor sensitivity are independent of the number of cells in the nucleus. *Brain Research Bulletin, 27,* 163-168.

Berry, C. A., Shaywitz, S. E., & Shaywitz, B. A. (1985). Girls with attention deficit disorder: A silent minority: A report on behavioral and cognitive characteristics. *Pediatrics, 76,* 801-804.

Bielajew, C., & Shizgal, P. (1982). Behaviorally derived measures of conduction velocity in the substrate for rewarding medial forebrain bundle stimulation. *Brain Research, 237,* 107-119.

Bielajew, C., & Shizgal, P. (1986). Evidence implicating descending fibers in self-stimulation of the medial forebrain bundle. *The Journal of Neuroscience, 6,* 919-929.

Black, J. P., Belluzzi, J. D., & Stein, L. (1985). Reinforcement delay of one second severely impairs acquisition of brain self-stimulation. *Brain Research, 359,* 113-119.

Boehme, R. E., & Ciaranello, R. D. (1981). Dopamine receptor binding in inbred mice: Strain differences in mesolimbic and nigrostriatal dopamine binding sites. *Proceedings of the National Academy of Sciences, 78,* 3255-3259.

Bornstein, R. A., Baker, G. B., Carroll, A., King, G., Wong, J. T. F., & Douglass, A. B. (1990). Plasma amino acids in attention deficit disorder. *Psychiatry Research, 33,* 301-306.

Bozarth, M. A. (1987). Neuroanatomical boundaries of the reward-relevant opiate-receptor field in the ventral tegmental area as mapped by the conditioned place preference method in rats. *Brain Research, 414,* 77-84.

Bozarth, M. A., & Wise, R. A. (1981). Intracranial self-administration of morphine into the ventral tegmental area of rats. *Life Sciences, 28,* 551-555.

Brady, K., Brown, J. W., & Thurmond, J. B. (1980). Behavioral and neurochemical effects of dietary tyrosine in young and aged mice following cold-swim stress. *Pharmacology, Biochemistry, and Behavior, 12,* 667-674.

Braun, A. R., & Chase, T. N. (1986). Obligatory D_1/D_2 receptor interaction in the generation of dopamine agonist related behaviors. *European Journal of Pharmacology, 131,* 301-306.

Breese, G. R., Cooper, B. R., & Mueller, R. A. (1974). Evidence for an involvement of 5-hydroxytryptamine in the actions of amphetamine. *British Journal of Pharmacology, 52,* 307-319.

Breese, G. R., & Mueller, R. A. (1985). SCH 23390 antagonism of a D_2 dopamine agonist depends upon catecholaminergic neurons. *European Journal of Pharmacology, 113,* 109-114.

Bugbee, N. M., & Goldman-Rakic, P. S. (1981). Functional 2-deoxyglucose mapping in association cortex: Prefrontal activation in monkeys performing a cognitive task. *Society for Neuroscience Abstracts, 7,* 239.

Butcher, S. P., Liptrot, J., & Aburthnott, G. W. (1991). Characterization of methylphenidate and nomifensine induced dopamine release in rat striatum using in vivo brain microdialysis. *Neuroscience Letters, 122,* 245-248.

Cador, M., Taylor, J. R., & Robbins, T. W. (1991). Potentiation of the effects of reward-related stimuli by dopaminergic-dependent mechanisms in the nucleus accumbens. *Psychopharmocology* (Berlin), *104,* 377-385.

Carboni, E., Imperato, A., Perezzani, L., & DiChiara, G. (1989). Amphetamine, cocaine, phencyclidine, and nomifensine increase extracellular dopamine concentrations preferentially in the nucleus accumbens of freely moving rats. *Neuroscience, 28,* 653-661.

Carlsson, A., & Lindqvist, M. (1978). Dependence of 5-HT and catecholamine synthesis on concentrations of precursor amino-acids in rat brain. *Naunyn-Schmiedebergs Archives of Pharmacology* (Berlin), *303,* 157-164.

Carr, G. D., & White, N. M. (1983). Conditioned place preference from intra-accumbens but not intra-caudate amphetamine injections. *Life Sciences, 33,* 2551-2557.

Carr, G. D., & White, N. M. (1986). Anatomical disassociation of amphetamine's rewarding and aversive effects: An intracranial microinjection study. *Psychopharmacology, 89,* 340-346.

Cass, W. A., Zahniser, N. R., Flach, K. A., & Gerhardt, G. A. (1993). Clearance of exogenous dopamine in rat dorsal striatum and nucleus-accumbens: Role of metabolism and effects of locally applied uptake inhibitors. *Journal of Neurochemistry, 61,* 2269-2278.

Castaneda, E., Becker, J., & Robinson, T. E. (1988). The long-term effects of repeated amphetamine treatment in vivo on amphetamine, Kcl, and electrical stimulation evoked striatal dopamine release in vitro. *Life Sciences, 42,* 2447-2456.

Castellanos, F. X., Elia, J., Kruesi, M. J., Gulotta, C. S., Mefford, I. N., Potter, W. Z., Ritchie, G. F., & Rapoport, J. L. (1994). Cerebrospinal fluid monoamine metabolites in boys with attention-deficit hyperactivity disorder. *Psychiatry Research, 52,* 305-316.

Castellanos, F. X., Giedd, J. N., Eckburg, P., Marsh, W. L., Vaituzis, A. C., Kaysen, D., Hamburger, S. D., & Rapoport, J. L. (1994). Quantitative morphology of the caudate nucleus in attention deficit hyperactivity disorder. *American Journal of Psychiatry, 151,* 1791-1796.

Castellanos, F. X., Giedd, J. N., Marsh, W. L., Hamburger, S. D., Vaituzis, A. C., Dickstein, D. P., Sarfatti, S. E., Vauss, Y. C., Snell, J. W., Lange, N., Kaysen, D., Krain, A. L., Ritchie, G. F., Rajapakse, J. C., & Rapoport, J. L. (1996). Quantitative brain magnetic resonance imaging in attention-deficit hyperactivity disorder. *Archives of General Psychiatry, 53,* 607-616.

Chiel, H. J., & Wurtman, R. J. (1981). Short-term variations in diet composition change the pattern of spontaneous motor activity in rats. *Science, 213,* 676-678.

Chiueh, C. C., & Moore, K. E. (1975). Blockade by reserpine of methylphenidate-induced release of brain dopamine. *Journal of Pharmacology and Experimental Therapeutics, 193,* 559-563.

Ciaranello, R. D., Barchas, R., Kessler, S., & Barchas, J. D. (1972). Catecholamines: Strain differences in biosynthetic enzyme activity in mice. *Life Sciences, 2,* 565-572.

Clarke, P. B. S., & Pert, A. (1985). Autoradiographic evidence for nicotine receptors on nigrostriatal and mesolimbic dopaminergic neurons. *Brain Research, 348,* 355-358.

Clarke, P. B. S., Pert, C. B., & Pert, A. (1984). Autoradiographic distribution of nicotinic receptors in rat brain. *Brain Research, 323,* 390-395.

Cloninger, C. R., Adolfsson, R., & Svrakic, N. M. (1996). Mapping genes for human personality. *Nature Genetics, 12,* 3-4.

Cloninger, C. R., Svrakic, D. M., & Przybeck, T. R. (1993). A psychobiological model of temperament and character. *Archives of General Psychiatry, 50,* 975-990.

Cocores, J. A., Patel, M. D., Gold, M. S., & Pottash, A. C. (1987). Cocaine abuse, attention deficit disorder, and bipolar disorder. *Journal of Nervous and Mental Disease, 175,* 431-432.

Colle, L. M., & Wise, R. A. (1988). Effects of nucleus accumbens amphetamine on lateral hypothalamic brain stimulation reward. *Brain Research, 459,* 361-368.

Conners, C. K. (1990). *Manual for Conners' Rating Scales.* Toronto: Multi-Health Systems.

Conners, K. C., Eisenberg, L., & Barcai, A. (1967). Effect of dextroamphetamine on children. *Archives of General Psychiatry, 17,* 478-485.

Cook, E. H., Stein, M. A., Drajowsi, M. D., Cox, W., Olkon, D. M., Kieffer, J. E., & Leventhal, B. L. (1995). Association of attention-deficit disorder and the dopamine transporter gene. *American Journal of Human Genetics, 56,* 993-998.

Crawley, J. N. (1991). Cholecystokinin-dopamine interactions. *Trends in Pharmacological Sciences, 12,* 232-236.

Crawley, J. N. (1992). Subtype-selective cholecystokinin receptor antagonists block cholecystokinin modulation of dopamine-mediated behaviors in the rat mesolimbic pathway. *Journal of Neuroscience, 12,* 3380-3391.

Davis, W. M., & Smith, S. G. (1975). Effect of haloperidol on (+)- amphetamine self-administration. *Journal of Pharmacy and Pharmacology, 27,* 540-542.

Delgado, J. M. R., Roberts, W. W., & Miller, N. E. (1954). Learning motivated by electrical stimulation of the brain. *American Journal of Physiology, 179,* 587-593.

Di Chiara, G., & North, R. A. (1992). Neurobiology of opiate abuse. *Trends in Pharmacological Sciences, 13,* 185-193.

Domesick, V. B. (1988). Neuroanatomical organization of dopamine neurons in the ventral tegmental area. *Annals of the New York Academy of Sciences, 537,* 10-26.

Douglas, V. I. (1983). Attention and cognitive problems. In M. Rutter (Ed.), *Developmental neuropsychiatry* (pp. 280-329). New York: Guilford.

Dulcan, M. K. (1990). Using psychostimulants to treat behavioral disorders of children and adolescents. *Journal of Child and Adolescent Psychiatry, 1,* 7-20.

Dupaul, G. J., & Barkley, R. A. (1990). Medication therapy. In R. A. Barkley (Ed.), *Attention deficit hyperactivity disorder: A handbook for diagnosis and treatment* (pp. 573-612). New York: Guilford.

During, M. J., Acworth, I. N., & Wurtman, R. J. (1988). Effects of systemic l-tyrosine on dopamine release from rat corpus striatum and nucleus accumbens. *Brain Research, 452,* 378-380.

Dworkin, S. I., & Bimie, C. (1989). 6-hydroxydopamine lesions of the nucleus accumbens attenuate the discriminative stimulus effects of d-amphetamine. *Drug Development Research, 16,* 435-441.

Ebstein, R. P., Novick, O., Umansky, R., Priel, B., Osher, Y., Blaine, D., Bennett, E. R., Nemanov, L., Katz, M., & Belmaker, R. H. (1996). Dopamine D4 receptor (D4DR) exon III polymorphism associated with the human personality trait of novelty seeking. *Nature Genetics, 12,* 78-80.

Elia, J. (1991). Stimulants and antidepressant pharmacokinetics in hyperactive children. *Psychopharmacology Bulletin, 27,* 411-415.

Ellison, G. D., Eison, M. S., Huberman, H. S., & Daniel, F. (1978). Long-term changes in dopaminergic innervation of caudate nucleus after continuous amphetamine administration. *Science, 201,* 276-278.

El Mestikawy, S., Glowinski, J., & Hamon, M. (1983). Tyrosine hydroxylase activation in depolarized dopaminergic terminals-involvement of Ca^{2+}-dependent phosphorylation. *Nature, 302,* 830-832.

El Mestikawy, S., & Hamon, M. (1985). Mechanism of tyrosine hydroxylase activation by dopamine autoreceptor blockade in depolarized dopaminergic terminals. *Journal of Neurochemistry* (Supplement), *44,* S111.

Ennis, M., & Aston-Jones, G. (1986). Evidence for self- and neighbor-mediated postactivation inhibition of locus coeruleus neurons. *Brain Research, 374,* 299-305.

Ennis, M., & Aston-Jones, G. (1987). Two physiologically distinct populations of neurons in the ventrolateral medulla innervate the locus coeruleus. *Brain Research, 425,* 275-282.

Erenberg, G., Cruse, R. P., & Rothner, D. A. (1985). Gilles de la Tourette's syndrome: Effects of stimulant drugs. *Neurology, 35,* 1346-1348.

Eriksson, T., & Carlsson, A. (1988). β-Adrenergic control of brain uptake of large neutral amino acids. *Life Sciences, 42,* 1583-1589.

Esposito, R. U., Faulkner, W., & Kornetsky, C. (1979). Specific modulation of brain stimulation reward by haloperidol. *Pharmacology, Biochemistry, and Behavior, 10,* 937-940.

Fallon, J. H. (1988). Topographic organization of ascending dopaminergic projections. In P. W. Kalivas & C. B. Nemeroff (Eds.), *The mesocorticolimbic dopamine system* (Annals of the New York Academy of Sciences, Vol. 537, pp. 1-9). New York: The New York Academy of Sciences.

Faraone, S., Biederman, J., Chen, W. J., Krifcher, B., Keenan, K., Moore, C., Sprich, S., & Tsuang, M. T. (1992). Segregation analysis of attention-deficit hyperactivity disorder: Evidence for single gene transmission. *Psychiatric Genetics, 2,* 257-276.

Faraone, S. V., Biederman, J., Keenan, K., & Tsuang, M. T. (1991). A family-genetic study of girls with DSM-III attention deficit disorder. *American Journal of Psychiatry, 148,* 112-117.

Feldman, R. S., Meyer, J. S., & Quenzer, L. (1996). *Principles of neuropsychopharmacology.* Sunderland, MA: Sinauer Associates.

Feldman, R. S., & Quenzer, L. (1984). *Fundamentals of neuropsychopharmacology.* Sunderland, MA: Sinauer Associates.

Fernstrom, J. D. (1983). Role of precursor availability in control of monoamine biosynthesis in brain. *Physiological Reviews, 63,* 484-546.

Fernstrom, J. D., & Wurtman, R. J. (1971). Brain serotonin content: Physiological dependence on plasma tryptophan levels. *Science, 173,* 149-152.

Fernstrom, J. D., & Wurtman, R. J. (1974). Nutrition and the brain. *Scientific American, 230,* 84-91.

Ferris, R. M., & Tang, F. L. M. (1979). Comparison of the effects of the isomers of amphetamine, methylphenidate, and deoxypipradrol on the uptake of 1-[3H]norepinephrine and [3H]dopamine by synaptic vesicles from rat whole brain, striatum, and hypothalamus. *Journal of Pharmacology and Experimental Therapeutics, 210,* 422-428.

Ferris, R. M., Tang, F. L. M., & Maxwell, R. A. (1972). A comparison of the capacities of isomers of amphetamine, deoxypipradrol, and methylphenidate to inhibit the uptake of tritiated catecholamines into rat cerebral cortex slices, synaptosomal preparations of rat cerebral cortex, hypothalamus, and striatum and into adrenergic nerves of rabbit aorta. *Journal of Pharmacology and Experimental Therapeutics, 181,* 407-416.

Fink, J. S., & Reis, D. J. (1981). Genetic variations in midbrain dopamine cell number: Parallel with differences in responses to dopaminergic agonists and in naturalistic behaviors mediated by central dopaminergic systems. *Brain Research, 222,* 335-349.

Fink, J. S., Swerdloff, A., Joh, T. H., & Reis, D. J. (1979). Genetic differences in ^{3}H-spiroperidol binding in caudate nucleus and cataleptic response to neuroleptic drugs in inbred mouse strains with different numbers of midbrain dopamine neurons. *Neuroscience Abstracts, 5,* 647.

Fischer, J. F., & Cho, A. K. (1979). Chemical release of dopamine from striatal homogenates: Evidence for an exchange diffusion model. *Journal of Pharmacology and Experimental Therapeutics, 208,* 203-209.

Fouriezos, G., Hansson, P., & Wise, R. A. (1978). Neuroleptic-induced attenuation of brain stimulation reward. *Journal of Comparative and Physiological Psychology, 92,* 661-671.

Freeman, W., & Watts, J. W. (1950). *Psychosurgery* (2nd ed.). Springfield, IL: Charles C Thomas.

Fuller, R. W., Perry, K. W., Bymaster, F. P., & Wong, D. T. (1978). Comparative effects of pemoline, amfonelic acid, and amphetamine on dopamine uptake and release in vitro and on brain 3,4-dihydroxyphenylacetic acid concentration in spiperone-treated rats. *Journal of Pharmacy and Pharmacology, 30,* 197-198.

Fuller, R. W., & Snoddy, H. D. (1979). Synergistic elevation of brain 3,4-dihydroxyphenylacetic acid concentration by methylphenidate and spiperone in control but not reserpine-pretreated rats. *Journal Pharmacy and Pharmacology, 31,* 339.

Fuster, J. M. (1973). Transient memory and neuronal activity in the thalamus. In K. H. Pribram & A. R. Luria (Eds.), *Psychophysiology of the frontal lobes* (pp. 157-165). New York: Academic Press.

Fuster, J. M. (1980). *The prefrontal cortex: Anatomy, physiology, and neuropsychology of the frontal lobe.* New York: Raven Press.

Fuster, J. M. (1981). Prefrontal cortex in motor control. In *Handbook of physiology, section 1: The nervous system* (Vol. 2, pp. 1149-1178). Washington, DC: American Physiological Society.

Gallistel, C. R., & Davis, A. J. (1983). Affinity for the dopamine D_2 receptor predicts neuroleptic potency in blocking the reinforcing effect of MFB stimulation. *Pharmacology, Biochemistry, and Behavior, 19,* 867-872.

Gallistel, C. R., & Karras, D. (1984). Pimozide and amphetamine have opposing effects on the reward summation function. *Pharmacology, Biochemistry, and Behavior, 20,* 73-77.

Gelenberg, A. J., Wojcik, J. D., Growdon, J. H., Sved, A. F., & Wurtman, R. J. (1980). Tyrosine in the treatment of depression. *American Journal of Psychiatry, 137,* 622-623.

Geller, I., & Seifter, J. (1960). The effects of meprobamate, barbiturates, d-amphetamine, and promazine on experimentally induced conflict in the rat. *Psychopharmacologia, 1,* 482-492.

Gibson, C. J., & Gelenberg, A. (1983). Tyrosine for the treatment of depression. In H. M. van Praag & J. Mendlewicz (Eds.), *Management of depressions with monoamine precursors, advances in biological psychiatry* (Vol. 10, pp. 148-159). New York: Karger.

Gittelman, R., Mannuzza, S., Shenker, R., & Bonagura, N. (1985). Hyperactive boys almost grown up. *Archives of General Psychiatry, 42,* 937-947.

Glickman, S. E., & Schiff, B. B. (1967). A biological theory of reinforcement. *Psychological Review, 74,* 81-109.

Goeders, N. E., Dworkin, S. I., & Smith, J. E. (1986). Neuropharmacological assessment of cocaine self-administration into the medial prefrontal cortex. *Pharmacology, Biochemistry, and Behavior, 24,* 1429-1440.

Goeders, N. E., Lane, J. D., & Smith, J. E. (1984). Self-administration of methionine enkephalin into the nucleus accumbens. *Pharmacology, Biochemistry, and Behavior, 20,* 451-455.

Goeders, N. E., & Smith, J. E. (1983). Cortical dopaminergic involvement in cocaine reinforcement. *Science, 221,* 773-775.

Goeders, N. E., & Smith, J. E. (1986). Reinforcing properties of cocaine in the medial prefrontal cortex: Primary action on presynaptic dopaminergic terminals. *Pharmacology, Biochemistry, and Behavior, 25,* 191-199.

Goldsmith, H. (1983). Genetic influences on personality from infancy to adulthood. *Child Development, 54,* 331-355.

Golinko, B. E. (1984). Side effects of dextroamphetamine and methylphenidate in hyperactive children: A brief review. *Progress in Neuropsychopharmacology and Biological Psychiatry, 8,* 1-8.

Gonzalez-Mora, J. L., Maidment, N. T., Guadalupe, T., & Mas, M. (1989). Post-mortem dopamine dynamics assessed by voltammetry and microdialysis. *Brain Research Bulletin, 23,* 323-327.

Gratton, A., & Wise, R. A. (1985). Hypothalamic reward mechanism: Two first-stage fiber populations with a cholinergic component. *Science, 227,* 545-548.

Gratton, A., & Wise, R. A. (1988). Comparisons of refractory periods for medial forebrain bundle fibers subserving stimulation-induced feeding and brain stimulation reward: A psychophysical study. *Brain Research, 438,* 256-263.

Green, A. R., & Nutt, D. J. (1983). Antidepressants. In D. G. Grahame-Smith & P. J. Cowen (Eds.), *Psychopharmacology I, part I: Preclinical psychopharmacology* (pp. 1-37). Amsterdam: Excerpta Medica.

Grey Walter, W. (1973). Human frontal lobe function in sensory-motor association. In K. H. Pribram & A. R. Luria (Eds.), *Psychophysiology of the frontal lobes* (pp. 109-122). New York: Academic Press.

Gross, G., Gothert, M., Ender, H. P., & Schumann, H. J. (1981). ^{3}H-Imipramine binding sites in the rat brain. *Archives of Pharmacology, 317,* 310-314.

Gudelsky, G. A. (1981). Tuberoinfundibular dopamine neurons and the regulation of prolactin secretion. *Psychoneuroendocrinology, 6,* 3-16.

Hadjiconstantinou, M., & Neff, N. H. (1983). Ascorbic acid could be hazardous to your experiments: A commentary on dopamine receptor binding studies with speculation on a role for ascorbic acid in neuronal function. *Neuropharmacology, 22,* 939-943.

Haenlein, M., & Caul, W. F. (1987). Attention deficit disorder with hyperactivity: A specific hypothesis of reward dysfunction. *Journal of the American Academy of Child and Adolescent Psychiatry, 26,* 356-362.

Haycock, J. W. (1987). Stimulation-dependent phosphorylation of tyrosine hydroxylase in rat corpus striatum. *Brain Research Bulletin, 19,* 619-622.

Haycock, J. W., & Haycock, D. A. (1991). Tyrosine hydroxylase in rat brain dopaminergic nerve terminals: Multiple-site phosphorylation in vivo and in synaptosomes. *Journal of Biological Chemistry, 266,* 5650-5657.

Hechtman, L. (1994). Genetic and neurobiological aspects of attention deficit hyperactive disorder: A review. *Journal of Psychiatry and Neuroscience, 19,* 193-201.

Helmeste, D. M., & Seeman, P. (1982). Amphetamine-induced hypolocomotion in mice with more brain D2 dopamine receptors. *Psychiatry Research, 7,* 351-359.

Hernandez, L., Lee, F., & Hoebel, B. G. (1987). Simultaneous microdialysis and amphetamine infusion in the nucleus accumbens and striatum of freely moving rats: Increase in extracellular dopamine and serotonin. *Brain Research Bulletin, 19,* 623-628.

Hiroi, N., & White, N. M. (1990). The resperpine-sensitive dopamine pool mediates (+)–amphetamine-conditioned reward in the place preference paradigm. *Brain Research, 510,* 33-42.

Hoebel, B. G., Monaco, A., Hernandez, L., Aulisi, E., Stanley, B. G., & Lenard, L. (1983). Self-injection of amphetamine directly into the brain. *Psychopharmacology, 81,* 158-163.

Hokfelt, T., Ljungdahl, A., Terenius, L., Elde, R., & Nilsson, G. (1987). Coexistence of peptides with classical neurotransmitters. *Experientia, 43,* 768-780.

Hokfelt, T., Skirboll, J. F., Rehfeld, M., & Goldstein, K. (1980). A subpopulation of mesencephalic dopamine neurons projecting to limbic areas contains a cholecystokinin-like peptide: Evidence from immunohistochemistry combined with retrograde tracing. *Neuroscience, 5,* 2093-2124.

Hubner, C. B., & Koob, G. F. (1987). Ventral pallidal lesions produce decreases in cocaine and heroin self-administration in the rat. *Proceedings of the Society for Neuroscience,* New Orleans, LA, p. 1717.

Huessy, H. R., Cohen, S. M., Blair, C. L., & Rood, P. (1979). Clinical explorations in adult minimal brain dysfunction. In L. Bellak (Ed.), *Psychiatric aspects of minimal brain dysfunction in adults* (pp. 19-36). New York: Grune & Stratton.

Hynd, G. W., Hern, K. L., Novey, E. S., Eliopulos, D., Marshall, R., Gonzalez, J. J., & Voeller, K. K. (1993). Attention deficit-hyperactivity disorder and asymmetry of the caudate nucleus. *Journal of Child Neurology, 8,* 339-347.

Hynd, G. W., Semrud-Clikeman, M., Lorys, A., Novey, E. S., & Eliopulos, D. (1990). Brain morphology in developmental dyslexia and attention deficit disorder/hyperactivity. *Archives of Neurology, 47,* 919-926.

Iversen, L. L., & Mackay, A. V. P. (1979). Pharmacodynamics of antidepressants and antimanic drugs. In E. S. Paykel & A. Coppen (Eds.), *Psychopharmacology of affective disorders* (pp. 60-90). New York: Oxford University Press.

Jenck, F., Gratton, A., & Wise, R. A. (1987). Opioid receptor subtypes associated with ventral tegmental facilitation of lateral hypothalamic brain stimulation reward. *Brain Research, 423,* 34-38.

Joseph, M. H., Peters, S. L., Prior, A., Mitchell, S. N., Brazell, M. P., & Gray, J. A. (1990). Chronic nicotine administration increases tyrosine hydroxylase selectively in the rat hippocampus. *Neurochemistry International, 16,* 269-273.

Kandel, E. R. (1991). Disorders of thought: Schizophrenia. In E. R. Kandel, J. H. Schwartz, & T. M. Jessell (Eds.), *Principles of neural science* (3rd ed., pp. 853-868). New York: Elsevier.

Kandel, E. R., Schwartz, J. H., & Jessell, T. M. (1991). *Principles of neural science* (3rd ed.). New York: Elsevier.

Kelley, A. E., & Delfs, J. M. (1991a). Dopamine and conditioned reinforcement, I. Differential effects of amphetamine microinjections into striatal subregions. *Psychopharmacology, 103,* 187-196.

Kelley, A. E., & Delfs, J. M. (1991b). Dopamine and conditioned reinforcement, II. Contrasting effects of amphetamine microinjections into the nucleus accumbens with peptide microinjection into the ventral tegmental area. *Psychopharmacology, 103,* 197-203.

Khantzian, E. J. (1983). An extreme case of cocaine dependence and marked improvement with methylphenidate treatment. *American Journal of Psychiatry, 140,* 784-785.

Khantzian, E. J. (1985). Self-medication hypothesis of addictive disorders: Focus on heroin and cocaine dependence. *American Journal of Psychiatry, 142,* 1259-1264.

Khantzian, E. J., Gawin, F., Kleber, H. D., & Riordan, C. E. (1984). Methylphenidate (Ritalin) treatment of cocaine dependence: A preliminary report. *Journal of Substance Abuse Treatment, 1,* 107-112.

Kinomura, S., Larsson, J., Gulyas, B., & Roland, P. E. (1996). Activation by attention of the human reticular formation and thalamic intralaminar nuclei. *Science, 271,* 512-515.

Klein, R. G., & Mannuzza, S. (1988). Hyperactive boys almost grown up: III. Methylphenidate effects on ultimate height. *Archives of General Psychiatry, 45,* 1131-1134.

Klein, R. G., & Mannuzza, S. (1991). Long-term outcome of hyperactive children: A review. *Journal of the American Academy of Child and Adolescent Psychiatry, 30,* 383-387.

Kohlert, J. G., & Bloch, G. J. (1993). A rat model for attention deficit-hyperactivity disorder. *Physiology and Behavior, 53,* 1215-1218.

Koob, G. R. (1992). Drugs of abuse: Anatomy, pharmacology and function of reward pathways. *Trends in Pharmacological Sciences, 13,* 177-184.

Kuczenski, R. (1983). Biochemical actions of amphetamine and other stimulants. In I. Creese (Ed.), *Stimulants: Neurochemical, behavioral, and clinical perspectives* (pp. 31-61). New York: Raven Press.

Kuczenski, R., & Segal, D. S. (1989). Concomitant characterization of behavioral and striatal neurotransmitter response to amphetamine using in vivo microdialysis. *The Journal of Neuroscience, 9,* 2051-2065.

Kurumiya, S., & Nakajima, S. (1988). Dopamine D_1 receptors in the nucleus accumbens: Involvement in the reinforcing effect of tegmental stimulation. *Brain Research, 448,* 1-6.

LaHoste, G. J., Swanson, J. M., Wigal, S. B., Glabe, C., Wigal, T., King, N., & Kennedy, J. T. (1996). Dopamine D_4 receptor gene polymorphism is associated with attention deficit hyperactivity disorder. *Molecular Psychiatry, 1,* 121-124.

Lander, E., & Kruglyak, L. (1995). Genetic dissection of complex traits: Guidelines for interpreting and reporting linkage results. *Nature Genetics, 11,* 214-247.

Leutwyler, K. (1996). Viral tracers: Neuroscientists use viruses to map out pathways in the brain. *Scientific American, 274,* 18.

Levy, F. (1991). The dopamine theory of attention deficit hyperactivity disorder (ADHD). *Australian and New Zealand Journal of Psychiatry, 25,* 277-283.

Li, Y. Q., Rao, Z. R., & Shi, J. W. (1989). Serotoninergic projections from the midbrain periaqueductal gray to the nucleus accumbens in the rat. *Neuroscience Letters, 98,* 276-279.

Liang, N. Y., & Rutledge, C. O. (1982). Comparison of the release of [^{3}H]dopamine from isolated corpus striatum by amphetamine, fenfluramine, and unlabelled dopamine. *Biochemical Pharmacology, 31,* 983-992.

Lieberman, H. R., & Banderet, L. E. (1990). Tyrosine protects humans from the adverse effects of acute exposure to hypoxia and cold. *Society for Neuroscience Abstracts, 16,* 272.

Lombroso, P. J., Pauls, D. L., & Leckman, J. F. (1994). Genetic mechanisms in childhood psychiatric disorders. *Journal of the American Academy of Child and Adolescent Psychiatry, 33,* 921-938.

Lou, H. C., Henriksen, L., Bruhn, P., Borner, H., & Nielsen, J. B. (1989). Striatal dysfunction in attention deficit and hyperkinetic disorder. *Archives of Neurology, 46,* 48-52.

Lucki, I., & Harvey, J. A. (1979). Increased sensitivity to d- and l-amphetamine action after midbrain raphe lesions as measured by locomotor activity. *Neuropharmacology, 18,* 243-249.

Luria, A. R. (1973). *The working brain: An introduction to neuropsychology.* New York: Basic Books.

Luria, A. R. (1980). *Higher cortical functions in man* (2nd ed.). New York: Basic Books.

Luthman, J., Fredriksson, A., Lewander, T., Jonsson, G., & Archer, T. (1989). Effects of d-amphetamine and methylphenidate on hyperactivity produced by neonatal 6-hydroxy-dopamine treatment. *Psychopharmacology, 99,* 550-557.

Lyness, W. H., Friedle, N. M., & Moore, K. E. (1979). Destruction of dopamine nerve terminals in nucleus accumbens: Effect on d-amphetamine self-administration. *Pharmacology, Biochemistry, and Behavior, 11,* 553-556.

Mabry, P. D., & Campbell, B. A. (1973). Serotonergic inhibition of catecholamine induced arousal. *Brain Research, 49,* 381-391.

Mack, F., & Bonisch, H. (1979). Dissociation constants and lipophilicity of catecholamines and related compounds. *Naunyn-Schmiedebergs Archives of Pharmacology, 310,* 1-9.

MacLean, P. D. (1973). A triune concept of the brain and behavior. In T. J. Boag & D. Campbell (Eds.), *A triune concept of the brain and behavior: The Clarence M. Hincks memorial lectures* (pp. 4-66). Toronto: University of Toronto Press.

Magoun, H. W. (1969). *The waking brain* (2nd ed.). Springfield, IL: Charles C Thomas.

Maher, T. J. (1988). Tyrosine and brain function. *ISI Atlas of Science: Biochemistry, 1,* 150-154.

Malison, R. T., McDougle, C. J., van Dyck, C. H., Scahill, L., Baldwin, R. M., Seibyle, J. P., Price, L. H., Leckman, J. F., & Innis, R. B. (1995). [123I]b-CIT SPECT imaging of striatal dopamine transporter binding in Tourette's disorder. *American Journal of Psychiatry, 152,* 1359-1361.

Mann, H. B., & Greenspan, S. I. (1976). The identification and treatment of adult brain dysfunction. *American Journal of Psychiatry, 133,* 1013-1017.

Mannuzza, S., Klein, R. G., & Addalli, K. A. (1991). Young adult mental status of hyperactive boys and their brothers: A prospective follow-up study. *Journal of the American Academy of Child and Adolescent Psychiatry, 30,* 743-751.

Mannuzza, S., Klein, R. G., Bessler, A., Malloy, P., & LaPadula, M. (1993). Adult outcome of hyperactive boys: Educational achievement, occupational rank, and psychiatric status. *Archives of General Psychiatry, 50,* 565-576.

Masserano, J. M., Vulliet, P. R., Tank, A. W., & Weiner, N. (1989). The role of tyrosine hydroxylase in the regulation of catecholamine synthesis. In U. Trendelenburg & N. Weiner (Eds.), *Handbook of experimental pharmacology* (Vol. 90/II, pp. 427-469). Berlin: Springer-Verlag.

Matochik, J. A., Liebenauer, L. L., King, A. C., Szymanski, H. V., Cohen, R. M., & Zametkin, A. J. (1994). Cerebral glucose metabolism in adults with attention deficit hyperactivity disorder after chronic stimulant treatment. *American Journal of Psychiatry, 151,* 658-664.

Matochik, J. A., Nordahl, T. E., Gross, M., Semple, W. E., King, A. C., Cohen, R. M., & Zametkin, A. J. (1993). Effects of acute stimulant medication on cerebral metabolism in adults with hyperactivity. *Neuropsychopharmacology, 8,* 377-386.

Mattes, J. A., & Gittelman, R. (1983). Growth of hyperactive children on maintenance regimen of methylphenidate. *Archives of General Psychiatry, 40,* 317-321.

Mattiace, L. A., Baring, M. D., Manaye, K. F., Mihailoff, G. A., & German, D. C. (1989). Mesostriatal projections in BALB/c and CBA mice: A quantitative retrograde neuro-anatomical tracing study. *Brain Research Bulletin, 23,* 61-68.

Maurer, R. A. (1980). Dopaminergic inhibition of prolactin synthesis and prolactin messenger RNA accumulation in cultured pituitary cells. *Journal of Biological Chemistry, 255,* 8092-8097.

Mauron, C., & Wurtman, R. J. (1982). Co-administering tyrosine with glucose potentiates its effect on brain tyrosine levels. *Journal of Neural Transmission, 55,* 317-321.

McGee, R., Williams, S., & Silva, P. A. (1987). A comparison of girls and boys with teacher-identified problems of attention. *Journal of the American Academy of Child and Adolescent Psychiatry, 26,* 711-717.

Milich, R., Wolraich, M., & Lindgren, S. (1986). Sugar and hyperactivity: A critical review of empirical findings. *Clinical Psychology Review, 6,* 493-513.

Milner, J. D., & Wurtman, R. J. (1985). Tyrosine availability determines stimulus-evoked dopamine release from rat striatal slices. *Neuroscience Letters, 59,* 215-220.

Milner, J. D., & Wurtman, R. J. (1986). Catecholamine synthesis: Physiological coupling to precursor supply. *Biochemical Pharmacology, 35,* 875-881.

Mogenson, G. J. (1987). Limbic-motor integration. *Progress in Physiological Psychology, 12,* 117-170.

Mogenson, G. J., Jones, D. L., & Yim, C. Y. (1980). From motivation to action: Functional interface between the limbic system and the motor system. *Progress in Neurobiology, 14,* 69-97.

Mogenson, G. J., & Yang, C. R. (1991). The contribution of basal forebrain to limbic-motor integration and the mediation of motivation to action (Review). *Advances in Experimental Medicine and Biology, 295,* 267-290.

Mogenson, G. J., Yang, C. R., & Yim, C. Y. (1988). Influence of dopamine on limbic inputs to the nucleus accumbens. *Annals of the New York Academy of Sciences, 537,* 86-100.

Moghaddam, B., & Bunney, B. S. (1989). Differential effect of cocaine on extracellular dopamine levels in rat medial prefrontal cortex and nucleus accumbens: Comparison to amphetamine. *Synapse, 4,* 156-161.

Moghaddam, B., Roth, R. H., & Bunney, B. S. (1990). Characterization of dopamine release in the rat medial prefrontal cortex as assessed by in vivo microdialysis: Comparison to the striatum. *Neuroscience, 36,* 669-676.

Montgomery, A. M. J., Rose, I. C., & Herberg, L. J. (1991). 5-HT$_{1A}$ agonists and dopamine: The effects of 8-OH-DPAT and buspirone on brain-stimulation reward. *Journal of Neural Transmission, 83,* 139-148.

Muir, J. L., Dunnett, S. B., Robbins, T. W., & Everitt, B. J. (1992). Attentional functions of the forebrain cholinergic systems: Effects of intraventricular hemicholinium, physostigmine, basal forebrain lesions, and intracortical grafts on a multiple-choice serial reaction time task. *Experimental Brain Research, 89,* 611-622.

Nakahara, D., Ozaki, N., Miura, Y., Miura, H., & Nagatsu, T. (1989). Increased dopamine and serotonin metabolism in rat nucleus accumbens produced by intracranial self-stimulation of medial forebrain bundle as measured by in vivo microdialysis. *Brain Research, 495,* 178-181.

Nakajima, S. (1986). Suppression of operant responding in the rat by dopamine D$_1$ receptor blockade with SCH 23390. *Physiological Psychology, 14,* 111-114.

Nakajima, S., & McKenzie, G. M. (1986). Reduction of the rewarding effect of brain stimulation by a blockade of dopamine D$_1$ receptor with SCH 23390. *Pharmacology, Biochemistry, and Behavior, 24,* 919-923.

Neill, D. B., Grant, L. D., & Grossman, S. P. (1972). Selective potentiation of locomotor effects of amphetamine by midbrain raphe lesions. *Physiology and Behavior, 9,* 655-657.

Noback, C. R., & Demarest, R. J. (1977). *The nervous system: Introduction and review.* New York: McGraw-Hill.

Nomikos, G. G., Damsma, G., Wenkstern, D., & Fibiger, H. C. (1990). In vivo characterization of locally applied dopamine uptake inhibitors by striatal microdialysis. *Synapse, 6,* 106-112.

Olds, J., & Milner, P. (1954). Positive reinforcement produced by electrical stimulation of septal area and other regions of rat brain. *Journal of Comparative and Physiological Psychology, 47,* 419-427.

Olds, M. E., & Olds, J. (1963). Approach-avoidance analysis of rat diencephalon. *Journal of Comparative Neurology, 120,* 259-295.

Parada, M., Hernandez, L., Schwartz, D., & Hoebel, B. G. (1988). Hypothalamic infusion of amphetamine increases serotonin, dopamine, and norepinephrine. *Physiology and Behavior, 44,* 607-610.

Parker, E. M., & Cubeddu, L. X. (1988). Comparative effects of amphetamine, phenylethylamine, and related drugs on dopamine efflux, dopamine uptake, and mazindol binding. *Journal of Pharmacology and Experimental Therapeutics, 245,* 199-210.

Pavlov, I. P. (1928). *Lectures on conditioned reflexes: Twenty-five years of objective study of the higher nervous activity (behavior) of animals* (W. H. Gantt & G. Volborth, trans.) (Vol. 1, pp. 363-391). New York: International Publishers.

Pfaus, J. G., Damsma, G., Nomikos, G. G., Wenkstern, D., Blaha, C. D., Phillips, A. G., & Fibiger, H. C. (1990). Sexual behavior enhances central dopamine transmission in the male rat. *Brain Research, 530,* 345-348.

Phillips, A. G. (1984). Brain reward circuitry: A case for separate systems. *Brain Research Bulletin, 12,* 195-201.

Phillips, A. G., Atkinson, L. J., Blackburn, J. R., & Blaha, C. D. (1993). Increased extracellular dopamine in the nucleus accumbens of the rat elicited by a conditional stimulus for food: An electrochemical study. *Canadian Journal of Physiology and Pharmacology, 71,* 387-393.

Phillips, A. G., & LePiane, F. G. (1980). Reinforcing effects of morphine microinjection into the ventral tegmental area. *Pharmacology, Biochemistry, and Behavior, 12,* 965-968.

Phillips, A. G., Mora, F., & Rolls, E. T. (1981). Intracerebral self-administration of amphetamine by rhesus monkeys. *Neuroscience Letters, 24,* 81-86.

Pickel, V. M., Towle, A. C., Joh, T. H., & Chan, J. (1988). Gamma-aminobutyric acid in the medial rat nucleus accumbens: Ultrastructure localization in neurons receiving monosynaptic input from catecholaminergic afferents. *Journal of Comparative Neurology, 272,* 1-14.

Pijnenburg, A. J., Honig, W. M., Van der Heyden, J. A., & Van Rossum, J. M. (1976). Effects of chemical stimulation of the mesolimbic dopamine system upon locomotor activity. *European Journal of Pharmacology, 35,* 45-58.

Porrino, L. J., Domer, F. R., Crane, A. M., & Sokoloff, L. (1988). Selective alterations in cerebral metabolism within the mesocorticolimbic dopaminergic system produced by acute cocaine administration in rats. *Neuropsychopharmacology, 1,* 109-118.

Porrino, L. J., Esposito, R. U., Seeger, T. F., Crane, A. M., Pert, A., & Sokoloff, L. (1984). Metabolic mapping of the brain during rewarding self-stimulation. *Science, 224,* 306-309.

Porrino, L. J., & Lucignani, G. (1987). Different patterns of local brain energy metabolism associated with high and low doses of methylphenidate: Relevance to its action in hyperactive children. *Biological Psychiatry, 22,* 126-138.

Porrino, L. J., Lucignani, G., Dow-Edwards, D., & Sokoloff L (1984). Correlation of dose-dependent effects of acute amphetamine administration on behavior and local cerebral metabolism in rats. *Brain Research, 307,* 311-320.

Porteus, S. D. (1973). *Porteus maze test: Fifty years application* (pp. 30-54). Palo Alto: Pacific Books.

Pribram, K. H. (1961). A further experimental analysis of the behavioral deficit that follows injury to the primate frontal cortex. *Journal of Experimental Neurology, 3,* 432-466.

Pribram, K. H. (1973). The primate frontal cortex-executive of the brain. In K. H. Pribram & A. R. Luria (Eds.), *Psychophysiology of the frontal lobes* (pp. 293-314). New York: Academic Press.

Quay, H. C. (1988). The behavioral reward and inhibition systems in childhood behavior disorder. In L. M. Bloomingdale (Ed.), *Attention deficit disorder* (Vol. 3, pp. 176-186). New York: Pergamon.

Reimherr, F. W., Wender, P. H., Ebert, M. H., & Wood, D. R. (1984). Cerebrospinal fluid homovanillic acid and 5-hydroxyindoleacetic acid in adults with attention deficit disorder, residual type. *Psychiatry Research, 11,* 71-78.

Reinstein, D. K., Lehnert, H., & Wurtman, R. J. (1985). Dietary tyrosine suppresses the rise in plasma corticosterone following acute stress in rats. *Life Sciences, 37,* 2157-2163.

Reis, D. J., Baker, H., Fink, J. S., & Joh, T. H. (1979). A genetic control of the number of central dopamine neurons in relationship to brain organization, drug responses, and behavior. In E. Usdin, I. J. Kopin, & J. Barchas (Eds.), *Catecholamines: Basic and clinical frontiers* (Vol. 1, pp. 23-33). New York: Pergamon.

Reis, D. J., Baker, H., Fink, S. J., & Joh, T. H. (1981). Chapter 16. In E. S. Gershon, S. Matthysse, X. O. Breakefield, & R. D. Ciaranello (Eds.), *Genetic research strategies in psychobiology and psychiatry* (pp. 215-229). Pacific Grove, CA: Boxwood.

Reis, D. J., Fink, S. J., & Baker, H. (1983). Genetic control of the number of dopamine neurons in the brain: Relationship to behavior and response to psychoactive drugs. In S. S. Kety, L. P.

Rowland, R. L. Sidman, & S. W. Matthysse (Eds.), *Genetics of neurological and psychiatric disorders* (pp. 55-75). New York: Raven.

Richard, F., Faucon-Biguet, N., Labatut, R., Rollet, D., Mallet, J., & Buda, M. (1988). Modulation of tyrosine hydroxylase gene expression in rat brain and adrenals by exposure to cold. *Journal of Neuroscience Research, 20,* 32-37.

Richtand, N. M., Inagami, T., Misono, K., & Kuczenski, R. (1985). Purification and characterization of rat striatal tyrosine hydroxylase: Comparison of the activation by cyclic AMP-dependent phosphorylation and by other effectors. *Journal of Biological Chemistry, 260,* 8465-8473.

Risner, M. E., & Jones, B. E. (1976). Role of noradrenergic and dopaminergic processes in amphetamine self-administration. *Pharmacology, Biochemistry, and Behavior, 5,* 477-482.

Robbins, T. W., & Everitt, B. J. (1982). Functional studies of the central catecholamines. *International Review of Neurobiology, 23,* 303-365.

Robbins, T. W., Everitt, B. J., Marston, H. M., Wilkinson, J., Jones, G. H., & Page, K. J. (1989). Comparative effects of ibotenic acid- and quisqualic acid-induced lesions of the substantia innominata on attentional function in the rat: Further implications for the role of the cholinergic neurons of the nucleus basalis in cognitive processes. *Behavioral Brain Research, 35,* 221-224.

Robbins, T. W., Everitt, B. J., Muir, J. L., & Harrison, A. (1992). Understanding the behavioral functions of neurochemically defined arousal systems. *International Brain Research Organization News, 20,* 7.

Robinson, T. E., Jurson, P. A., Bennett, J. A., & Bentgen, K. M. (1988). Persistent sensitization of dopamine neurotransmission in ventral striatum (nucleus accumbens) produced by prior experience with (+)–amphetamine: A microdialysis study in freely moving rats. *Brain Research, 462,* 211-222.

Roland, P. E. (1993). *Brain activation.* New York: Wiley-Liss.

Role, L. W., & Kelly, J. P. (1991). The brain stem: Cranial nerve nuclei and the monoaminergic systems. In E. R. Kandel, J. H. Schwartz, & T. M. Jesell (Eds.), *Principles of neural science* (3rd ed., pp. 683-699). New York: Elsevier.

Rompre, P. P., & Gratton, A. (1993). Mesencephalic microinjections of neurotensin-(1-13) and its C-terminal fragment, neurotensin-(8-13), potentiate brain-stimulation reward. *Brain Research, 616,* 154-162.

Rompre, P. P., & Wise, R. A. (1989). Opioid-neuroleptic interaction in brainstem self-stimulation. *Brain Research, 477,* 144-151.

Rosenzweig, M. R., Leiman, A. L., & Breedlove, S. M. (1996). *Biological psychology.* Sunderland, MA: Sinauer.

Ross, R. A., Judd, A. B., Pickel, V. M., Joh, T. H., & Reis, D. J. (1976). Strain-dependent variations in number of mid-brain dopaminergic neurons. *Nature, 264,* 654-656.

Routtenberg, A.(1978). The reward system of the brain. *Scientific American, 239,* 154-164.

Safer, D. J., & Krager, J. M. (1994). The increased rate of stimulant treatment for hyperactive/inattentive students in secondary schools. *Pediatrics, 94,* 462-464.

Sagvolden, T., Metzger, M. A., & Sagvolden, G. (1993). Frequent reward eliminates differences in activity between hyperkinetic rats and controls. *Behavioral and Neural Biology, 59,* 225-229.

Sagvolden, T., Metzger, M. A., Schiorbeck, H. K., Rugland, A. L., Spinnangr, I., & Sagvolden, G. (1992). The spontaneously hypertensive rat (SHR) as an animal model of childhood hyperactivity (ADHD): Changed reactivity to reinforcers and to psychomotor stimulants. *Behavioral and Neural Biology, 58,* 103-112.

Samson, H. H., & Harris, R. A. (1992). Neurobiology of alcohol abuse. *Trends in Pharmacological Sciences, 13,* 206-211.

Sanghera, M. K., Crespi, F., Martin, K. F., Heal, D. J., Buckett, W. R., & Marsden, C. A. (1990). Biochemical and in vivo voltammetric evidence for differences in striatal dopamine levels in inbred strains of mice. *Neuroscience, 39,* 649-656.

Sato, M. (1986). Acute exacerbation of methamphetamine psychosis and lasting dopaminergic supersensitivity—a clinical survey. *Psychopharmacology Bulletin, 2,* 751-756.

Sato, M., Chen, C. C., Akiyama, K., & Otsuki, S. (1983). Acute exacerbation of paranoid psychotic state after long-term abstinence in patients with previous methamphetamine psychosis. *Biological Psychiatry, 18,* 429-440.

Satterfield, J. H., & Cantwell, D. P. (1975). Psychopharmacology in the prevention of antisocial and delinquent behavior. *International Journal of Mental Health, 4,* 227-237.

Satterfield, J. H., Hoppe, C. M., & Schell, A. M. (1982). A prospective study of delinquency in 110 adolescent boys with attention deficit disorder and 88 normal adolescent boys. *American Journal of Psychiatry, 139,* 795-798.

Schaefer, G. J. (1988). Opiate antagonists and rewarding brain stimulation. *Neuroscience and Biobehavioral Reviews, 12,* 1-17.

Schaefer, G. J., & Michael, R. P. (1980). Acute effects of neuroleptics on brain self-stimulation thresholds in rats. *Psychopharmacology, 67,* 9-15.

Schotte, A., & Leysen, J. E. (1989). Autoradiographic evidence for the localization of high affinity neurotensin binding sites on dopaminergic nerve terminals in the nigrostriatal and mesolimbic pathways in rat brain. *Journal of Chemical Neuroanatomy, 2,* 253-257.

Schvehla, T. J., Mandoki, M. W., & Sumner, G. S. (1994). Clonidine therapy for comorbid attention deficit hyperactivity disorder and conduct disorder: Preliminary findings in a children's inpatient unit. *Southern Medical Journal, 87,* 692-695.

Schwarz, R. D., Uretsky, N. J., & Bianchine, J. R. (1980). The relationship between the stimulation of dopamine synthesis and release produced by amphetamine and high potassium in striatal slices. *Journal of Neurochemistry, 35,* 1120-1127.

Seeman, P., Grigoriadis, D. E., & Niznik, H. B. (1986). Selectivity of agonists and antagonists at D2 dopamine receptors compared to D1 and S2 receptors. *Drug Development Research, 9,* 63-69.

Seiden, L. S., Sabol, K. E., & Ricaurte, G. A. (1993). Amphetamine: Effects on catecholamine systems and behavior. *Annual Review of Pharmacology and Toxicology, 32,* 639-677.

Semrud-Clikeman, M., Filipek, P. A., Biederman, J., Steingard, R., Kennedy, D., Renshaw, P., & Bekken, K. (1994). Attention-deficit hyperactivity disorder: Magnetic resonance imaging morphometric analysis of the corpus callosum. *Journal of the American Academy of Child and Adolescent Psychiatry, 33,* 875-881.

Severson, J. A., Randall, P. K., & Finch, C. E. (1981). Genotypic influences on striatal dopaminergic regulation in mice. *Brain Research, 210,* 201-215.

Shaywitz, B. A., Cohen, D. J., & Bowers, M. B. (1977). CSF monoamine metabolites in children with minimal brain dysfunction: Evidence for alteration of brain dopamine. *Journal of Pediatrics, 90,* 67-71.

Shenker, A., Bergstrom, D. A., & Walters, J. R. (1990). Methylphenidate and pemoline inhibit the firing rate of rat substantia nigra dopamine neurons. *Society for Neuroscience Abstracts, 16,* 1048.

Shih, T. M., Khachaturian, Z. S., & Barry, H. (1974). Evidence for cholinergically mediated effect of methylphenidate hydrochloride in the central nervous system. *The Pharmacologist, 16,* 242.

Shih, T. M., Khachaturian, Z. S., Barry, H., & Hanin, I. (1976). Cholinergic mediation of the inhibitory effect of methylphenidate on neuronal activity in the reticular formation. *Neuropharmacology, 15,* 55-60.

Shih, T. M., Khachaturian, Z. S., Barry, H., & Reisler, K. (1975). Differential effects of methylphenidate on reticular formation and thalamic neuronal activity. *Psychopharmacologia* (Berlin), 44, 11-15.

Shih, T. M., Khachaturian, Z. S., & Hanin, I. (1977). Involvement of both cholinergic and catecholaminergic pathways in the central action of methylphenidate: A study utilizing lead-exposed rats. *Psychopharmacology, 55,* 187-193.

Shizgal, P., Bielajew, C., Corbet, D., Skelton, R., & Yeomans, J. S. (1980). Behavioral methods for inferring anatomical linkage between rewarding brain stimulation sites. *Journal of Comparative and Physiological Psychology, 94,* 227-237.

Shizgal, P., Bielajew, C., & Kiss, I. (1980). Anodal hyperpolarization block technique provides evidence for rostro-caudal conduction of reward related signals in the medial forebrain bundle. *Society for Neuroscience Abstracts, 6,* 422.

Shizgal, P., Schindler, D., & Rompre, P.-P. (1989). Forebrain neurons driven by rewarding stimulation of the medial forebrain bundle in the rat: Comparison of psychophysical and electrophysiological estimates of refractory periods. *Brain Research, 499,* 234-248.

Shue, K. L., & Douglas, V. I. (1992). Attention deficit hyperactivity disorder and the frontal lobe syndrome. *Brain and Cognition, 20,* 104-124.

Sibley, D. R. (1991). Cloning of a D3 receptor subtype expands dopamine receptor family. *Trends in Pharmacological Sciences, 12,* 7-9.

Sibley, D. R., & Monsma, F. J. (1992). Molecular biology of dopamine receptors. *Trends in Pharmacological Sciences, 13,* 61-69.

Sieg, K. G., Gaffney, G. R., Preston, D. F., & Hellings, J. A. (1995). SPECT brain imaging abnormalities in attention deficit hyperactivity disorder. *Clinical Nuclear Medicine, 20,* 55-60.

Smith, S. J., & Augustine, G. J. (1988). Calcium ions, active zones, and synaptic transmitter release. *Trends in Neuroscience, 11,* 458-464.

Sokoloff, P., Giros, B., Martres, M. P., Bouthenet, M. L., & Schwartz, J. C. (1990). Molecular cloning and characterization of a novel dopamine receptor (D3) as a target for neuroleptics. *Nature, 347,* 146-151.

Sonuga-Barke, E. J. S., Taylor, E., Sembi, S., & Smith, J. (1992). Hyperactivity and delay aversion, I: The effect of delay on choice. *Journal of Child Psychology and Psychiatry, 33,* 387-398.

Soubrie, P. (1986). Reconciling the role of central serotonin neurons in human and animal behavior. *The Behavioural and Brain Sciences, 9,* 319-364.

Starkstein, S. E., Moran, T. H., Bowersox, J. A., & Robinson, R. G. (1988). Behavioral abnormalities induced by frontal cortical and nucleus accumbens lesions. *Brain Research, 473,* 74-80.

Stein, L. (1964). Reciprocal action of reward and punishment mechanisms. In R. G. Heath (Ed.), *The role of pleasure in behavior* (pp. 113-139). New York: Harper & Row.

Stein, L. (1968). Chemistry of reward and punishment. In *Psychopharmacology: A review of progress, 1957-1967* (pp. 105-123). Washington, DC: Government Printing Office.

Stein, L., & Belluzzi, J. D. (1989). Cellular investigations of behavioral reinforcement. *Neuroscience and Biobehavioral Reviews, 13,* 69-80.

Stein, L., & Wise, C. D. (1970). Behavioral pharmacology of central stimulants. In W. G. Clark & J. del Giudice (Eds.), *Principles of psychopharmacology* (pp. 313-325). New York: Academic Press.

Stein, L., Wise, C. D., & Belluzzi, J. D. (1977). Neuropharmacology of reward and punishment. In L. Iverson, S. D. Iverson, & S. H. Snyder (Eds.), *Handbook of psychopharmacology* (Vol. 8, pp. 25-53). New York: Plenum.

Stein, L., Wise, C. D., & Berger, B. (1973). Antianxiety action of benzodiazepines: Decrease in activity of serotonin neurons in the punishment system. In S. Garattini, E. Mussini, & L. O. Randall (Eds.), *The benzodiazapines* (pp. 229-325). New York: Raven.

Stein, L., Xue, B. G., & Belluzzi, J. D. (1993). A cellular analogue of operant conditioning. *Journal of the Experimental Analysis of Behavior, 60,* 41-53.

Stein, L., Xue, B. G., & Belluzzi, J. D. (1994). In vitro reinforcement of hippocampal bursting: A search for Skinner's atoms of behavior. *Journal of the Experimental Analysis of Behavior, 61,* 155-168.

Steinbusch, H. W. M. (1984). Serotonin-immunoreactive neurons and their projections in the CNS. In A. Bjorklund & T. Hokfelt (Eds.), *Handbook of chemical neuroanatomy* (Vol. 3, pp. 68-125). Amsterdam: Elsevier.

Stellar, J. R., & Corbett, D. (1989). Regional neuroleptic microinjections indicate a role for nucleus accumbens in lateral hypothalamic self-stimulation reward. *Brain Research, 477,* 126-143.

Stellar, J. R., Kelley, A. E., & Corbett, D. (1983). Effects of peripheral and central dopamine blockade on lateral hypothalamic self-stimulation: Evidence for both reward and motor deficits. *Pharmacology, Biochemistry, and Behavior, 18,* 433-442.

Steriade, M. (1984). The excitatory-inhibitory response sequence in thalamic and neocortical cells: State-related changes and regulatory systems. In G. M. Edelman, W. E. Gall, & W. M. Cowan (Eds.), *Dynamic aspects of neocortical function* (pp. 107-150). New York: John Wiley.

Stevenson, J. (1992). Evidence for a genetic etiology in hyperactivity in children. *Behavior Genetics, 22,* 337-344.

Stevenson, R. D., & Wolraich, M. L. (1989). Stimulant medication therapy in the treatment of children with attention deficit hyperactivity disorder. *Clinical Pharmacology and Therapeutics, 36,* 1183-1197.

Stoof, J. C., & Kebabian, J. W. (1981). Opposing roles for the D-1 and D-2 dopamine receptors in efflux of cyclic AMP from rat neostriatum. *Nature, 294,* 366-368.

Sulzer, D., Maidment, N. T., & Rayport, S. (1993). Amphetamine and other weak bases act to promote reverse transport of dopamine in ventral midbrain neurons. *Journal of Neurochemistry, 60,* 527-535.

Sulzer, D., & Rayport, S. (1990). Amphetamine and other psychostimulants reduce pH gradients in midbrain dopaminergic neurons and chromaffin granules: A mechanism of action. *Neuron, 5,* 797-808.

Sunahara, R. K., Guan, H.-C., O'Dowd, B. F., Seeman, P., Laurier, L. G., Ng, G., George, S. R., Torchia, J., van Tol, H. H., & Niznik, H. B. (1991). Cloning of the gene for a human dopamine D_5 receptor with higher affinity for dopamine than D_1. *Nature, 350,* 614-619.

Sved, A. F., Baker, H. A., & Reis, D. J. (1984). Dopamine synthesis in inbred mouse strains which differ in numbers of dopamine neurons. *Brain Research, 303,* 261-266.

Sved, A. F., Baker, H., & Reis, D. J. (1985). Number of dopamine neurons predicts prolactin levels in two inbred mouse strains. *Experientia, 41,* 644-646.

Tam, S.-Y., Elsworth, J. D., Bradberry, C. W., & Roth, R. H. (1990). Mesocortical dopamine neurons: High basal firing frequency predicts tyrosine dependence of dopamine synthesis. *Journal of Neural Transmission, 81,* 97-110.

Taylor, J. R., & Robbins, T. W. (1984). Enhanced behavioral control by conditioned reinforcers following microinjections of d-amphetamine into the nucleus accumbens. *Psychopharmacology, 84,* 405-412.

Taylor, J. R., & Robbins, T. W. (1986). 6-hydroxydopamine lesions of the nucleus accumbens, but not of the caudate nucleus, attenuate enhanced responding with reward-related stimuli produced by intro-accumbens d-amphetamine. *Psychopharmacology* (Berlin), *90,* 390-397.

Trujillo, K. A., Belluzzi, J. D., & Stein, L. (1986). Naloxone suppression of self-stimulation is independent of response difficulty. *Pharmacology, Biochemistry, and Behavior, 33,* 147-155.

Trujillo, K. A., Belluzzi, J. D., & Stein, L. (1989). Opiate antagonists and self-stimulation: Extinction-like response patterns suggest selective reward deficit. *Brain Research, 492,* 15-28.

Vadasz, C., Baker, H., Joh, T. H., Lajtha, A., & Reis, D. J. (1982). The inheritance and genetic correlation of tyrosine hydroxylase activities in the substantia nigra and corpus striatum in the CXB recombinant inbred mouse strains. *Brain Research, 234,* 1-9.

Vaeth, J. M., MacNeill Horton, A., Koretzky, M., Shapiro, S., Civiello, C., & Anilane, J. (1988). Alcoholism and attention deficit disorder: MMPI collelates. *International Journal of Neuroscience, 35,* 1-5.

van Praag, H. M., & Mendlewicz, J. (Eds.). (1983). *Advances in biological psychiatry: Vol. 10. Management of depressions with monoamine precursors.* New York: Karger.

van Tol, H. H. M., Bunzow, J. R., Guan, H. C., Sunahara, R. K., Seeman, P., Niznik, H. B., & Civelli, O. (1991). Cloning of the gene for a human dopamine D_4 receptor with high affinity for the antipsychotic clozapine. *Nature, 350,* 610-614.

Vulto, A. G., Sharp, T., Ungerstedt, U., & Versteeg, D. H. G. (1988). Rapid postmortem increase in extracellular dopamine in the rat brain as assessed by brain microdialysis. *Journal of Neurochemistry, 51,* 746-749.

Walters, J. R., Bergstrom, D. A., Carlson, J. H., Chase, T. N., & Braun, A. R. (1987). D_1 dopamine receptor activation required for postsynaptic expression of D_2 agonists effects. *Science, 236,* 719-722.

Wedzony, K., Limberger, N., Spath, L., Wichmann, T., & Starke, K. (1988). Acetylcholine release in rat nucleus accumbens is regulated through dopamine D2-receptors. *Naunyn-Schmiedebergs Archives of Pharmacology, 338,* 250-255.

Weiss, G., & Trokenberg-Hechtman, L. (1986). *Hyperactive children grown up* (pp. 84-141). New York: Guilford.

Weiss, R. D., Pope, H. G., & Mirin, S. M. (1985). Treatment of chronic cocaine abuse and attention deficit disorder, residual type, with magnesium pemoline. *Drug and Alcohol Dependence, 15,* 69-72.

Wender, P. H. (1971). *Minimal brain dysfunction in children.* New York: John Wiley.

Wender, P. H. (1975). Speculations concerning a possible biochemical basis of minimal brain dysfunction. *International Journal of Mental Health, 4,* 11-28.

Wender, P. H. (1978). Minimal brain dysfunction: An overview. In M. A. Lipton, A. DiMascio, & K. F. Killan (Eds.), *Psychopharmacology: A generation of progress* (pp. 1429-1435). New York: Raven Press.

Wender, P. H. (1986). Concurrent therapy with d-amphetamine and adrenergic drugs. *American Journal of Psychiatry, 143,* 259-260.

Wender, P. H. (1987). *The hyperactive child, adolescent, and adult: Attention deficit disorder through the lifespan.* New York: Oxford University Press.

Wender, P. H., Reimherr, F. W., & Wood, D. R. (1981). Attention deficit disorder (minimal brain dysfunction) in adults. *Archives of General Psychiatry, 38,* 449-456.

Wender, P. H., Reimherr, F. W., Wood, D., & Ward, M. (1985). A controlled study of methylphenidate in the treatment of attention deficit disorder, residual type, in adults. *American Journal of Psychiatry, 142,* 547-552.

Wenkstern, D., Pfaus, J. G., & Fibiger, H. C. (1993). Dopamine transmission increases in the nucleus-accumbens of male-rats during their 1st exposure to sexually receptive female rats. *Brain Research, 618,* 41-46.

West, T. E. G., & Wise, R. A. (1988). Nucleus accumbens opioids facilitate brain stimulation reward. *Society for Neuroscience Abstracts, 14,* 1102.

Westerink, B. H. C., Damsma, G., Rollema, H., de Vries, J. B., & Horn, A. S. (1987). Scope and limitation of in vivo brain dialysis: A comparison of its application to various neurotransmitter systems. *Life Sciences, 41,* 1763-1776.

Westerink, B. H. C., & de Vries, J. B. (1988). Characterization of in vivo dopamine release as determined by brain microdialysis after acute and subchronic implantations: Methodological aspects. *Journal of Neurochemistry, 51,* 683-687.

Westerink, B. H. C., Hofsteede, R. M., Tuntler, J., & de Vries, J. B. (1989). Use of calcium antagonism for the characterization of drug-evoked dopamine release from the brain of conscious rats determined by microdialysis. *Journal of Neurochemistry, 52,* 722-729.

Westerink, B. H. C., Tuntler, J., Damsma, G., Rollema, H., & de Vries, J. B. (1987). The use of tetrodotoxin for the characterization of drug-enhanced dopamine release in conscious rats studied by brain dialysis. *Naunyn-Schmiedebergs Archives of Pharmacology, 336,* 502-507.

White, F. J. (1987). D-1 dopamine receptor stimulation enables the inhibition of nucleus accumbens neurons by a D-2 receptor agonist. *European Journal of Pharmacology, 135,* 101-105.

White, F. J., & Wang, R. Y. (1986). Electrophysiological evidence for the existence of both D-1 and D-2 dopamine receptors in the rat nucleus accumbens. *Journal of Neuroscience, 6,* 274-280.

White, N. M., Packard, M. G., & Hiroi, N. (1991). Place conditioning with dopamine D1 and D2 agonists injected peripherally or into nucleus accumbens. *Psychopharmacology* (Berlin), *103,* 271-276.

Wilcox, R. A., Robinson, T. E., & Becker, J. B. (1986). Enduring enhancement in amphetamine-stimulated striatal dopamine release in vitro produced by prior exposure to amphetamine or stress in vivo. *European Journal of Pharmacology, 124,* 375-376.

Wilens, T. E., Biederman, J., & Spencer, T. (1994). Clonidine for sleep disturbances associated with attention-deficit hyperactivity disorder. *Journal of the American Academy of Child and Adolescent Psychiatry, 33,* 424-426.

Wise, C. D., Berger, B. D., & Stein, L. (1973). Evidence of alpha-noradrenergic reward receptors and serotonergic punishment receptors in the rat brain. *Biological Psychiatry, 6,* 3-21.

Wise, R. A. (1980). The dopamine synapse and the notion of pleasure centers in the brain. *Trends in Neuroscience, 3,* 91-95.

Wise, R. A. (1987). The role of reward pathways in the development of drug dependence. *Pharmacology and Therapeutics, 35,* 227-263.

Wise, R. A. (1989). Opiate reward: Sites and substrates. *Neuroscience and Biobehavioral Reviews, 13,* 129-133.

Wise, R. A., & Bozarth, M. A. (1984). Brain reward circuitry: Four circuit elements "wired" in apparent series. *Brain Research Bulletin, 12,* 203-208.

Wise, R. A., & Bozarth, M. A. (1987). A psychomotor stimulant theory of addiction. *Psychological Review, 94,* 469-492.

Wise, R. A., & Rompre, P. P. (1989). Brain dopamine and reward. *Annual Review of Psychology, 40,* 191-225.

Woods, S. K. (1990). *Potentiation of the methylphenidate-induced release of dopamine in the nucleus accumbens as measured by in vivo microdialysis.* Unpublished doctoral dissertation, University of Massachusetts, Amherst.

Woods, S. K., & Meyer, J. S. (1991). Exogenous tyrosine potentiates the methylphenidate-induced increase in extracellular dopamine in the nucleus accumbens: A microdialysis study. *Brain Research, 560,* 97-105.

Wu, M., Brudzynski, S. M., & Mogenson, G. J. (1993). Functional interaction of dopamine and glutamate in the nucleus accumbens in the regulation of locomotion. *Canadian Journal of Physiology and Pharmacology, 71,* 407-413.

Wurtman, R. J. (1982). Nutrients that modify brain function. *Scientific American, 246,* 50-59.

Wurtman, R. J., Hefti, F., & Melamed, E. (1981). Precursor control of neurotransmitter synthesis. *Pharmacological Reviews, 32,* 315-335.

Yakovlev, P. I., & Lecours, A. R. (1967). The myelogenetic cycles of regional maturation of the brain. In A. Minkowski (Ed.), *Regional development of the brain in early life* (pp. 3-70). Oxford: Blackwell.

Yamauchi, T., & Fujisawa, H. (1981). Tyrosine 3-monooxygenase is phosphorylated by Ca^{2+}–calmodulin-dependent protein kinase, followed by activation by activator protein. *Biochemical and Biophysical Research Communications, 100,* 807-813.

Yamauchi, T., Nakata, H., & Fujisawa, H. (1981). A new activator protein that activates tryptophan 5-monooxygenase and tyrosine 3-monooxygenase in the presence of Ca^{2+}-, calmodulin-dependent protein kinase. *Journal of Biological Chemistry, 256,* 5404-5409.

Yellin, A. M., Hopwood, J. H., & Greenberg, L. M. (1982). Adults and adolescents with attention deficit disorder: Clinical and behavioral responses to psychostimulants. *Journal of Clinical Psychopharmacology, 2,* 133-136.

Yeomans, J. S. (1989). Two substrates for medial forebrain bundle self-stimulation: Myelinated axons and dopamine axons. *Neuroscience and Biobehavioral Reviews, 13,* 91-98.

Yeomans, J. S., Kofman, O., & McFarlane, V. (1985). Cholinergic involvement in lateral hypothalamic self-stimulation. *Brain Research, 329,* 19-26.

Yeomans, J. S., Maidment, N. T., & Bunney, B. S. (1988). Excitability properties of medial forebrain bundle axons of A9 and A10 dopamine cells. *Brain Research, 450,* 86-93.

Yeomans, J. S., Mercouris, N., & Ellard, C. (1985). Refractory period estimates are lengthened by reducing electrode tip exposure or increasing current. *Behavioral Neuroscience, 99,* 913-928.

Yokel, R. A., & Wise, R. A. (1976). Attenuation of intravenous amphetamine reinforcement by central dopamine blockade in rats. *Psychopharmacology, 48,* 311-318.

Zaczek, R., Culp, S., & De Souza, E. B. (1991). Interactions of [^{3}H] amphetamine with rat brain synaptosomes: II. Active transport. *Journal of Pharmacology and Experimental Therapeutics, 257,* 830-835.

Zetterstrom, T., Sharp, T., Collin, A. K., & Ungerstedt, U. (1988). In vivo measurement of extracellular dopamine and DOPAC in rat striatum after various dopamine-releasing drugs; implications for the origin of extracellular DOPAC. *European Journal of Pharmacology, 148,* 327-334.

Zigmond, R. E. (1985). Biochemical consequences of synaptic stimulation: The regulation of tyrosine hydroxylase activity by multiple transmitters. *Trends in Neurosciences, 8,* 63-69.

Zigmond, R. E., Schwarzschild, M. A., & Rittenhouse, A. R. (1989). Acute regulation of tyrosine hydroxylase by nerve activity and by neurotransmitters via phosphorylation. *Annual Review of Neuroscience, 12,* 415-461.

Index

Aburthnott, G. W., 60, 64
Activity level, heritability of, 40
Acworth, I. N., 75, 76
Addalli, K. A., 48
Adderall, 50, 69
ADHD:
  combined type, 47
  definition of, 174
  diagnostic criteria for, 46-47
  gender and, 48
  genetic component, 39
  predominantly hyperactive-impulsive type,
    47
  predominantly inattentive type, 47
  prevalence rates, 48
  See also Hyperkinetic syndrome; Minimal
    brain dysfunction
ADHD adults:
  and therapist bond, 133-134
  as social misfits, 135
  concentration problems, 133
  empathy problems, 133
  extreme sense of panic, 140
  hypermotor behavior, 133
  immature behavior, 134
  inner world of, 135
  organization problems, 133
  outer world functioning, 134-135
  PMS symptom increase in female, 137

self-control problems, 133
self-image problems, 134
spontaneous lessening of symptoms in, 136
useful medications for, 49-50
visual spatial problems, 139
See also ADHD adults, treatment of;
  ADHD individuals; ADHD individuals,
  behavior of; ADHD symtomatology
  (general)
ADHD adults, treatment of:
  direct approach, 134
  humor in, 134
  individual maturity level and, 139-140
  long-term, 134
  significant others' cooperation in, 138-139
ADHD children:
  at home, 47
  inner world of, 112, 122-123
  in one-on-one situations, 47
  in school, 47
  needing direct experience, 120
  not treating, 48
  pets for, 122
  poor self-image, 119
  potential alcohol abuse in, 124
  potential antisocial behavior in, 124
  potential drug abuse in, 124
  processing psychic feeling, 112
  weight problems, 122

205

About the Authors

Sandra K. Woods is a psychotherapist, neuroscientist, and member of the adjunct faculty of the Psychology Department, University of Massachusetts at Amherst. She met her co-author, Willis H. Ploof, in the late 1960s, following her early graduate training in clinical psychology. She and Dr. Ploof have been collaborating on various projects ever since. After more than 20 years in the field, during which time she worked as a psychotherapist, psychometrist, director of a sheltered workshop for the developmentally disabled, school psychologist, and consultant to various social service agencies, she returned to graduate school at the University of Massachusetts, earning her Ph.D. in neuroscience in 1990.

Dr. Woods currently divides her time between her outreach work for a community-based mental health clinic, her writing, and her private practice. She specializes in the diagnosis and treatment of children and adults with ADHD. She has also taught writing to undergraduate psychology majors at the University of Massachusetts.

Willis H. Ploof recently retired from private practice in psychiatry to concentrate on his writing and died as this book was being completed. During his long professional career, he was responsible for the establishment of two community-based mental health clinics, one in Holyoke, Massachusetts, and the other in Kingsport, Tennessee. During the Korean War, he served as chief psychiatrist at the Army Disciplinary Barracks in Harrisburg, Pennsylvania. For many years, he served as consultant to the Massachusetts Rehabilitation Commission and to the Youthful Offender Program at Goodwill Industries, Springfield, Massachusetts.

In the late 1960s, Dr. Ploof established and supervised the Pupil Adjustment Program for the Springfield School Department, a comprehensive program designed to treat children with symptoms of ADHD. He received his M.D. from the Boston University School of Medicine and did his training in the practice of child, adolescent, and adult psychiatry under Elvin Semrad, Felix Deutch, and Joseph Weinreb.

Postscript: During his lifetime, Dr. Ploof helped many mature to adulthood. Words are inadequate to describe what he meant to me and to those who received his healing. This manuscript is only partly reflective of the person, his capacities, and his life's work.

SANDRA K. WOODS